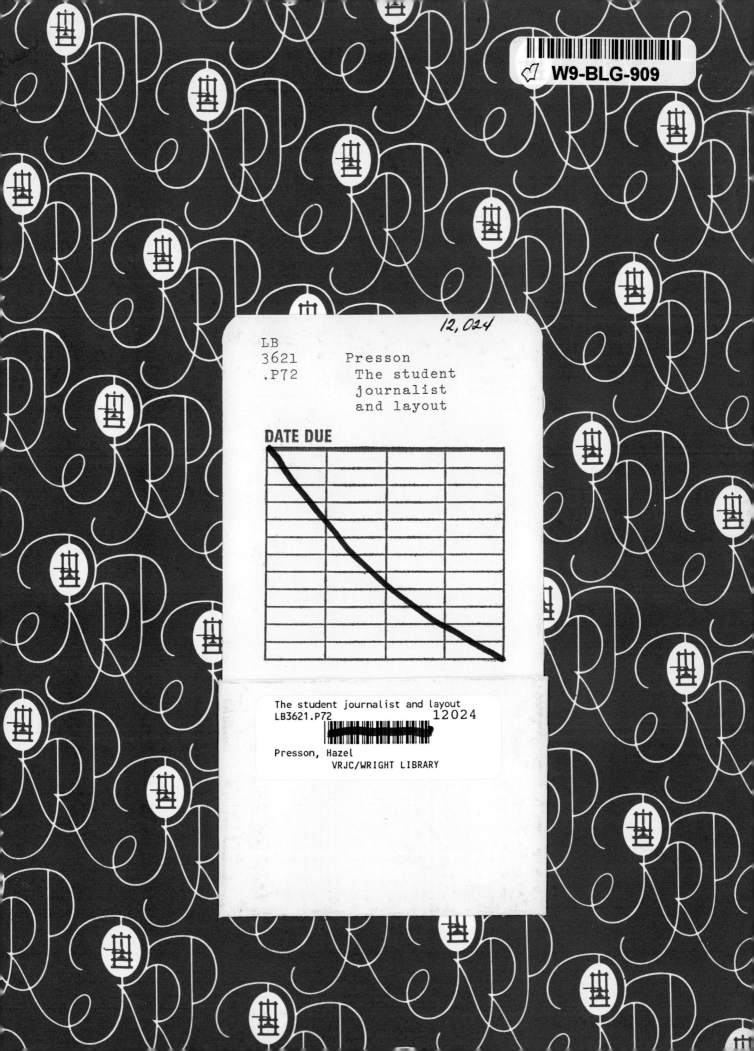

THE STUDENT JOURNALIST
AND LAYOUT

It's not all moonlight and roses with the layout editor—but there are wonderful moments when the pre-planning pays off, and the photographer submits a series of pictures that not only fit the layout but tell the story and tell it well.

THE STUDENT JOURNALIST AND LAYOUT

Hazel Presson

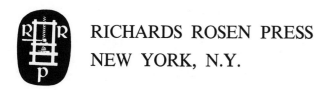

RICHARDS ROSEN PRESS
NEW YORK, N.Y.

Standard Book Number: 8239–0253–6
Library of Congress Catalog Card Number: 72–163949

Published in 1972 by Richards Rosen Press, Inc.
29 East 21st Street, New York City, N.Y. 10010

Revised Edition

Manufactured in the United States of America

ABOUT THE AUTHOR

Hazel Presson is a combination adviser-teacher-author whose experience with high school newspapers dates back to a sunny spring morning when the editor of the school paper dashed into a freshman English class in search of someone who could read proof in an emergency.

"That was a much more important day than it seemed at the time," she observes. "The teacher recommended me—and I've been associated with school publications ever since."

Miss Presson now is head of the journalism department at Northside High School in Fort Smith, Arkansas, teaching journalism and serving as adviser of the newspaper and yearbook, both of which hold medalist ratings from the Columbia Scholastic Press Association and all-American ratings from the National Scholastic Press Association.

"We never have a dull moment," she says, "for in newspaper work you wake up every day in a new world. It's exciting to know what's going on —and fun to pass the news on to others."

A member of Phi Beta Kappa, Miss Presson holds an M.A. degree from the University of Arkansas and has done additional work in journalism at the University of Oklahoma as a Newspaper Fund Fellow and at Columbia University under a grant from *Life* magazine. Active in the work of the scholastic press associations, she holds the Gold Key from the Columbia Scholastic Press Association, the Pioneer Award from the National Scholastic Press Association and is a member of the National Council of School Press and Adviser Associations and the Mid-America Council of Secondary School Press Associations. Extending her teaching efforts beyond her own classroom, she participates in a range of con-

vention programs and in various workshops sponsored during the summer by colleges and universities for student journalists.

After school hours the adviser-teacher becomes the author, being presently engaged in work on a light, contemporary novel, following a

historical novel that grew out of research for *The Story of Arkansas,* a history now being used as a state text. Preceding this volume, she has contributed a number of articles to scholastic and professional magazines. She is the author of the books *The Student Journalist and News Reporting* and *The Student Journalist and Interviewing,* also published by Richards Rosen Press.

CONTENTS

ACKNOWLEDGMENTS

Student journalists and their advisers are an unusual group of people in many respects. They are distinguished by an enthusiasm for their work and by their generosity in sharing their experiences with others. They range from those who say, "I don't know what I'm doing but I want to do it," to those who offer such specific help as "We tried it this way and it worked."

Thus, the writer of a book for newspaper and yearbook staffs owes much to the many persons he meets from day to day. In this instance, I would like to acknowledge my gratitude to the students in my high school classes at Northside, who are my chief purpose for being in this work, and to the teachers and students in the numerous workshops and meetings across the country where we have encountered and attempted to solve many of the problems common to us all.

Also, I am indebted to the journalism teachers, the specialists and consultants, and the professional journalists with whom I have worked in a wide range of situations; to the newspaper and yearbook advisers whom I have met and whose publications have come to my attention; to those in the local school system—the board of education, the superintendent, and the principal—who provide the setting and encouragement for this kind of educational program; and to those responsible for the publication of this series, Ruth and Richard Rosen, who saw the need for help for the beginning student and his adviser and who have endeavored to get that help into print.

Among the many whom I would like to mention specifically are Colonel Joseph M. Murphy, director emeritus of the Columbia Scholastic Press Association; Charles R. O'Malley, director of CSPA; James F. Paschal, executive director of the Future Journalists of America; Dr. Max R. Haddick, director of the Interscholastic Press League Conference, and Rex Jobe, assistant director, University of Texas; K. J. Austin, director of special field services, Taylor Publishing Company; Martha Hankins, Paris High School, Paris, Texas; Benjamin W. Allnutt, Bethesda–Chevy Chase High School, Bethesda, Maryland; William D. Downs, director of the Arkansas High School Press Association; Dr. Robert Knight, director of the Missouri High School Press Association; Harvey Jacobs, director of the School of Journalism, New Mexico State University; Lester Benz, executive secretary of Quill and Scroll; and those who would never suspect that what they have done or said might have contributed to this total effort, including Mrs. Shelton Jones, Starkville, Mississippi; William Oglesby, Springdale, Arkansas; Paul S. Swensson, Princeton, New Jersey; Foster Harris, University of Oklahoma; Mrs. Frank McGehee, Little Rock, Arkansas; and Mrs. Ben Jaramillo, Albuquerque, New Mexico.

Special recognition goes to a group of advisers who prepared specific helps for this presentation: Mrs. Hazel Aldridge, Central High School, Muskogee, Oklahoma; Mrs. Ruth Marie Griggs, Broad Ripple High School, Indianapolis, Indiana; Elizabeth Hurley, Pampa High School, Pampa, Texas; Mrs. Lorine Lay, Chaffin Junior High School, Fort Smith, Arkansas; Mrs. Verna Powers, Waverly High School, Waverly, Nebraska; Mrs. Marjorie Robinson, Loudonville High School, Loudonville, Ohio; and I. E. Clark, Schulenburg, Texas.

PREFACE

Can a new adviser and an inexperienced staff of student journalists find happiness publishing a school yearbook or newspaper?

Is it possible for an "old" teacher who doesn't know the first thing about journalism to have the yearbook or newspaper dumped into his lap and live to enjoy the school year?

Can a group of high school seniors who have never worked on a yearbook enlist the aid of a teacher who will help them produce a volume that will be a credit to the school and a pleasure to the student body?

Sound familiar?

As one more volume in the Student Journalist series for beginners who want the answers to all these questions to be "yes," I have designed a book that I hope will be not only a help in making those seeming impossibilities come true but also an introduction to many pleasant experiences for the staff and adviser.

For some time, I have been visiting with advisers and staffs in many areas, observing them as they encounter and solve their problems, listening to their tales of woe and of joy. I have consulted with specialists and experts in both the scholastic and related professional fields, and I have studied student publications nationwide. It is a fascinating study and a rewarding one, as the total view is one of enthusiasm for the job—and the total product is good.

Publication of a school yearbook or newspaper is an investment in work and money that should be successful by all the standards we could name.

The secret to that success lies, as in every endeavor, in knowing what to do and how to get it done.

In light of the need for knowing what to do in putting the parts of a publication together, the purpose of this volume is to offer guidance in the area of layout and design. In both the yearbook and the newspaper, the matter of layout is of importance, because as has been said, "Layout is like dress: it is the 'total look' of the publication" —and the success of the publication is linked with that "total look."

When student journalists and advisers get together for a meeting, the subject of layout is usually discussed with considerable interest—sometimes formally, as in previously planned sessions at which specialists lecture or give instruction, sometimes informally in groups in which ideas are exchanged and questions discussed.

The subject attracts both young people and their teachers, perhaps for two reasons. One is that people basically have a feeling for pattern and design and, as in listening to music, just have an urge to "get with it." The other reason is that in putting the school yearbook or paper together, some plan is necessary so the parts can be assembled with a pleasing effect.

Basic considerations involved in that "some plan" are presented in this volume for inexperienced staffs and their advisers venturing for the first time into school publications.

Hazel Presson

PART I

Developing an Understanding

CHAPTER I

KNOW WHAT THE WORDS MEAN

This is a book for beginners. It is a very simple approach to one of the problem areas in student publications—layout.

Why a problem area? (1) Because students, even the inexperienced, are often expected to produce publications that compare favorably with the work of professional layout people; (2) because beginners especially are overwhelmed with the necessity of doing something with words and pictures, though not knowing what to do; and (3) because frequently staffs and advisers have to cope with inadequacies and insufficiencies.

Summary guidelines set down here are designed to help you who are inexperienced student journalists develop an understanding of layout and design and to help you learn about layout by producing layouts effectively as you work on your yearbooks and newspapers.

Such development of understanding is basic, since layout is actually only a secondary part of something larger. By definition the purpose of layout is to display. Obviously, if there is nothing to display, then no layout is necessary. Conversely, what we are to display should determine the display.

We put it this way: Our purpose in a student publication is to communicate ideas—and our means of communication is the display of words and pictures on pages of white space.

To state it differently: We have ideas that we communicate through display designed (1) to attract the reader, (2) to indicate relationships to him, and (3) to provide him with an understanding of our meaning.

It is assumed that if we understand the basic principles involved, we can explore other possibilities, even to experimenting, when we have sufficient experience and background.

What are called "basic principles" are derived from purposes. "Rules" are not rules as such. They are actually a summary of practices understood to be successful in a wide variety of situations and under varying conditions.

"Being successful" means that the layout has served the purpose intended: that is, to communicate the message to be conveyed to the reader not only so it is clear but also in such a way that the communication is a pleasing presentation in itself.

Specific Terms

"That speech would have been a lot of help if I had just known what all the words meant."

That comment heard at the close of a session at a state convention holds the secret to many of our difficulties: Unless we know what the words mean, we cannot comprehend ideas being presented.

Therefore, we shall begin here with a quick look at some of the terms commonly used in discussing yearbook and newspaper layout.

Words of a general nature include those referring to the way your publication is printed. *Mimeographed* and *duplicated* are terms familiar enough as ways to print newspapers—they are never used for yearbooks—but there are other ways to print both newspapers and yearbooks. These include two popular processes:

(1) *Letterpress printing*—A method of printing in which the impression is made directly upon

the paper by "raised" and "hot" type, engravings, and so forth. This "raised" type consists of individual letters set by hand into lines of type. (They are usually metal, but are of wood if very large.) "Hot" type comes from a typesetting machine called a Linotype machine, which casts lines of type on slugs of molten metal.

Lines of type are locked securely into a metal frame and inked. Paper is then placed over the inked type and a roller is pressed upon it, thus making the impression that we read.

(2) *Offset printing*—Related to the old art of lithography. In old-style lithographic printing, the design is drawn on a flat surface, usually a stone, with a special crayon. The first impression is a reverse print, which is then transferred to a second surface—the paper on which the readable impression is printed. Today's offset printing is the process of printing from a flat surface—such as a picture or a block of type—employing photographic techniques.

In that method, the impression is not transferred directly to the paper, as in letterpress printing, but is first transferred to a rubber blanket and then to the paper. Obviously, a press used for letterpress printing and one for offset (or lithographic) printing would not be alike.

Fortunately for the school publications staff, the difference between the two printing processes does not make much difference, since the contract signed with the printing company names one or the other of the processes as the one used.

Terms having to do generally with layout, design, and display:

Makeup—Frequently used as a synonym for layout.

Paste-up—The actual blocks of type and pictures pasted on an accurately drawn layout sheet ready for printing. (Not all staffs are required to do their own paste-ups, as some contracts include this as part of the shop work.)

Format—Refers to the total design of your publication.

Specifications—The list of all the details making up the format. It includes size of publication, kind of type, width of columns, and so on.

Typography—A term referring to the use of type in making impressions on paper; the art and science of printing design. It includes the kind of type used, size, and such.

Dummy—The rough sketch of your layout plan. Newspaper staffs send either a dummy or a paste-up to their printing shop. Yearbook staffs use the dummy as their own guide to perfecting their layout sheets, which must be accurate when sent to the printing company.

Style sheet or *style book*—A complete guide for the publications staff's use to ensure consistency in spelling, punctuation, width of pictures, headline forms, and so forth. Every staff should have such a style sheet, working it out to be as complete as possible for their publication so that all details will be consistent.

Terms having to do with the use of type:

Boldface—Also called blackface; a kind of heavy-faced type—as distinguished from lightface.

Caps—Capital letters.

Condensed type—Type characters with faces narrow in proportion to their height.

Cursive—A kind of type similar to script, designed to look like handwriting.

Display type—Type faces designed for headings, headlines, special effects, advertisements, and the like—larger and heavier than the body type.

Gothic—The plainest, simplest style of type face, with lines of unvarying width and no serifs or other decorative strokes on the letters.

Italic—The style of letters that slope forward, as distinguished from upright letters.

Letter spacing—Additional spacing between letters in a line of type.

Lightface—A kind of type with light lines in letters, as distinguished from boldface.

Linotype—A machine that sets type in lines up to five inches in length. As the operator "types" on a keyboard, the words are cast on a slug of hot metal.

Lithotype—A kind of type set by a machine similar to a typewriter. The face frequently resembles a typewriter face.

Lower case—Letters that are not capitals. Caps and lc and clc are abbreviations used to mean caps and lower case.

Pica—A term used to indicate measure of type

in the point system. There are approximately 72 points in an inch. There are 12 points in a pica. Therefore a pica is approximately one sixth of an inch.

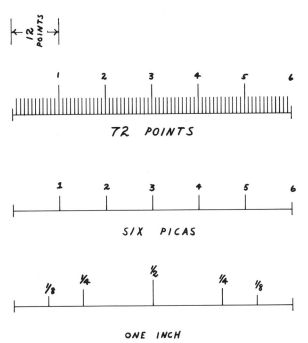

This diagram shows the relationship between points, picas, and inches. In student publications, the term "point" is generally used in speaking of type or of spacing—as, "the headline is 24-point type," or "the body copy is to be set in 10-point type with 2-point spacing." The word "pica" is used of widths, as "the column is 14 picas wide," or in designating measure of pictures or space, as "the picture is cropped to 20 picas wide by 30 picas deep and reduced to fit a space 14 picas wide by 21 picas deep."

Point system—Type is measured according to a point system worked out long ago for standardization in type design. *A point* is approximately one seventy-second of an inch. The sizes of type designed and then cast by type foundries are graduated on the point scale. The term refers to the height of letters. For example, school papers use about 9-point type for body copy, with headlines ranging from about 12 point to 48 or 60 point for major stories. Most yearbooks use 10 point for body copy, with 24 or 30 or 36 point for headlines, depending on the heaviness of the type face selected.

Roman—A face of type distinguished by thick and thin strokes and by serifs. Also (usually not

capitalized) the common form of letter face for general use, as distinguished from italic, cursive, and text.

Sans serif—Type designed without any kind of decorative lines on the letters.

Script—A kind of type similar to cursive, designed to look like handwriting.

Serif—Decorative line on letters, such as a tiny finishing stroke on major lines.

Type face—A general term referring to the appearance of a type, especially with reference to its shape, form, or character.

Type family—A term used to indicate the various forms and sizes of a basic design. Type families are divisions of type races, each named for easy identification. Some are named for their designer, as Garamond; others are general, as Century. Families are made up of *series*. This enables us to indicate a variation in the form of a letter, as Garamond italic.

Type races—The many styles of type are divided into six general groups called races. They are roman, text, square serif, sans serif, script, and ornamented.

Type series—A term used to describe variations in the form of a letter. A series consists of all the sizes in a particular letter style. For example, for headlines a staff may choose the Bodoni family, and then in the Bodoni italic series —which includes a number of sizes—select the 30 point.

Type size—Measurement of type is determined by the point system.

Type weight—The lightness or darkness of a given type face. Weight is measured in terms of light, medium, bold, extra bold, and ultra bold.

Typewriter type—An imitation of copy produced by a typewriter—in which every character, including space and punctuation, is the same width.

Terms having to do with use of words in type:

Body copy—Written material covering content, as opposed to headline copy, caption copy, ad copy, and the like.

By-line—Line at the beginning of a story giving the name of the person who wrote it. (Not used in yearbooks.)

Caption—Yearbook: descriptive copy accompanying a picture. Newspaper: heading above any illustration.

Copy—Written material, as for newspaper stories or yearbook coverage, headlines, captions, ads.

Copy block—A term referring to the area covered by copy.

Cutlines—Newspapers: explanatory copy accompanying a picture.

Flush—A term referring to position of copy. Any copy—body, head, or the like—flush left is set so that all lines are aligned against an imaginary line on the left; this leaves the right side irregular. Copy set flush right is lined up evenly on the right, leaving the left irregular.

Identification—Yearbook: caption giving names only, as naming club members in a group picture.

Justify—A term referring to position of copy within a copy area. To justify a line is to set the type with necessary spacing so it fills the line. To justify a column is to space the type so that the column area is filled completely.

Leading—Adding space between lines. Pronounced *ledding*.

Set solid—To set type with no spacing between lines.

Widow—A term referring to the last line in a block of copy. A widow is a short last line. Formerly editors and printers made every effort to avoid widows, defining a widow as less than half a line. Generally now short last lines are not considered objectionable unless they are very short, as only a word or so. However, if the last line of a paragraph is a very short line, it should not be carried over to become the first line of the next column.

Terms having to do with headlines:

Center—To space evenly between right- and left-hand margins.

Character—A letter of the alphabet, numeral, mark of punctuation, and so on, used in typesetting. In character count, all characters count as one space, except for capital letters, which count two.

Count—Checking by some predetermined method to see that the amount of copy being pre-

pared for a certain space has been properly estimated and will exactly fit that space.

Downstyle—A term referring to the use of as few capital letters as necessary. Many professional newspapers today are using headlines in downstyle. Capitalization in such heads is as in normal sentence writing. Downstyle is increasingly popular in school newspapers and yearbooks.

Flush left, flush right—Headlines set flush left are aligned on the left. Flush right heads are aligned on the right. Flush left is considered more readable and is the favored newspaper style. Both styles are popular in the contemporary yearbook.

Headline—A statement that summarizes the body copy or entices the reader to continue into the body copy. The most meaningful headlines usually have a subject and a predicate, either of which may be understood.

Headline schedule—This term refers to the complete headline plan worked out for a publication. Some staffs paste examples of all their heads on a large sheet of poster board and display it for easy reference. Others include it in their style book. The headline schedule should give complete information as to kind of type, size of head, count, when used, and such.

Kicker—A small headline that is placed above the main head. Sometimes called a tag. Usually about half the point size of the main head.

Label—A heading that does not make a statement as a headline does but merely names something, as Football Team.

Reverse kicker—Large short headline above a smaller main headline. Usually about twice the point size of the main head.

Tombstone—A term referring to the placing of headlines. When headlines of the same size or nearly the same size are placed side by side, they are said to be tombstoned.

Unit count—This method of counting headlines is based on a scale that has been worked out previously, by which width of characters is more closely estimated than by character count. For example, in unit count in some type styles the capital *W* is six times as wide as the lower case *i*. The unit count ensures a more accurate estimate of copy to fit the space intended and usually leads to a more orderly and trimmer look. With both the unit and the character count methods the staff must work out a careful estimate of width of copy needed. That is, if the editor tells you that the headline must count 30 to 33 by the unit count, he must know that this is the length of head that will be most attractive in the space intended.

Terms having to do with photographs:

Bleed—To extend a picture off one or more margins of a page.

Center of interest—Focal point of attention in a picture, page, or spread. The center of interest should determine the proper cropping of a picture.

Crop—To eliminate unwanted areas of a picture. A photograph is never actually cut. You indicate what you want to eliminate by using crop marks in the margin.

Montage—A composite picture made up of a number of smaller pictures or parts of pictures blended together with no spacing between the component parts.

Mortise—An area removed from a printing plate, usually a picture, so that type can be set in.

Photo essay, photo poem, picture story— Terms used to indicate the combination of words and pictures to convey certain kinds of ideas, in a "creative" way.

Screen—A term usually used in reference to engravings or plates for offset. Screen is a device employed by engravers so that pictures can be reproduced in print.

Terms having to do specifically with newspapers:

Anchor the corners—An old newspaper phrase meaning that the corners of a page should contain some attention-getting device, such as a headline, box, or picture.

Assignment sheet—The editor's list of stories and pictures assigned to staff members.

Banner—Unusually large headline that extends across the full page to indicate a story of great importance.

Box—A unit of type set to attract special notice by having borders of lines or extra space; sometimes set in boldface.

Catchline—Line of large type between picture and cutlines.

Cutoff rule—A thin horizontal line used when necessary to separate stories or pictures for clearness.

Ear—Small block of type that runs beside a nameplate.

Flag—The nameplate of a newspaper, the logo.

Fillers—Brief items used to fill out a column.

Folio lines—Lines giving newspaper name, date, and page number; usually run at the top of a page.

Hairline rule—Thinnest rule used in newspaper makeup.

Nameplate—The flag, the logo—the formal identification of the newspaper on the front page.

Overline—The line of display type over a picture.

Reading diagonal—The direction the eye normally follows in glancing over a page from top left to lower right.

Terms having to do with the parts of a yearbook:

Backbone—The back of a bound book connecting the front and back covers; also called the spine.

Double page spread—The two facing pages that the reader sees upon opening a book. In yearbook layout an effort should be made to consider as a unit the double page spreads that the reader sees as he leafs through the book.

Division pages—One or more pages designed to serve as dividers of content and help the reader understand the organization of the book.

End sheets—Those sheets of paper placed between the front and back covers and the body of the book to hold the pages within the cover. Half of each sheet is pasted to the cover; the other half serves as a fly leaf.

Foreword—The opening word that introduces the reader to the content of the yearbook.

Gutter—The center space between two facing pages.

Index—The listing of persons, organizations, advertisers, and so on, that appear in the yearbook.

Signature—Folded printing sheet forming one section of a book. Usually it is sixteen pages for yearbooks.

Basic elements in layout—The basic elements of layout are (1) white space, (2) type, and (3) pictures. That is, any layout is an arrangement of type and pictures on white space.

Structural principles of design:

(1) *Balance*—Refers to the arrangement of the basic elements in an effort to achieve pleasing distribution of weight within the layout. Balance may be formal or informal.

(2) *Eye direction*—Leading the reader from one element to another. This may be achieved by (1) the orderly repetition of some feature in the design, such as a shape, tone, or color, or (2) a line of some sort, either real or imaginary.

(3) *Proportion*—Concerns the amount of space given to each element to show the relative importance of each.

(4) *Unity*—Refers to grouping the elements so that they appear to be related to one another.

(5) *Contrast*—Avoiding monotony in the shape of elements and their arrangement.

(6) *Harmony*—Refers to the pleasing effect of the total design.

CHAPTER II

CONSIDER THE "TOTAL LOOK"

Designing your yearbook or newspaper is much like designing your school wardrobe—implying the need for thinking of the whole before you begin to choose parts. You want to have your total appearance one of harmony, pleasing to the beholder, contemporary in style, and—certainly—functional and practical.

You would never think of shopping for one item after another with no thought for the co-ordination of items. And you would not dress any morning for school by merely donning the first garment at hand and then reaching for just any old scarf or any old shoes.

(Admittedly there are those who do leave that impression. In many instances, the impression is one of choice, in others it is lack of care—and in both instances serves to prove the point.)

So with consideration of the overall effect in mind, the yearbook or newspaper staff must decide first what they want to create as their "total look."

The staff of the 1970's is much freer than even the staff of the 1960's; many of the old "rules" are being questioned, frequently dropped.

With the beginning of this decade, it is obvious that not only are students asking, "Why do we have to do it this way?" or "Who says so?"—they are mastering fundamentals so that they can answer their own questions.

For the last several years, research has been going on in the professional field, with leaders in all phases of the communications arts saying, "This is a new era. We will discard what is non-functional, what is merely subservient to somebody's rule of yesteryear."

They add: "We are seeking to make reading easier," and "We want the total effect of our publications to be bright and airy," and "We want to help the reader get the point sooner."

Leaders in the newspaper industry, for example, are conducting research in all areas and are attending workshops to try to improve their publications.

"The new look" may not be a new phrase, but it certainly has a new meaning for the 1970's. A new word has been coined at the workshops to accompany the term "readership." It is "looker-ship."

In yearbooks the changes are similarly marked, as publishing houses are teaming with colleges and universities in the conducting of workshops and seminars so that staffs can be given training in current design.

Publishers, incidentally, are cooperating in such instruction because they are people in the business of communication. They are interested in seeing that the printed word and picture are offered to the public in the most pleasing package possible.

Your View

When you are considering the total look of your publication, you might think of yourself as a kind of architect. Buildings today are simply designed—or else are so cleverly planned that they look streamlined, neat, trim. The architect planning a building makes an effort to create from the materials he chooses something with a look of simplicity, unity, consistency in detail.

Three qualities that characterize the scholastic publications of the 1970's are: (1) simplicity, (2) unity, (3) consistency.

Creating that kind of design is not necessarily simple—but neither does it mean that the staff room becomes a kind of disaster area where something is going on all the time but no one knows who is doing what or why. If the staff understands the total look, and if each staff member knows how to fit in so that he can produce his part of the work well and on time, then the result will be good.

Key persons here are the editor and the adviser. Both must know what they are trying to create, and both must know what every other member of the staff is contributing. All members, of course, should know—and fortunate the staff all of whom do know—and care. Fortunate, too, the staff with a feeling of harmony, fellowship, and understanding underlying the publication effort.

An Illustration

Recently at a press convention in one of the discussion sessions, this question was asked: "What do I do first as the staff member in charge of the sophomore class for the yearbook?"

The speaker reflected for a moment, then answered, "You meet with the others on the staff, and all of you in charge of doing the class sections discuss the total design of your book to see what kind of basic plans you want to make."

"But," the girl said, "we do not work this way. The editor just gave me the sophomore class and told me to do it."

Several in the group nodded in agreement.

"That's the way many staffs do both their newspaper and their yearbook," one boy added. "I know a school where everybody just gets a job and is supposed to work on their own."

"It's sad but true," another boy added. "I'm assigned to do the opening section of our yearbook. When I asked the editor what to put in it, he said, 'Oh, you know, the administration and all that sort of jazz.' I figured there must be a better way to go about it. That's why I'm here."

The speaker smiled. "There *is* a better way—and it's easier, too. Let's begin by . . ."

That little incident provides our starting point.

PART II

Designing the Yearbook

CHAPTER **III**

MATCH THE "TOTAL LOOK" WITH THE BASIC PLANS

Planning a yearbook is most effective when as many of the staff as are sincerely interested in doing the actual work of production can sit down for a period long enough to discuss possibilities and ideas.

Suggestion: Acquire some contemporary yearbooks to study so that you will know what kinds of books are being produced in other schools. Not necessarily "way-out" books, though some are—but just typical of today's reading, thinking, observing, discriminating teenagers. You can find lists of books in the contest ratings published annually in the scholastic press magazines. They may be obtained in two ways: by exchanging copies of your book or by paying the regular subscription price.

Study the books, noting the various characteristics and qualities that you consider impressive.

Make a list of the following considerations for your new book and be prepared to discuss each item with others on the staff when you meet again.

At the second meeting, discuss all suggestions, weigh them, and make decisions. As a guide in making your decisions, consider your budget first. *The outgo should never exceed the income.* And remember: There are always hidden costs and emergency needs.

Second, choose the style that is compatible with your school. A small school for girls, for example, should produce a book that the casual viewer would know immediately is not from a large military academy.

Third, reflect the contemporary scene. In this Bikini Age, some schools are producing yearbooks that would still blush to go for a swim in bloomers and long stockings. No generation gap exists in those schools as far as the yearbook and newspaper are concerned. They're still in the 1890's.

There is no objection to being traditional, and many books are consistently similar in many respects to their preceding volumes—but you can do so without being out-of-date and behind the times. *The secret lies in your total design.*

The List to Consider

(1) What size should our book be?
There are three popular sizes: 7¾" by 10½" _____ 8½" by 11" _____ and 9" by 12" _____

(2) What kind of "total look" do we want to achieve?
Quiet, conservative, dignified? _____ Bright, colorful, gay? _____ An attention-getter? _____ Traditional, school colors, mascot, etc.? _____ "Something different"? _____ "Something *a little* different"? _____ A complete change from last year? _____

(3) Since books are designed according to some sort of page plan, do we want a page plan that is filled with pictures and the necessary copy, with a trim, compact look? _____ or do we want a page that has considerable white space, with an open, airy look? _____
(Note: If the budget does not allow any more

pages than are actually needed, white space is a luxury that must be carefully considered.)

(4) As for type, do we want a generally light look in headline and body type? _____ or do we prefer bold headlines and a correspondingly heavier type?_____

Discuss the above questions and then briskly make your decisions, so you can begin work at once.

From this point on, *the staff must want to work on the book as a whole* instead of as a collection of parts that are likely to be unharmonious. This is necessary for *unity* and *rhythm* from page to page.

Actually, if the book is planned, and if the layout is worked out carefully by double spreads, there will be a flow from page to page as the reader peruses the completed volume.

Specifications First

As the above list suggests, we begin with actual measurements and specific statements regarding space and type so that we have a definite guide to follow. These are called *specifications* and serve the same purpose as a builder's specifications—that is, indication of what to do and EXACTLY how to do it. This is necessary to insure *consistency* and *unity.*

After the various decisions are made, and specifications are worked out, the adviser and editor should compile a guidebook with all this information gathered so that each staff member can have a copy at hand at all times.

The following example of a specifications sheet indicates what decisions have to be made early in designing your yearbook:

Designing a Yearbook—Specifications

(1) Size of book: 7¾″ by 10½″ _____ 8½″ by 11″ —— 9″ by 12″ _____

(2) Number of pages: _____

(3) Page layout method: 2 column _____ 3 column _____ other _____

(4) Page layout style: mosaic _____ geometric _____ fitted _____

(5) Page margins: gutter _____ top _____ outside _____ bottom _____

(6) Size of copy area: _____ Width of colmun _____

(7) Amount of equidistant spacing between all elements: _____

(8) Body type face _____ point _____ spaced _____ lines per vertical inch

(9) Theme copy type face _____ point _____ spaced _____ lines per vertical inch

(10) Caption type face _____ point _____ spaced _____ lines per vertical inch

(11) Headline type face _____ point _____

If measurements were given in inches, items (5), (6) and (7) would read thus:

(5) Page margins: gutter _____ top _____ outside _____ bottom _____

(6) Size of copy area: _____ Width of column _____

(7) Amount of equidistant spacing between all elements: _____

An Example

In order to show the care with which basic planning must be done, the following measurements have been worked out. It is necessary for measurements to be exact, and it is necessary for those working on layout to follow these exact measurements, since the pleasing effect of your finished layout is determined by the care put in on it.

Note: Let it be said again and again, however, that you do not need to be a slave to the basic plan. The plan is a guide. Layout affords opportunity for creativity by allowing deviation from the basic plan—*if you understand what you are doing.* That does not mean merely a random and careless disregard of detail.

For 7¾ by 10½ book on the 2-column plan: Total page is 7¾″ by 10½″. Margins: gutter—⅝″ . . . top—⅝″ . . . outside—⅞″ . . . bottom—1″. Equidistant spacing between all elements within the copy area—¼″.

Copy area is 6¼″ wide by 8¾″ deep.
Each of the 2 columns is 3″ wide.

Measured in picas, the total page is 46 picas wide by 63 picas deep.
Margins: gutter—3 picas . . . top—4 picas . . . outside—5 picas . . . bottom—6 picas.
Equidistant spacing between all elements within the copy area—2 picas.
Each of the 2 columns is 18 picas wide.
Copy area is 38 picas wide by 53 picas deep.

For 7¾ by 10½ book on the 3-column plan:
Total page is 7¾″ by 10½″.
Margins: gutter—¼″ . . . top—½″ . . . outside—½″ . . . bottom—½″.
Equidistant spacing between all elements within the copy area—¼″.
Copy area is 7″ wide by 9½″ deep.
Each of the 3 columns is 13 picas wide.

However, for an airier look, measure by picas:
Total page is 46 picas wide by 63 picas deep.
Margins: gutter—2 picas . . . top—4 picas . . . outside—5 picas . . . bottom—6 picas.
Equidistant spacing 1½ picas between all elements within the copy area.
Copy area is 39 picas wide by 53 picas deep.
Each of the 3 columns is 12 picas wide.

For an 8½ by 11 book on the 2-column plan:
Total page is 8½″ by 11″.
Margins: gutter—⅝″ . . . top—⁶⁄₈″ . . . outside—⅞″ . . . bottom—1″.
Equidistant spacing between all elements within the copy area—¼″.
Copy area is 7″ wide by 9¼″ deep.
Each of the 2 colums is 3⅜″ wide.

Measured in picas, the total page is 51 picas wide by 66 picas deep.
Margins: gutter—4 picas . . . top—5 picas . . . outside—5 picas . . . bottom—6 picas.
Equidistant spacing between all elements within the copy area—2 picas.
Copy area is 42 picas wide by 55 picas deep.
Each of the 2 columns is 20 picas wide.

For an 8½ by 11 book on the 3-column plan:
Total page is 8½″ by 11″.
Margins: gutter—⅜″ . . . top—⁶⁄₈″ . . . outside—⅞″ . . . bottom—1″.
Equidistant spacing between all elements within the copy area—¼″.
Copy area is 7¼″ wide by 9¼″ deep.
Each of the 3 columns is 2¼″ wide.

Measured in picas, the total page is 51 picas wide by 66 picas deep.
Margins: gutter—3 picas . . . top—5 picas . . . outside—6 picas . . . bottom—7 picas.
Equidistant spacing between all elements within the copy area—1½ picas.
Copy area is 42 picas wide by 54 picas deep.
Each of the 3 columns is 13 picas wide.

For a 9 by 12 book on the 2-column plan:
Total page is 9″ by 12″.
Margins: gutter—⅝″ . . . top—⁶⁄₈″ . . . outside—⅞″ . . . bottom—1″.
Equidistant spacing between all elements within the copy area—¼″.
Copy area is 7½″ wide by 10¼″ deep.
Each of the 2 columns is 3⅝″ wide.

Measured in picas, the total page is 54 picas wide by 72 picas deep.
Margins: gutter—3 picas . . . top—4 picas . . . outside—5 picas . . . bottom—6 picas.
Equidistant spacing between all elements within the copy area—2 picas.
Copy area is 46 picas wide by 62 picas deep.
Each of the 2 columns is 22 picas wide.

For a 9 by 12 book on the 3-column plan:
Total page is 9″ by 12″.
Margins: gutter—⅝″ . . . top—⁶⁄₈″ . . . outside—⅞″ . . . bottom—1″.
Equidistant spacing between all elements within the copy area—⅜″.
Copy area is 7½″ wide by 10¼″ deep.

Each of the 3 columns is 2¼″ wide.

Measured in picas, the total page is 54 picas wide by 72 picas deep.

Margins: gutter—3 picas . . . top—4 picas . . . outside—6 picas . . . bottom—6 picas.

Equidistant spacing between all elements within the copy area—1½ picas.

Copy area is 45 picas wide by 62 picas deep.

Each of the 3 columns is 14 picas wide.

Use of Space

The trend is now toward lighter and airier pages, so you will be seeing more and more use of space for special effect. As one professional layout consultant puts it, "Pages have an airier look these days, with less crowding."

That airy look, incidentally, is usually gained by putting the space at the corners. *It does not mean just any space, just anywhere.*

Outer margins have been planned to afford as much room as possible for columns of suitable width—but if you want to shift a little, you can add space to the outside margin. However, do not increase the gutter margin.

The gutter margin is generally being decreased instead of widened in order to hold the two pages of the double spread together. With many pictures crossing the gutter and so much effort to tie facing pages together, this is logical.

All planning now is being done by double spreads. Planning by double spreads means planning facing pages at one time, no matter how many separate people or organizations you have to cover there.

For example, if you have four clubs to be covered on two facing pages, then plan the coverage and layout for all four at the same time. Other-

PLANNING LADDER

		1	Title page	athletics	48	49 and intramurals
opening	2	3	section	"	50	51 "
"	4	5	"	"	52	53 "
Activities	6	7	Division	"	54	55 "
Student	8	9	life	"	56	57 "
"	10	11	"	"	58	59 "
"	12	13	"	Student Body	60	61 Division
"	14	15	"	seniors	62	63 including
clubs	16	17	and organizations	"	64	65 royalty, features, and
"	18	19	"	"	66	67 favorites
"	20	21	"	"	68	69 "
"	22	23	"	"	70	71 "
"	24	25	"	"	72	73 "
"	26	27	"	"	74	75 "
"	28	29	"	juniors	76	77 "
academic	30	31	including	"	78	79 "
faculty	32	33	and administration	"	80	81 "
"	34	35	"	"	82	83 "
"	36	37	"	sophomores	84	85 "
"	38	39	"	"	86	87 "
"	40	41	"	"	88	89 "
"	42	43	"	"	90	91 "
"	44	45	"	index	92	93 index
athletics	46	47	and intramurals	index	94	95 closing word
				blank	96	

The planning ladder is a means of seeing your book as a whole. In this example, the paging for the various sections is based on a study of averages in yearbooks across the country. Advertising, if included, would be additional.

wise, your pages will looked pieced together, like a so-called crazy quilt, or an old-fashioned picture album.

By thinking ahead, you can solve all those problems of coordination. That is the reason for such preplanning as working out your planning ladder well in advance of time to take the pictures.

(The planning ladder is a listing of page numbers by facing pages—thus: p. 1, pp. 2–3, pp. 4–5, pp. 6–7 and so forth. By drawing a vertical line down a ruled sheet of paper, you can easily list the paging for your entire book. Thus you have an overall view and can indicate sections by brackets. Note that odd numbers are righthand pages.)

More on Margins

Some staffs are experimenting with much wider margins. (This does not include the equidistant spacing between all elements within the copy area.) Formal guidelines in book making have long included a note that page margins should be wide enough to frame the reading matter on the page with enough white space that the reader is attracted to the page.

They specify that the widest margin be at the bottom of the page, the next widest at the outside, the next at the top and the narrowest at the gutter. In the case of textbooks, for example, each page is considered a separate unit, with no consideration given to the double spread, since the reader of text materials covers only one page at a time.

In this visual-minded age, however, with many magazines, brochures, and the like making extensive use of pictures, the page is no longer a separate unit. It is now a part of the total spread the viewer sees. For that reason, the term "lookership" is worth remembering. Our reader is also a "looker" and we are presenting material for readership AND lookership.

In another sense we have a twofold purpose: (1) to keep the reader on the spread until he has covered it fully and (2) to encourage him to turn the page to read more of the book. Knowing that margins can contribute to achieving those purposes, today's layout man considers them thoughtfully.

The bottom margin should generally be wider than the top, experts say, because the eye tends to think the content is going to drop off the page. If the top and bottom margins are the same width, the reader tends to think the bottom is narrower.

To remember about space: Space in yearbooks is so precious—and so expensive—that we need to make the best possible use of it. That is, don't experiment with extra wide margins—or even large expanses of white space for special effect—unless the space is worth more than what you could put into it.

No Instant Success

In yearbook layout there is no such thing as instant success, for success comes only with consistently fitting pieces into a master plan with painstaking care.

The creativity that we talk about and want to encourage comes in the formulating of that master plan. The time to think with imagination is the time when you are thinking pattern—thinking about *how to get the total idea of the total desired effect down in lines and figures so that the rest of the staff can make it come true.*

Like a house plan.

The architect does the creative thinking. He makes it original, if it is going to be original. Not the builder. The builder follows the plan. That's why the staff—as a whole and as a collection of individuals—must understand the total plan of the book and be agreed on how to produce the parts so that the total effect can come to pass.

Helpful Checklist

The surest way to produce your dream book—and produce it on time—is to adopt basic plans that have built-in foolproof measures, no pitfalls for unaware staffers, no gimmicks that can go wrong.

Check these points when making initial decisions:

_____(1) Is this plan easy to follow, even for beginners?

_____(2) Is it a plan easy to revise when necessary? (Even with the most careful planning, revision may be required if your coverage needs are altered or if your pictures do not turn out as expected.)

_____(3) Is it a plan easy to modify to ensure variety?

_____(4) Is it really basic, for structural strength and pleasing effect?

_____(5) Is it a simple, classic plan, always a good choice?

_____(6) Is it a plan that readers consistently like, that has proved its worth?

Note: In yearbook design, an understanding of the principles covered in general art courses is helpful.

CHAPTER **IV**

CHOOSE COLUMN PLAN AND LAYOUT STYLE

With all of the preliminary planning completed and your specifications worked out, you are ready for guiding principles to help you plan both coverage and display.

Your yearbook should be the story of the school year, told as fully and as accurately as you can do it—brightened with your interpretation of the events as to their significance for all concerned.

By looking at your yearbook, an outsider should be able to gain a summary idea of what sort of year it was at your school.

Many staffs, unfortunately, limit themselves to only partial coverage of the school year. If, for instance, you devote page after page to beauties and royalty and favorites, and cover none of the classroom pictures that could be a part of your book, then the reader would have reason to believe that nothing is considered significant at your school except beauties and royalty and favorites.

If you put only four seniors to a page and then group all the fifty children in the first grade in a picture three inches deep, even your reader will know that you are suffering "multigrande senioritis."

If you run nothing but portraits and group pictures, then it will be obvious to everyone that you did not care to show that many interesting things went on in your school in which the student body could be pictured. Those who say that nothing interesting goes on in the classroom are merely playing ostrich and hiding their heads in mug shots, so to speak.

If you make the effort to cover the campus from day to day, looking for activity in the class-

room, you can get as many pictures as you can use. Remember: *Where there are people, there is action—and where there is action, there is reaction.* The key is the action.

This is what gives your layout sparkle—because these are the pictures that have special meaning and therefore offer opportunity for special display. An example is the close-up, showing some emotion that is really worth playing up, running as a dominant picture on a spread. (In the classroom coverage, it might be a picture of the class as the teacher returns exam papers. One jubilant student may thrust his paper toward his neighbor with a wink that says, "I made an A!")

(To repeat: The subject of coverage and picture content is frequently mentioned in this work because the very nature of layout assumes the presence of something to display. Many staffs put out page after page of dullness and dreariness because they have no pictures except portraits or groups or trite poses. To get meaningful pictures requires effort—and effort goes hand in hand with ideas.)

Column Plan

In connection with specifications and total design, we continually use the term "column plan." It is a basic term, like page, or double spread, or copy block.

Briefly it is this: The copy area on a page is divided evenly into vertical spaces so copy blocks, pictures, and even bodies of white space will be of fixed width. That fixed width (1) assures an overall appearance of neatness and orderliness,

(2) makes the setting of copy uniform and therefore avoids possible problems, and (3) allows for harmonious relationships in double- and triple-column arrangements.

In yearbooks both the two-column and the three-column plans are suitable. A popular variation is the five-column plan, which considers the entire double spread as a page. Other variations can be worked out. However, for beginners either the two-column or the three-column is best, since any experimenting can then be done with using the half column. It is correct on both the two-column and the three-column to divide a column vertically, if you like, and also to cross the gutter in order to gain width. Thus many variations are possible.

The choice of column plan is a matter of taste. It is related to your concept of your total design. The column plan is a guide to aid you in arranging your pictures and words in keeping with your layout style.

Layout Style

An understanding of style in general will help the beginner see what is meant here regarding the yearbook. We use the word to express an idea that is not too easy to define. But we understand one another when we say, "She wears her clothes with style," or "I like the style of this writer," or "That singer has style." It has to do with certain effects achieved.

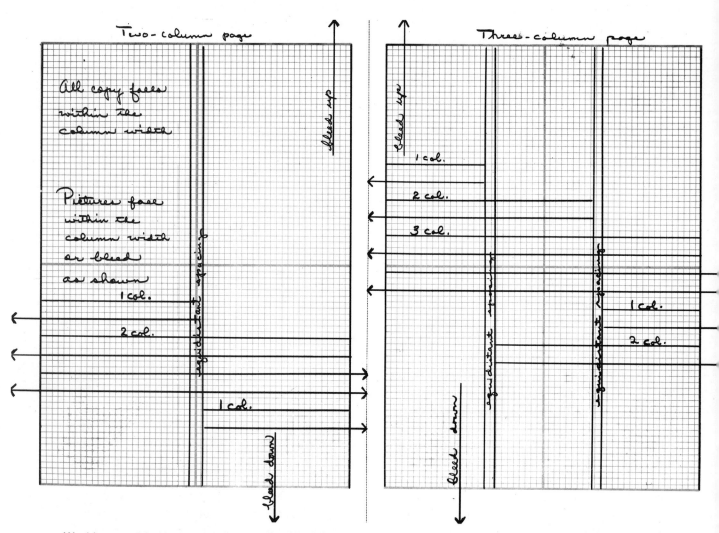

Working out this kind of detailed guide will help you as a quick reference for measurements and will ensure consistency. Post this guide where all who are working on layout can see it easily. These examples are based on the dimensions given in the sample specification sheet for a 7¾ by 10½ book.

Although there is much to know, the beginner in yearbook work can assume his earliest responsibilities with confidence if he understands three general styles in layout: mosaic, geometric, fitted.

To repeat: "certain effects achieved"—mosaic effect, geometric effect, fitted effect.

In studying other yearbooks, you will find that sometimes a book is planned so that two of those styles are combined to afford a change of pace. Such combinations would be a geometric or mosaic style for the opening section in a fitted-page book, or perhaps mosaic pages for features and special effect in a book that uses geometric throughout. Or an opening section in geometric for a mosaic basic design. Or geometric dividers and special pages in a mosaic book, or vice versa.

HOWEVER, a beginner should be careful about combinations. Keep your layouts consistent, harmonious, compatible. The secret: *Avoid too much variety.* If you stay as close as possible to one style, you will achieve unity in your completed book.

Mosaic Style

Briefly defined, mosaic layout is one in which a pleasing effect is created by grouping pictures of various sizes and shapes around a dominant picture. They are clustered at the gutter so the deepest part of the design formed by the pictures is at

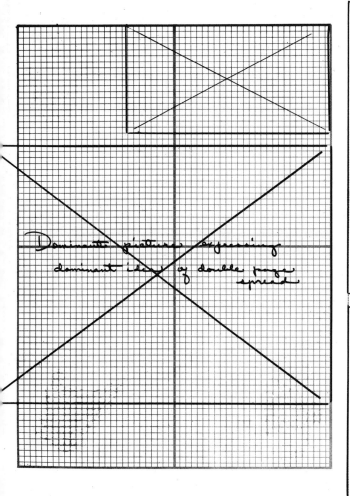

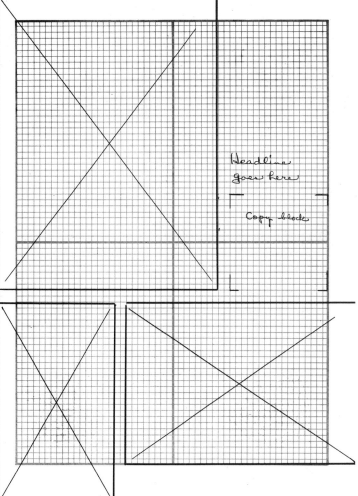

Mosaic layout is built around a dominant picture that expresses the dominant idea of the double page spread. Smaller pictures are arranged to guide the reader around the spread with supporting ideas. Copy may be justified or unjustified. (Note that this is designed on a two-column page plan.)

the gutter. The corners are open. It has been described as an "oval makeup." That is, the entire grouping is oval-shaped, either a horizontal oval, which would extend wide across the double spread, or a vertical oval, which would be deep at the gutter and then not so wide at the sides. In both the horizontal and vertical ovals, the design would be deepest at the gutter.

In mosaic style, it is important to have a large dominant picture to begin with. One difficulty is that sometimes it is hard to get a dominant picture in both size and quality that is also dominant in meaning. Smaller pictures are arranged around the dominant picture so that the reader is guided to see every picture on the spread.

The dominant picture may be either a horizontal, a vertical, or a square. Remember: Square shapes are not as pleasing to the viewer as are horizontal and vertical shapes, so give thought to careful cropping before using many squares. Make as many shapes rectangular as possible. Some very shallow horizontals and some very narrow verticals will give your layouts variety and sparkle.

About cropping: Study your picture carefully before cropping so that if possible the meaning of the picture is enhanced by what you decide to eliminate. Cropping should be determined by center of interest, eye direction, proper framing, and amount of background or setting needed to

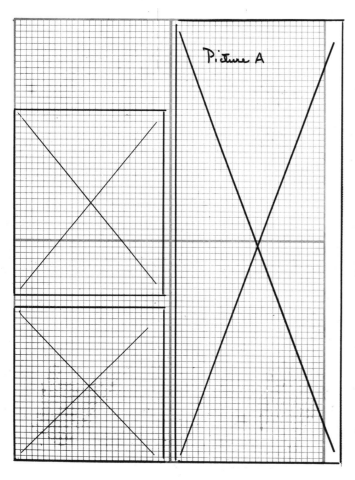
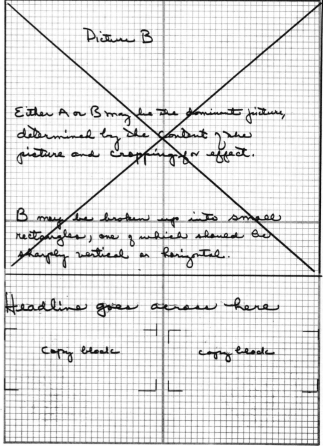

In geometric layout—either modular or mondrian—the columns form vertical spaces. Horizontal lines drawn across the double page spread then define rectangles that are combined for picture and copy areas. Space usually falls to the outside, though not necessarily so. Copy may fall to the outside or fill an inside block that adjoins an outer margin.

tell the story properly. A picture is not necessarily a vertical, for example, just because it is printed on a rectangular piece of paper that you can stand on one end.

In mosaic layout, pictures may bleed if the meaning of the picture or the shape of it is enhanced by running off the edge of the page. Remember: Bleed only for effect. The trend now is toward less bleeding. With less bleeding, those pictures that do bleed are more effective.

In all styles of layout, you are guided by your column plan. Thus, in arranging a mosaic spread, you know what widths your pictures may be. It is helpful to make a diagram giving all the possible picture widths for you to glance at as you plan

for enlargement or reduction after the proper cropping.

The mosaic layout has been defined as the pinwheel approach, since the eye must be guided from the first picture around the design to the last. (By design, we mean the total pattern, not anything like a symbol or a figure that would be recognizable. In fact, if the pictures as a group form any kind of recognizable shape, the layout is a failure.)

In mosaic layout, the gutter margin is minimized. Usually the dominant picture crosses the gutter. If it does not, then smaller pictures bleed into the gutter in an effort to hold the entire cluster together with no attention called to gutter

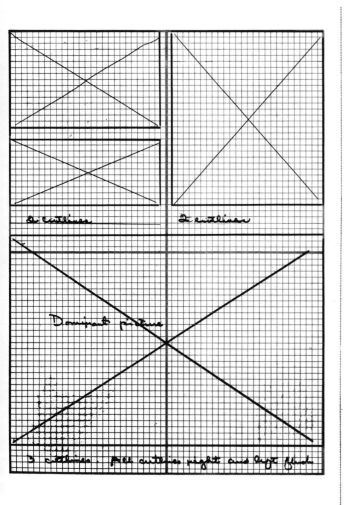 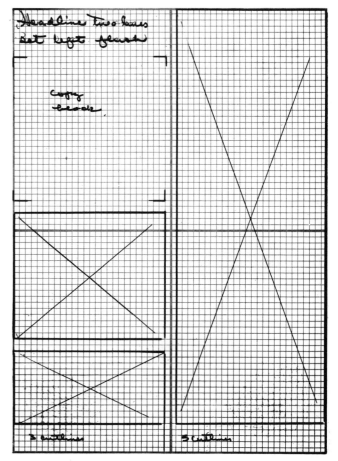

This fitted page layout is characterized by a dominant picture supported by other pictures and copy arranged to fill the entire body page. This design gains an open look with copy in column three on a

four-column double page spread. Cutlines trimly tailored along the bottom margin and cutlines separating pictures within the body page also help create an airy appearance.

space. However, do not bleed into the gutter from both the right-hand and left-hand pages, as this causes confusion and spoils the effect of both pictures.

Captions, headlines, and copy are kept to the outside of the picture grouping. Frequently the captions are clustered, perhaps in one block, perhaps in two or three. Nothing violates the equidistant spacing between the elements.

One of the secrets of successful mosaic layout is in the ability to achieve pleasing balance. That means you need to have sufficient pictures to choose from so that you can select those with suitable tone, density, and shape—and then you must be able to arrange them properly. If you study magazine layouts, especially the advertising designed by professional artists, you can develop an eye for design.

Geometric Style

Geometric layout styles are increasingly popular with yearbook staffs who are willing to study the principles and then give care to the preparation of the spreads. The styles include modular and mondrian approaches to layout. As in mosaic, space is generally to the outside of the grouped pictures, as are also captions and copy.

In modular layout, you begin by dividing your double spread so that you have one major rectangle. It may be either horizontal or vertical. After you have cropped your pictures, so that you know what shapes you have, you arrange them and your copy and captions to fill the rectangle. Obviously, as in the mosaic, you must have a variety of pictures to choose from, including not only variety in shape but in tone, in composition, in possibility for enlargement, and the like.

The modular style requires large dominant pictures to be effective. Whereas in the mosaic, a group of small pictures can be arranged to balance a dominant picture, in modular your layout will fail if you have too many small pictures or if they are too much alike in content. Variety and contrast in size, shape, tone, density, and composition are required.

Also as in mosaic, the column widths must be observed, equidistant spacing must be observed, and no captions should fall between the pictures.

Horizontal lines to determine your initial rec-

tangle may be placed wherever you like. Remember: White space is an element of layout like pictures and type and can be used to balance pictures and type. Be sure all your white space is to the outside of your pictures. An exception is the use of a block of white space to balance pictures or type.

A related layout style is known as the isolated element—a style used to draw attention to a certain picture by pulling it away from the remainder of the group. The isolated element is set off from the other pictures by a frame of white space. The isolated element may bleed.

Mondrian layout is a style named for the Dutch painter Pieter Mondriaan, whose paintings have influenced contemporary design in all areas in which geometric patterns are used, from magazine format to linoleum floors.

To work out an arrangement in mondrian style, you begin with establishing horizontal and vertical lines that will define the areas in which you will place pictures and type. The vertical lines, as in all styles, are framed by the columns. The horizontals are placed wherever you need them, as determined by the shape and size of your pictures after you have cropped them suitably and have them proportioned. Here again it is necessary to have large pictures. Also, copy and white space fall to the outside of the picture groupings. Captions are clustered, since the equidistant spacing between elements is not violated.

In a mondrian layout, pictures may bleed if necessary, and pictures may take up as many as necessary of the rectangles created by the intersecting horizontal and vertical lines.

Fitted Style

A third kind of layout has been used successfully for a long time—the fitted page. The effectiveness of this style lies in the care with which all the elements on the page are fitted together to meet all the requirements of the structural principles of basic design.

Fitted layout requires precision in cropping pictures and in fitting copy. To arrange a double spread according to the fitted-page style, you follow many of the same steps as in mosaic and geometric.

Beginning with a dominant picture, which may

be displayed anywhere on the spread, you add other pictures and type, observing equidistant spacing, so that you meet every margin all the way on every side. That means there is no extra white space whatsoever.

At the gutter you may bleed on the left-hand or the right-hand page in order to minimize the width of the gutter margin and make the spread look more unified. Or you may begin by crossing the gutter with your dominant picture. Captions may fall between the pictures, either above or below.

Note: Extreme care must be taken to keep zigzags from occurring across the spread. That means you must choose pictures of widely varying sizes, especially some narrow verticals and some shallow horizontals. Pictures may be of any depth. However, avoid breaking a page across the middle. Generally it is best to divide a page horizontally by thirds or by fifths.

The fitted layout is especially suitable—and valuable—if you must make every inch of space count. It has been a longtime favorite.

One advantage that gives this style variety and relief from book after book of mosaic and geometric is the use of body copy between pictures, giving prominence to pictures and an open look to the page.

Preplanning Suggested

Whatever your layout style, it will be a help to you to use pieces of colored paper—medium gray is a good choice—as a guide in arranging your pictures. After marking your column lines and drawing in your horizontals, cut the paper the size of the pictures you intend to use and then experiment with the placement.

Since the pictures will have a quality the colored paper does not have, be mindful of the horizontal and vertical lines in the pictures, as well as of tone and density. The eye will follow an imaginary line as quickly as a drawn line.

It will also help if you spread your pictures on a table before deciding on how to place them, in order to see how the eye follows from one to another. Try a number of arrangements in order to find the pattern that seems most effective. If you cannot get your prints in time to do this, try cutting from magazines pictures similar to those

you will use and experiment with them before you draw the final layout.

Helpful Guidelines

(1) Do not run too many close-cropped pictures side by side. Strive for variety in picture content.

(2) Avoid crowding. Give your pages some space, either white space, or some background (suitable, of course) in the pictures.

(3) Always follow the column lines. An exception occasionally is allowable—if planned to enhance the layout, but *never just at random*.

(4) Avoid "zigzags and little joggles." Arrange the pictures and type so that the content of the page seems to fall into large, easily defined blocks.

(5) Faithfully heed the old slogan, "Line something up with something." That will help you establish strong horizontals, which will give your spreads a pleasing effect. The "something" may be a line that the eye can follow, or it may be an imaginary line.

(6) Vary your strong horizontals with a narrow vertical or a dominant vertical for a quick change of pace.

(7) Generally keep the number of elements per spread to about six, or fewer. It will help avoid the cluttered look. "Element" includes copy. It also includes picture units. (A picture unit is a group of small pictures related in meaning and held together by spacing narrower than the equidistant spacing used on the spread.)

(8) Check carefully to see that you use a wide variety of picture sizes from page to page, in order to avoid monotony.

(9) See that every page includes type—generally body or theme copy, headlines, and captions. There is a trend now toward no headline on many spreads. *Note:* To omit a headline means to overlook an important way (1) to gain the reader's attention by directly speaking to him in large type and (2) to achieve variety and contrast on the spread.

(10) Check to see that every spread has a dominant element. It is usually a picture, which should be dominant in meaning for the spread as well as in quality and interest.

VARSITY BASKETBALL TEAM—Front Row: Raymond O'Connell, John Thomas, Randy Rice, Richard Kometic, Terry Damweber. **Second Row:** Dennis Finnegan, Dennis Sharkazy, Scott Oberholtzer, Dennis Podorsky, Frank Szoke. **Third Row:** Dale Poe, assistant coach; Dreux Daumer, Bruce Hetrich, Patrick Rothdeutsch, Joseph Epstein, Frederick Kimock, head coach.

In the game against Palmerton, Zephyrs Pat Rothdeutsch and Dennis Podorsky battle for a rebound with Blue Bombers Mike Samok and Joseph Valo on Whitehall's home court. Whitehall won 56—40.

League title held steady
Tribute to basketball team
Unusual skill

Varsity Cagers Capture First Crown in 8 Years

Capturing its first Lehigh Valley League basket-ball title since 1959, Whitehall whipped Stroudsburg, 68—54, in Muhlenberg's Memorial Hall.

Coach Frederick Kimock's cagers had a few exciting moments at the start of the fourth quarter of the play-off game when Stroudsburg, trailing 47—39, reeled off seven straight points to move within one with 6:15 to play. Whitehall settled the issue with 2:22 remaining when Dennis Podorsky, intentionally fouled while making a layup, added two free throws. Patrick Rothdeutsch led the scoring and rebounding for the Zephyrs with 21 points and 14 rebounds. Stroudsburg led only three times in the game—at 2—0, 26—25, and 28—27.

Mahanoy Area downed the Zephyrs, 61—53, to cancel Whitehall's bid for the District XI crown. Clarence Mack led the Golden Bears with 22 points.

In league play Raymond O'Connell sank three clutch free throws in the final 26 seconds ensuring the Zephyrs' victory over Stroudsburg, 70—68, to tie for second half honors. Frank Szoke and Podorsky led the way with 17 points each and Rothdeutsch followed with 16. Stroudsburg's Hal Watson was high scorer with 25.

The Zephyrs, who closed the season with a 14—1 league record and 19—4 overall slate, placed Roth-deutsch, first team; Szoke and John Thomas, second team; and Podorsky and Randy Rice, honorable mention; on the Lehigh Valley All-Star teams.

Key defensive player Randy Rice tops the ball from an unidentified William Allen cager as Canary Vic Berliant, 40, watches. Allen nipped the stubborn Zephyrs in an exhibition game, 68—54, behind Berliant's 17 points.

This version of geometric approach to layout (from *The Whitehall,* Whitehall High School, Hokendauqua, Pennsylvania) and reversal of pattern rely on strong dominant pictures for effect, enhanced by the variety in the other pictures and thoughtful cropping. Blocks of moderately light type add contrast. These pages are good examples of careful planning to guide the reader by eye direction. Most staffs feel that they cannot afford to use this much white space for general coverage throughout the book, so reverse this kind of design for special effects occasionally.

Endurance and strength
Track team ends strenuous year
Untiring efforts

Senior Thinclad Captures 7th Place in State Finals

After taking first place in the mile event in the Lehigh Valley League track meet at Emmaus, senior Joseph Yudt became eligible for participation in the District XI tournament which led him to state finals. Yudt, who received the Zephyr award in track, placed seventh in the two-mile event in state finals at Pennsylvania State University.

New coach H. Richard Hamilton's thinclads posted a 2—5 league record at the end of the season occupying sixth place in league standing.

Visiting Bombers crushed the Zephs, 60—35, taking all the field events. Peter Nush and Frank Groller picked up sweeps in the 220 and 100, respectively.

Host Whitehall trounced Stroudsburg, 60—35, as Yudt set a school record of 4:44 in the mile run.

Parkland's Jim Ott broke a school record in the Trojans' defeat of the Zephs, 68—22. Ott, a District XI cross-country champion, won the mile event in 4:29.4. Parkland won nine of the 10 events with Nush gaining Whitehall's only first by winning the 220.

Yudt was a double winner for the Zephyrs in their tight 52—43 win over Catasauqua taking the 880 and the mile. Ed Leggett turned in a triple-win performance for the Rough Riders, capturing firsts in three field events—the long jump, high jump, and pole vault.

In the last league meet of the season Northampton nipped the Zephs, 49—46. Double winner Frank Groller placed first in both the 100 and 220.

Leaping as far as possible Charles Malinauskas takes third place in the broad jump during the Catasauqua track meet. The Zephyr thinclads defeated the Rough Riders, 52—43, in the first meet of the season.

TRACK TEAM—Front Row: James Stellar, Thomas Kubinsky, Barry Gogel, Richard Yudt, Richard Lerch, Neil Marushak, Joseph McDonald, Russell Oplinger. **Second Row:** Todd Kanishock, James Potrako, Joseph Yudt, co-captain; Steve Gober, Barry Sheets, Gary Dornblaser, Denton Stettler, James Kerin, Gregory Poffenbarger. **Third Row:** Thomas Lerch, manager; Peter Nush, captain; Daniel Hartzell, Daniel Haines, John Kubinsky, Robert Koval, co-captain; Richard Deutsch, James Fenstermaker, Richard Kometic. **Fourth Row:** Morgan Jones, coach; William Gross, John Miller, Michael Harakal, Keith Mosser, Paul Malinauskas, Roger Derr, Dale Parker, Frank Groller, David Vandegrift, H. Richard Hamilton, coach.

High jumper James Duran hurdles the bar during the meet with the Rough Riders. Catasauqua's Edward Leggett took first in this event and also won the long jump and pole vault for a triple win performance.

"ARMS AND THE MAN" / Satire

A chocolate cream soldier and his young counterpart introduced conflict between two ideas of war in South's winter drama, "Arms and the Man." The play, by George Bernard Shaw, shoots down the romantic image of war through two soldiers, Sergius (Steve Abbott), and Bluntschli (Dave White).

Shaw's satire opens when Bluntschli, the epitome of a poor soldier, seeks refuge in the home of an ostentatiously wealthy family, the Petkoffs. Bluntschli is aided by Raina (Devona Legler), the Petkoff's naive daughter who is engaged to Sergius, the typical romantic war hero. Senior

Penn Wallace took the role of Major Petkoff who thought that war was just a game. His wife Katherine, played by junior Megan O'Connor, was more hypocritical while strictly guided by her social class. Also a part of the comedy were Jeff Salisbury, the proper Petkoff butler, Judy Gravos, the proud Petkoff maid, and Am Smith, a Russian soldier.

Director Kim Brewster called the anti-war satire "timely and applicable" and referred to the play as "drama which is pertinent today and which presents a challenge to both audience and actor." Lavish sets designed by technical director Dave Sherman aided the cast in achieving the Victorian atmosphere which prevailed in the February production.

The use of one pattern with near reversals (these from *The Eugenean,* South Eugene High School, Eugene, Oregon) is popular with many staffs, since it ensures consistency from page to page. These spreads illustrate the geometric approach to design, with emphasis on prominent horizontal and vertical pictures. Note the unusual kind of heading on these pages. The light type helps create an airy look for the layout.

GUIDE THE WAY / Leaders

In a year of struggle for identity and peaceful co-existence, the job of the school leaders, that of running a smooth student government, was a challenge. To meet the demands of a nearly 1550 enrollment, yet compromise with the administration and the community, communication became the important goal.

In early November, President Dave Ouellette began with an historical all-student assembly, without faculty attendance. Controversial topics were the dress code, smoking in the parking lot, and racial prejudice. After nearly three hours of open discussion, students found a new understanding. Few opinions were changed yet communication was achieved and, to the surprise of some, there was even a degree of consent.

An awareness of responsibility and an active interest in all school activities was important. Recognizing South's shrinking funds, Secretary Janet Newman and Co-Auditor Kathy Martin conducted a study on budgets at other Eugene high schools to discover new means of making money. Historian Ann Henderson, in addition to compiling the scrapbook, maintained the school news bulletin board in the office. The task of planning and co-ordinating the annual Charity Drive belonged to Vice-President John Pennington. Student Manager Dave Husk, who sold a record number of season tickets for football and basketball, was also involved in setting up assemblies during the year.

Key clubbers donate time to community

After completing 528 man-hours of work painting Broad Ripple Park's train the "old 587" last summer, Key Club members started the school year off with a bang by sponsoring the second annual Key Club Dance-After-The-First-Football-Game.

Contributing to the school by helping Orange Aid's "Stash the Trash" campaign, Key Club also served the community in projects ranging from testing hamburgers for Walker Research to doing recreational work at an inner-city school on Saturday afternoons.

Sponsored by the Northside Kiwanis Club, Key Club participated in District and State workshops. Ripple senior Hudson Cooney was elected Lt. Governor of the fourth district.

Enthusiastic supporters of the basketball team, Key Club officers Mark MacLucas, Brian Blair, Dave Johnson, Pat Barnes, and John Owen prepare a victory hoop.

Student Council—BACK ROW: Jay Cohen, Mark Stephens, Blair Austin, Ben McCormick, John Hudson Cooney, Clyde Lieberman, Steve Shuel, Bill Cordell, Dave Johnson, Brian Welch, Neil Baker, Bill Silvey, Phil Whistler, Mark MacLucas. SECOND ROW: Kate Mullane, Marilyn Myers, Ann Cooney, Laurie Gustafson, Susan Peck, Jody Brafford, Mary Jo van het Erve, Jane Sellery, Dori Patterson, Peggy Weber, Betsy Marsh, Janet Negley, Alicia Hill. FRONT ROW: Julie Houk, Cheryl Pierson, Holly Hughes, Mary Carnell, Dee Dee Frazin, Marcia Miles, Susie Grills, Ann Chivington, Beth Wood, Janet Griffin, Kathy Wilson, Linda Culclasure. Eight new freshman members were selected in November to represent the freshman class.

Key Club—BACK ROW: John Hudson Cooney, Neil Baker, Gary Larson, Brian Welch, Paul Dryden, Jeff Stevens, David Johnson, Bill Cordell, Al Baumgart, Tom Hougham, Todd Sammons, Clyde Lieberman. THIRD ROW: Gary Carlson, John Owen, Blair Austin, Phil Whistler, Pat Barnes, Bruce Paltman, David King, Dan Morris, Dave Lancaster, Jim Erwin, Ben McCormick. SECOND ROW: Brian Blair, Steve Daily, Ed Guion, Russell Rice, Mark MacLucas, John Chivington, Larry Lett, Jim Jansen, Rick Turney, Dave Carr. FRONT ROW: Jay Cohen, Bill Cooper, Dan Evard, Dan Goldstein, Mark Walsh, Gary Swim, Larry Minnix, Jack Keene, Stan Peters, Mr. Warren Jackson. Members are selected on the basis of leadership, scholarship, and citizenship.

Orange Aid urges pupils to 'stash the trash'

Intensive "Stash the Trash" campaigning went into full swing when members of Orange Aid, Ripple's oldest organization, donned badges and exhibited posters urging students to have school pride and to help keep Broad Ripple clean.

Keeping with tradition, Orange Aid sponsored the Big-Little Sister program, Christmas caroled at the Harris Sanitorium, and operated the newly built used bookstore.

Bright balloons and colorful backdrops set the stage for the OA style show, "Up, Up, and Away."

Striving to better the relationship between pupils at Broad Ripple, Student Council gave the starting boost to a Human Relations Forum.

A newly formed Agenda Committee increased the efficiency of the council and informed the student body of the council's activities.

Members sold AFS tags on the first annual AFS Tag Day and at the APT Carnival to raise funds to support the AFS program.

Two picnics, a Christmas progressive dinner, and a dance sparked the Student Council's social season.

Selling used books is "old hat" to OA officers Betsy Marsh, Pam Retterer, Judy Barnes, Ann Chivington, and Dee Dee Frazin as they plan their main project.

These fitted page designs (from *The Riparian,* Broad Ripple High School, Indianapolis, Indiana) follow the long-favored arrangement of all elements to fill the entire body page. With type between the pictures, the pages have an open appearance, and each picture thus framed by type or space draws attention. This plan allows opportunity for extensive use of shallow horizontal pictures and both narrow and chunky verticals. The heavy headline type and rather heavy body type give the spread a bold look.

Election year enlivens facts for students

The '68 campaign fever and election provided a view of governmental clockwork in action for Social Studies students. U.S. History and Government classes recorded the important issues and events of the campaign and analyzed the results in term papers and scrapbooks. Complying with Indiana state laws, government students taped a series of speeches on election processes and presented them to the student body over the P.A. system.

During the spring semester, an experimental sociology course was offered to junior and senior students. The purpose of this new course was to develop a better understanding of human relationships and to prepare students for more effective participation in all aspects of society. The course covered such problems as race relations, the population explosion, urban development, and adolescent rebellion, better known as the generation gap.

In preparation for the hour lectures on the U.S. election, Carolyn Collins and Allen Harmon wait to record their speeches as Margaret Burres discusses party caucuses.

Judge Fran Murchie listens intently as plaintiff Gerry Thomas explains her case to attorney Ted Weesner. Clerk Susan Jansen records this verbal battle taking place in a realistic court session presented by a U.S. History II class.

Explaining forces to a seventh grade pupil at a neighboring grade school, Connie Kleindorfer participates in the Exploratory Teaching program.

Who's Who, Encyclopedia Britannica, and other detailed reference materials provide World History I students John Cheffy and Susan Spangler with background information on explorers for their reports on the "Age of Exploration."

For a class demonstration on logical thinking, Psychology pupil Mike Stanfill decides how to bring suspended strings together without moving his body.

CHAPTER V

MAKE FRIENDS WITH TYPE

In designing your layout plan, you need to know something about type.

Many yearbook staffs overlook the use of type —probably for two reasons. For one thing, they do not understand about the kinds of type and their possible uses. For another, they do not want to take the trouble to write copy and headlines. It is easier to say that no one reads copy than it is to write words that everyone will read with pleasure as part of the record of the year.

Most printing plants offer a variety of type faces, which they present in a type catalogue. You simply look at them, choose what you like, and then try to use that type effectively for the words you want to print.

Some years ago there were generally accepted practices about what kinds of type were suitable for certain purposes and what kinds of type could be used together in good taste.

The trend today is toward less restriction, the practice being simply to use "what is good taste." To beginners that is not much help, for they have no experience to aid them.

For that reason, the following suggestions are made to help the inexperienced make choices that will be in good taste and also easy to manage:

(1) Choose type faces that are generally popular because of easy readability and simple lines. (Face means the actual design of the letter.) Avoid fancy or novelty type faces.

(2) Choose only one or two type faces for all your type needs.

(3) You may combine serif and sans serif faces if you like, provided that you do not shift at random from one to another, as in body copy.

Favorite combinations include the following:

Garamond for body copy and captions, with Spartan for headlines.

Vogue for body copy and captions, with Bodoni for headlines.

Garamond for body copy with vogue for captions and news gothic for headlines.

Those, of course, are only a few of the faces available, but they show the combination of a serif face for body copy and sans serif for headlines, or a sans serif face for body copy and a serif face for headlines.

It is also correct to combine sans serif faces for captions, body copy, and the headlines—or serif faces for all your type needs.

The choice is somewhat complicated by the fact that no one printer has all faces. Therefore, you must see what faces are available with boldface or italics, since you will need either boldface or italics to use in your captions to afford contrast. Note: Boldface is a better choice than italics for opening words of captions as it affords more contrast in the small body of type. Either is correct.

A note about theme copy: Usually theme copy is set in a face different from the body copy—as, say, vogue, if the body copy is Garamond. That is to show the reader at a glance that there is a difference between your theme copy and your body copy. If not in a different face, then the theme copy can be set in italics.

Remember, however, that italic type is not easy to read in large blocks, so do not use italics for body copy or captions. In fact, it is better not to use italics for headlines.

The matter of type face is settled for those who have a standard contract with most printers, as a certain kind of type face is generally specified for body copy and captions in their standard books. A choice is usually possible in headline type.

Measuring Type

Printers use two words that every student journalist should know from the first. One is the word *pica*. A pica is approximately one sixth of an inch. For all practical purposes, picas and inches can be used interchangeably for short distances.

The pica is a horizontal measure, as for lines. A column would be three inches wide, or 18 picas wide. Rulers are available giving measurement in inches on one side and in picas on the other. They are very helpful in the yearbook staff room. Printers call them pica sticks or line gauges.

The second word in measurement is *point*. It is a term that printers use to designate the height of letters or lines. That is, it is a vertical measure. There are 72 points in an inch. There are 12 points in a pica.

In headline type for yearbooks, the most common size is 24 point, which means that the letters are designed on a block that is 24 points high, which would be two picas. Sometimes yearbook headlines are 30 point, occasionally 36 point.

In body copy, we generally use 10-point type, spaced a little between the lines so it is more readable. The amount of spacing is usually two points per line, so that each line that has letters designed on a 10-point block would thus require 12 points of space. Printers describe this by saying "copy set 10 on 12." Since each line occupies 12 points of vertical space, this would be one pica of vertical space, or one sixth of an inch. That makes measurement of copy blocks easy, as every six lines of copy in the correct width would occupy a vertical inch of space. Conversely, if we have an inch of space to fill with copy, we know that we need six lines of copy, obviously in the correct width.

Captions are usually set in 8 point, spaced slightly. This is said to be "copy set 8 on 9." That means we can count on having eight lines of caption copy per vertical inch.

Headline Style

The headline can be one of the most attractive elements on a spread if the staff wants to go to the trouble to do three things: (1) plan a suitable headline style—and follow it painstakingly, (2) write colorful statements based on specific ideas, and (3) place the headline on the layout in such a way that it attracts the reader.

Headline planning should be carefully con-

sidered so that adequate headings will be available for any display desired. The headings, as a group, are called the headline schedule. The headline schedule should be posted on the bulletin board, or a copy should be made for every staff member, perhaps to be included in the style book mentioned earlier. It should include not only an example of each headline to be used and the description, but also the count.

Height of the headline is given in points. The trend now is toward smaller and lighter headlines than heretofore. Now the 24-point headline is used generally, especially in all but the largest books—and even the largest books are now scaling down their sizes. Also, whereas headlines were formerly often double page, now they are generally only a page, or across a double spread, of perhaps a page and a column.

Two widths are adequate for most books on the two-column plan: (1) one line across two columns, usually measuring about 30 to 36 picas, depending on the size of the copy area, and (2) two lines across one column, each line averaging 15 to 18 picas, depending on the width of the column as determined by the size of the book.

For a three-column plan, headlines could be one, two, and three columns wide, or only two and three columns wide. On a three-column page, the one-column headlines are difficult to write since the space is limited.

If your total plan includes subdivision pages, you will want a 30-point or a 36-point headline, perhaps crossing the gutter. If crossing the gutter, come to within one fourth of an inch on each side.

Headline Count

Some staffs set up their own unit count for headlines by consulting with their printers. For beginners, however, it is adequate to use a unit count generally standard and therefore suitable for most kinds of type chosen for yearbooks. It is based on the average width of the lower case letters of the alphabet.

In working out your headline schedule, you need to know the average width of the lower case letters in the face and size of the type you chose. You have to consult your printer for that.

If you cannot find out what the average is, you

can estimate—but at best this is only an estimate. Should you be in that position, choose a face such as news gothic, selecting the 24 point for most of your headlines—or all of them. In that face, as in a number of others that are popular for headlines, the average width of the lower case letters approximates one pica. Therefore, if you want a line 18 picas wide, you simply use 18 as your unit count. Remember: this is only an estimate.

Example: Suppose in the copy for your academic section, you need a headline for the English Department. It is to be two lines, one column wide, not to exceed 18 picas, your column width being 3½″, or 21 picas wide.

Since you chose news gothic, your unit count for the line is 18 as a maximum.

After several efforts at trying to condense the meaning of your copy into a statement, you arrive at this summary thought:

English Department
offers new courses

Since this appears to be about the right number of units, you count letter by letter according to the chart given below:

$$E \quad n \, g \, l \quad i \, s \, h \quad D \quad e \, p \, a \, r \, t \, m \, e \, n \, t$$
$$1½ \; 1 \; 1 \; ½ \; ½ \; 1 \; 1 \; 1 \; 1½ \; 1 \; 1 \; 1 \; 1 \; ½ \; 1½ \; 1 \; 1 \; ½ \; = 17½$$

$$o \, f \, f \, e \, r \, s \quad n \, e \, w \quad c \, o \, u \, r \, s \, e \, s$$
$$1 \; 1 \; 1 \; 1 \; 1 \; 1 \; 1 \; 1 \; 1 \; 1 \; 1½ \; 1 \; 1 \; 1 \; 1 \; 1 \; 1 \; 1 \; = 18½$$

This exceeds the maximum, so we substitute the word *classes* for *courses* and have 18. Note the downstyle in capitalization, which is increasingly popular.

The standard unit count:

1 unit for all lower case letters *except*

½ unit for *f, l, i, t* and *j and except*

1½ for *m* and *w.*

For capital letters—1½ units each *except*

1 unit for capital I and L *and except*

2 units for capital M and W.

For punctuation—1 unit each *execpt* 2 units for dash.

For spacing—1 unit for space between words.

Summary:

(1) Headlines should usually be placed to read into the copy block, because this aids the reader. However, there are some variations.

(2) Headlines should be specific, based on specific copy. A good slogan to adopt: "Let us write our headlines so that no other staff in any other school or in any other school year could use this same headline."

(3) A colorful headline can help offset a poor picture.

(4) Every spread should have a headline—or if in the opening section, some wording in a contrasting larger type. This "rule" is frequently not followed. However, to omit the headline is to lose the contrast that headline type affords. A headline, like a dominant picture, has built-in reader attraction. Your spread suffers if you fail to make use of this device.

(5) Headlines are generally set flush left now. Centered heads are passing from the scene. Headlines with kickers, or tags, are increasing in popularity, especially in the academic and organization sections. The reason is that you can write a more complete headline. For example:

English Department
offers new courses

However, by using a tag, the headline can convey more specific information:

English Department
———————————

Courses broadened
with debate, drama

Note that with the tag, a rule is used. The tag is usually about half the point size of the main head. Therefore, since our main head would be 24 point, the tag would be 12 point. If the head is roman, the tag would probably be italic.

When tags are used, the main head is often indented slightly. For a one-column head, indent one pica; for a two column head, indent two

Innovations mark the '71 scene with dynamic force of new decade

As a new decade of historical change dawned, Americans braced themselves for the unpredictable forces which would shape all our lives.

Oklahomans kept pace with progress, although fate decreed that tragedy would necessarily be a part of life.

Termed the second top news event of 1970 was the tragic airplane crash October 2 in which 31 people including 24 Wichita State University football players were killed.

Four Oklahoma athletes were aboard the plane carrying players to Idaho for a game.

Oklahoma's Johnny Bench, catcher for the Cincinnati Reds, was awarded the Most Valuable Player of the Year Award by the National League.

A long time dream of state leaders was realized when the first barge sailed down the Arkansas River Jan-

uary 21 and docked at Tulsa's Port of Catoosa.

Last spring hundreds of U.S. universities exploded in protest over the Cambodian invasion and the Kent State killing.

Predictions of campus chaos in the fall were practically routine. However, the new term turned out to be relatively calm.

Headlines were made by stories covering women's lib, Apollo 14 moon flight, change in abortion laws, conflict between players and management in professional sports, pollution, and impact of the drug scene, ecology drives, banning of TV cigarette commercials, and the expansion of the war in Laos and Southeast Asia.

Knights anticipated joining the mainstream of life in the U.S. in the turbulent 70's as they viewed the steady flow of major news events with increasing interest and concern.

The following clippings from contemporary yearbooks illustrate the importance of type selection in the personality of your book. Note the various combinations of serif and sans serif faces for headlines and body copy. Headlines are being run either downstyle or with the first letter of all words capitalized. Two of the examples show unjustified copy —the "guidance" story unjustified on the left and the "business" story unjustified on the right. Note that in the "business" story sentence fragments are used, separated by suspension points. Periods are not usually used with headlines. Observe the attractiveness of italics when used for special effect.

Physics Society constructs machine designed for testing strength

A test which separated the men from the boys was administered by the Society of Physics Students during the annual campus Halloween event, the Carnival of the Great Pumpkin.

The group's contributing booth featured a "Test Your Strength" machine which in most cases helped PAC's male students make a good impression on their dates.

The society's top objective is to increase interest in the study of phys-

ics. It is from this group that prospective Sigma Pi Sigma members are selected.

Members of the society also hosted a meeting of the American Association of Physics Teachers in October and held an open house for high school teachers in early spring.

The organization was headed by Wallace Tuthill, president; William McClure, vice president; and Linda Fralick, secretary-treasurer.

Medics Prepare Themselves Through Volunteer Services

Continuing to inspire more students to undertake a career in medicine, the Medical Careers Club offered a year of suggestions and activities for all interested students. In addition to regular club activities, many members worked at the two city nursing homes as Blue Stripers and at Memorial Hospital as Candy Stripers.

With the help of the new male members, the first in the history of the club, the organization sold candles which were made and designed by the mentally retarded of the John F. Kennedy Flame of Hope Organization. Mrs. Mary Leigh Boisseau led the club in sponsoring a car wash.

With added funds from bake sales, the club was able to sponsor a spring trip to a nearby college. Thus the members had an opportunity to investigate a possible location for furthering their education in a medical direction. An annual spring banquet and a tour of Memorial Hospital completed the club's activities.

Blazettes

New Props, New Banner Add Variety and Spice

Dazzling performances of PHS Blazettes were enhanced by discs, umbrellas, capes, pom-poms, flags, cowgirl hats, and a new banner. These props added spice and sparkle to ten different, well-executed routines, parades, and football games.

Enthusiastic Blazettes performed at five pep assemblies, the Homecoming bonfire, basketball games, and a spring show entitled "A Day in the Life of a Blazette." Members worked in a one-week drill team school conducted by Kilgore Rangerette Lieutenant Frances Collins and worked at the Sonic Drive-In on Blazette Day to raise funds.

Dedication, work, loyalty, and a yen for variety were the ingredients that made the fifth year the best one yet. Before every performance, Blazette Director Miss Fran Hicks inspired all Blazettes with the words, "Stand Tall, Think, and SMILE!" Every member strived to fulfill her goal for perfection and variety in 1968.

FLUFFING their pom-poms to the "National Emblem March," forty-four Blazettes add color to assembly.

Tutoring Students Characterizes Future Educators' Agenda

The three R's—Reading, 'Riting, and 'Rithmetic—held unusual meaning for members of The Future Teachers of America. Looking forward to teaching careers at many different levels, these GW-ites, under the leadership of Miss Constance Winfield, sponsor, offered services to the local community and to the school, exploring the vast opportunities in Danville waiting for well-qualified teachers.

Among the many projects was a tutoring service. Members met individually with students, deficient in certain areas, during free periods or prior to school. Individual teachers were asked to tell their students of this special help that was available.

At Christmas, a party was given at the Richard Smith School for the mentally retarded. This afforded an opportunity for observing the teacher-student situation under unusual circumstances. It also was the club Christmas community project, along with participation in the Empty Stocking Fund.

Reorganized Guidance Department Improved Efficiency

Students in a quandary—
pondering a prospective vocation,
mulling over college choices,
despairing of academic difficulties—
turned to the Guidance Department for aid.
A structural reorganization
allowed each counselor to concentrate
on one grade level; private interviews
gave every student a better understanding
of his own achievements. Sound advice
helped confused boys and girls
to acquire the self-assurance
that would transform them
into young adults.
Diligent secretaries assisted counselors
in preparing transcripts and bulletins,
scheduling interviews, communicating with
parents. Faced with numerous problems,
Counselors solved them for each student.

Business courses develop skill and efficiency.

"How to Succeed in Business Without Really Trying" . . . general consensus: impossible! . . . business education: a mixture of 98% work and 2% natural dexterity . . . striving to reach goals in Shorthand and Typing . . . clacking away to the strains of John Phillip Sousa's marches . . . becoming accustomed to the idiosyncrasies of your typewriter . . . the temptation to look at the keys . . . the inky experience of a first ribbon change . . . having a whole line of "e's" because you held the key too long . . . relinquishing valued time to type up something for a teacher . . . Shorthand . . . as if you were learning a foreign language . . . acquiring the precision necessary to form the intricate curliques . . . hours of practice . . . an ever-present companion, the stenographer's notebook . . . listening to records on job hunting . . . tips on interviews . . . hearing guest speakers discuss various careers . . . Bookkeeping . . . maintaining records of financial transactions . . . the responsibility of accuracy . . . determining profit or loss . . . the frustration of ending up in the red . . . cost analysis, taxes . . . Office Practice—training in the fundamentals of grammar, shorthand, typing, and secretarial background . . . working Data Processing machines . . . photo-copying . . . calculating . . . the tragedy of a broken fingernail . . . the thrill of being a Diocesan Spelling Champion . . . working toward the highest degree of skill and efficiency . . . General Business . . . a general benefit . . . .

Columns 13 picas wide, set in 10-point Garamond with 2-point leading...
Character count 2.8 per pica = 13 x 2.8 = margins 10 - 47

Note to typist: Type within the lines shown, coming as near the right
line as possible. Try not to go more than 2 spaces short or 2 spaces
beyond this line. Hyphenate when necessary. Indent 3 spaces for paragraph.

If the back campus could talk, it
could tell many stories about the art
of judo at Northside this year.

On a pretty day after school, members of the Judo Club could be seen
dragging the mats outside for a practice
session. In bad weather, the mats were
spread out in gym A and practice continued.

The first thing a passer-by might
have noticed was that one of the ghi-
robed figures was reading directions
for holds and throws from a book while
the others listened and tried to carry
out the instructions. Although interested adults helped out occasionally,
the members had no instructor this year
and learned mainly by trial and error

Out-of-town shiahis were scheduled
for November, January and February.

Judokas try self teaching

If the back campus could talk, it could tell many stories about the art of judo at Northside this year.

On a pretty day after school, members of the Judo Club could be seen dragging the mats outside for a practice session. In bad weather, the mats were spread out in gym A and practice continued.

The first thing a passer-by might have noticed was that one of the ghi-robed figures was reading directions for holds and throws from a book while the others listened and tried to carry out the instructions. Although interested adults helped out occasionally, the members had no instructor this year and learned mainly by trial and error.

Out-of-town shiahis were scheduled for November, January and February.

This is the copy for the "judoka" story as it was typed on copy paper to go to the publisher. Note that a widow occurred in the printed story in the third line from the bottom and thus made a difference in the estimated line count. Protect yourself by careful editing of copy so the last line of a paragraph will be from half to three-fourths a line. The widow in line 9 could have been edited out, since it was obvious in the typed copy.

picas; for a three-column head, indent three picas. Be consistent in indention—indenting all heads with tags, or none.

Justify or Not?

This term refers to the appearance of copy blocks on your spread.

Two ways to set copy are now popular:

(1) One way is to set the body copy—and frequently the captions also—with all lines, except perhaps the last one, full column width. Indention for paragraphing is normal. That is the style used almost entirely in books, newspapers, and most magazines. Copy set thus is said to be *justified*. The columns in this book are justified. Copy fills the column space flush left and flush right.

(2) The second way is to set the copy flush left and ragged on the right. This is said to be *unjustified*.

For some years, theme copy has been set flush on one side—left or right, depending on the relationship to the pictures—and ragged on the other. Now, however, some books are running all copy flush on one side and ragged on the other.

For easy readability, it is suggested that the left side be flush and the right side ragged. (Sometimes, however, the layout seems to dictate the justified right and ragged left. That is more difficult to plan. With copy set ragged left, the headline is generally also ragged left. Both head and copy are thus flush right.)

Copy Fitting

Copy should be carefully planned so that it will fit exactly into the space intended. That space will be the column width and whatever depth your layout shows.

As was said earlier in this chapter, if you use 10-point type with two points of space between the lines—that is, 10 on 12—then every line of type and its accompanying space will fill one pica. Thus, for every six lines of type you will fill a vertical inch of space.

Thus, if your layout shows that you have a copy block three inches deep, you will need 18 lines of type. That is, six lines for each of the three vertical inches.

Conversely, if you write your copy before you plan your layout, you can tell how deep the copy block should be by counting your lines of copy—provided you have typed them the correct width. Thus for 15 lines of copy of the correct width, you will need to allow two and one-half inches of space on your layout.

Concerning the width of your copy: Use a character count guide for estimating the width of the copy you type. The width of the copy should be the column width. For beginners, this is a must.

You have to know the number of characters per pica in the kind of type you choose. Your printer can supply you with that information. The character count for the kinds of type used generally for body copy, for example, averages from 2.1 to 3.3 per pica.

Suppose the kind of type you are using averages three character counts per pica. Thus, every time you type three characters, you are filling one pica in your line of copy as it will appear in type in your book.

Suppose your column width is 18 picas. To fill a line of type, you will type three times 18—which will be 54 characters—and so your typewriter margins should be 10–64. Character count includes spaces, punctuation, and figures. Remember: this is an average.

Careful effort in character and line count will ensure a copy block that fits exactly as you want it to fit.

Captions

In addition to selecting the kind and size of type you think suitable for your captions, you also need to consider display style. You have several choices.

First, you decide between (1) single captions accompanying single pictures on the spread and (2) cluster captions.

The single caption with the single picture may be placed below the picture, beside it, or above it. The cluster caption is placed somewhere on the spread as one of the blocks fitting into the layout.

In the cluster caption, you identify pictures

carefully to help the reader easily associate the proper words with each picture. For example, if the cluster caption is at the lower right of the spread, the guide words for the reader must be thus: Far left . . . top center . . . bottom center . . . above . . . Obviously these guide words should be selected to aid the reader as much as possible. If carefully done, cluster captions can be satisfactory. BUT if the spread involves several pictures, or if many persons are to be identified, the result may be such a forbidding block of copy that the reader will skip it completely.

After deciding between single or cluster captions, you choose some way to attract the attention of the viewer so he will pause to read the captions as he looks at the pictures. Here you have a choice of boldface, or italics, or caps (or a combination, such as boldface caps) for the initial word or words of the captions, depending on the length of the line.

Captions, whether single or cluster, may be set as copy blocks are set, justified or unjustified. If unjustified, the caption is set flush with the picture. Thus, if the caption is at the left of the picture, the caption is set flush right. If the caption is at the right of the picture, the caption copy is set flush left.

Copy for captions must be counted as carefully for fit as is body copy. Copy widths are worked out as for body copy, and copy paper is prepared as for body copy. Some staffs count characters in their caption copy very carefully in order to be sure that the last line of the caption is full, or almost full. Widows in caption copy are generally considered undesirable. (In a block of copy, the last line is called a widow if it is less than half a line in width.) To ensure avoiding a widow, revise your caption copy until the last line is typed about three fourths full.

CHAPTER VI

PLAN THE DUMMY

Which comes first?

The old question of "the Chicken vs. the Egg" takes on a yearbooking look when the subject of designing layouts arises.

Question: "Do you design your layouts and then order your pictures and write your copy? Or do you get your pictures and write your copy and then design your layouts?"

Fortunately, the answer is easy. You design the layout.

BUT—and it is an important but—you work out your design based on (1) what you know to be the idea to be displayed by the layout, (2) what you estimate to be the amount of copy needed and the headline, and (3) what you would like to have—*and think you can obtain*—in picture coverage of the idea. Guesswork, you say.

Actually, it is what is called an "educated guess," because you sketch the layout in your imagination, basing your ideas on your experience. (If you have had no experience, you try to discuss the problem with someone who has had.)

Getting Started

You go about it this way:

(1) You decide exactly what is to be covered on the spread in question. For example, suppose it is the first pep rally of the football season.

Main idea: "Students assemble for pep making."

Since the pep making includes many students assembled in the stadium, the dominant picture in both idea and size would logically be a view of the student body. (This idea, and therefore the picture of this idea, has weight and meaning because it includes many people, occurs in a large place, and has scope in significance. This is another way of explaining dominance.)

Should that dominant picture for the spread be horizontal or vertical? In this instance, since the stadium is horizontal, the picture would probably seem most natural if horizontal. That forms the basis of your spread. Your dominant picture is thus your dominant idea.

Supporting features in a pep rally include the head cheerleader, other cheerleaders, the drum major or student director, the band, the football captain and team, possibly the president of the student body conducting the program, perhaps an alumnus, an ex-quarterback who is present to make a talk. Doubtless there will be banners, signs, and such, and possibly colorful skits.

Each feature, therefore, would be a possibility for a supporting picture. They would be smaller than the dominant picture because subordinate to the main idea.

(2) Using a miniature layout sketch pad, you pencil those ideas (possibilities for pictures) in around the dominant picture—possibly a vertical for the ex-quarterback, a horizontal for the director and some of the band, because this is a horizontal idea, horizontal for a banner perhaps, and a close-up of the radiant face of the head cheerleader or some student waving a pep sign, both of which should show the individual pep maker to give emotion to the spread.

(3) With those ideas sketched on a miniature dummy sheet, you talk them over with the photographer so that he knows exactly what you have in mind.

(4) You fill out photo assignment cards for him—and hope for the best.

(5) When you get the contact prints or the finished prints, you see whether he was able to capture your ideas as you had the spread planned and the design worked out.

(6) If he succeeded, then you are ready to draw a full-size, complete layout with exact

measurements so you can prepare your pictures and words—the body copy, the headline, and the captions—to send to the printer.

However, generally some modification of your sketch will be necessary when you see the contact prints or the finished prints. Often the activity will not be carried out as had been announced, or as you had expected it to be, so some of your pictures do not materialize.

Also, with changes in the program, there may be additional picture ideas, which the photographer has covered. SUGGESTION: Have it understood with the photographer that if something unexpected occurs, or if he sees a picture you did not order, you would like him to try to get a picture of it, perhaps from two angles and of more than one shape so you can have a choice in substitution.

Another also: Many times some of your picture ideas will not be as effective as you had expected, whereas others will be more usable. It is always a good idea to be flexible in your planning so that you can take advantage of something better—and can avoid using something that turns out to be weak or uninteresting.

"Yes, but," you say, "suppose you did all this planning—and then nothing turned out as you expected?"

If that happens to you—and it may—you study the pictures available, still considering your dominant idea and the need for a dominant picture. Fit in others as you can, once you have a dominant picture and know exactly what shape it is. (Lack of a dominant picture causes a spread to look like a page in a picture album or a postcard collection.)

It is possible that what the photographer brings you will not fit into your plan—or even into your idea—at all. In that event, study your pictures to see what kind of dominance and what idea can be worked out. The secret to success here—and to your enjoyment of the work—is to be aware that this can happen and to be confident that you can modify your layout or revise your thinking in order to make the best possible use of those pictures that will help tell the story of the year.

Briefly, then, the answer to the question, "Which comes first?" is:

(1) Consider the coverage from all angles,
(2) decide on your dominant impression,
(3) visualize the spread,
(4) sketch a miniature layout,
(5) order your pictures,
(6) study your pictures when you get them,
(7) revise your sketch as necessary, and
(8) transfer your sketch to a complete layout with exact measurements.

Fringe Benefit: To work out your layout ideas by considering the idea of the coverage on the spread, you are focusing on idea. Since the headline on the spread should be a statement of the idea on the spread, you are thus making it easy to compose your headline. A yearbook headline is usually a statement, with either subject or verb understood if necessary to make it count. Since your ideas are generally expressed in statements, the headline comes naturally—and it will be specific. All you need do is give some care to the wording, in order to avoid repetition from page to page and to offer the reader as colorful a statement as possible.

Reversal Bonus

After you have decided on your basic column plan and layout style, you will begin to sketch double spreads that seem both functional and pleasing to you. If you have some well-done yearbooks in your classroom library, you will be studying these to see what features of certain double spreads are most effective.

Here you must ask yourself:

(1) Is this a pleasing design?
(2) Does this design meet the standards of good layout?
(3) Will it be possible for us to get the kind of pictures necessary for such a layout?
(4) Will this meet our needs?

Once you have designed a layout that seems especially attractive and functional, you can use it many times throughout your book, since with different pictures and copy, the pattern will not be noticeable to your readers.

(In fact, one proof of good layout is that the reader is not at all aware of the layout as such. Remember: The purpose of the layout is to present an idea. If the reader gets the idea as you intend, then your layout has succeeded.)

ALSO, you can use the same layout in reversals: upside down and inside out.

With the modification demanded—or made possible—by the pictures you get plus the resulting reversals, you can lay out an entire book with only a few basic patterns.

For Overall Check

In an undertaking as large as putting a yearbook together, and one that is necessarily made up of so many parts, it is important to devise some method that will ensure a quick check on the overall look. You need to be sure that succeeding pages are not alike, or even too similar, for you want variety from page to page within a harmonious whole.

Get a small notebook—more than one if necessary—and number the pages as your yearbook is numbered. Then as you definitely decide on layouts, sketch them in, with a note about the content of the pictures and the headline written in. This will give you an easy-to-use record of your headlines, as well as of your layouts. Thus, you can check wording of headlines to be sure that you do not repeat such common words as frequently follow one another page by page—such as sponsor, students, seniors, projects, activities.

The miniature dummy that you make for quick reference is not, of course, the same dummy that you keep as an exact record of what you send to the printer. That dummy is for final and accurate check. What you need in preparing your total plan is a guide to help you easily turn through the pages or check page by page.

The editor or the adviser should keep the miniature at hand for constant reference. In addition, every section editor should keep his own section miniature dummy in order to control both consistency and variety.

Let it be said again: *Consistency* is gained by observing a carefully planned set of rules and basic patterns. *Variety* is gained by making use of (1) fresh ideas in picture content, (2) suitable cropping, and (3) contrast in the layout details within the total basic design.

PART III

Designing the Newspaper

CHAPTER VII

LOOK AT TODAY'S NEW TRENDS

Nothing can compare with the school paper. It is unique.

In the schools across the fifty states, it is good, it is bad; it is well done and poorly done; it is attractive, it is dull; it is a hodgepodge, it has impact; it is sloppy, it is orderly; it is bright, fresh, contemporary, or it is "old hat."

BUT—no matter what, it's important, it's worth the effort it takes, for it serves an honorable function and affords enthusiastic young people an opportunity to have a vigorous part in school life.

In many schools it is worthy of the best traditions in journalism.

Keeping Current

A survey of hundreds of school papers shows that many staffs are reflecting the trend in the professional papers to produce a sheet that is in keeping with the times. Over the past several years, dozens of staffs have been revising their format, following patterns set by dailies and weeklies always looking for some better way to attract and keep reader attention. Sometimes a major set of changes is involved, sometimes only slight variation.

Generally such a revision of format does not come at the beginning of a school year but after the staff has developed some ideas based on the experience of putting out several issues. One encouraging fact about updating is that it need not cost any money. The price comes in thought and effort on the part of the staff.

A fact not so encouraging is that most staffs are forced to use the type and comply with the procedures of the shop where the paper is printed or to consider the limiting factors of their duplicating equipment. One advantage that duplicated papers have is that the staff can better control their production.

Advisers who have had considerable experience in scholastic journalism would agree that practically no school paper would consider itself to have the best situation possible. Strangely, that does not seem to be a deterrent. It is apparent that editors gather their staffs around them—hopefully with an enthusiastic adviser—study the situation, and immediately begin to make the most of whatever is available.

For you who have been newly assigned to layout, with no experience, it may be helpful to begin by a survey of generalities:

Professional Proof

The professional press is so aware of the need for reader attention that money and effort are being devoted constantly to the problem of reaching the reader. Those efforts range from research to workshops for staff personnel and include the employing of trained experts in the plant. Note: The object of their concern is the design and layout of the paper.

Today's reader is much more a viewer than he was before the impact of television on his perception. That is why the term "lookership" becomes increasingly important.

True, we want the reader to read—and hopefully read every word we consider worth his time —*but he cannot read if he does not see first*.

No matter how good your copy is, you will

Hope To Revive Main Foyer Art Exhibits

By Linda Packer

Last November, while students and teachers walked through HPHS, a man and woman entered the school, walked to the art exhibition area by the front entrance and carried away several pieces of sculpture and prints to the tune of $1600.

The art exhibit committee decided to take no immediate action since this was the first major theft that had occurred since the series' inception. The next month, two bronze works, one 5½ feet tall and the other weighing almost 75 pounds, were also stolen.

And that proved to be the last anybody has seen of the art exhibits. Within a day, the rest of the plundered show was removed by the committee and the main foyer returned to the state which it had been in ten years earlier, before the displays were initiated.

"Area 'Looks Dead'

"It's just emptiness," said Mr. Tom Carbol, head of the art department, "and it looks dead."

Since the exhibits were dicontinued, he and the rest of the art department have been working with the PTA, headed by Mrs. Leonard Zieve and Mrs. Robert Babbin, to reopen the art exhibition area. Their plans have finally begun to materialize in the shape of a wall.

"Our main problem," stated Mr. Carbol, "is money. We're lacking funds. But what we'd like to do is to set up a wall blocking off the entrance to the area."

Intersecting part of the wall, like a gate, would be a set of double doors. "The ultimate would be for the doors to be glass — or for the whole wall to be glass," Mr. Carbol commented. "However, there just isn't that kind of money lying around.

"But I'm beginning to think that the type of wall we have in mind would be even better than glass. It would provide space for hanging art works on the inside, but, more important, we'd get student involvement and have students design the outside of the wall.

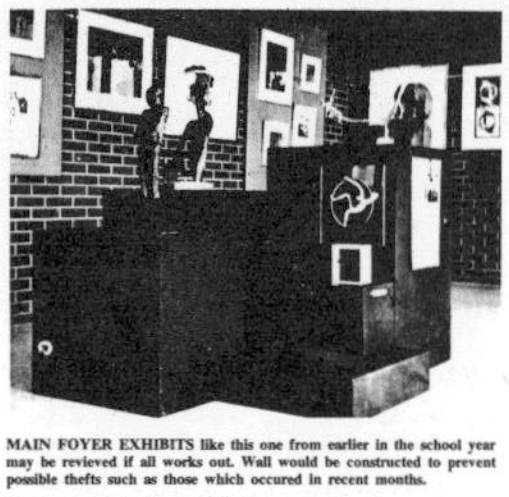

MAIN FOYER EXHIBITS like this one from earlier in the school year may be revieved if all works out. Wall would be constructed to prevent possible thefts such as those which occured in recent months.

Getting Cost Estimates

"This is still very much in the planning stages," he added. "I'm getting cost estimates and so on. We're also looking into the possibility of having a criss-cross metal gate instead of the wall, although I don't like that idea very much. To me, a metal gate says 'stay out,' not 'come in.'"

Although the wall would provide control, there would still be the problem of getting people to man the gallery. "We'd have to depend on student or PTA volunteers," Mr. Carbol pointed out. "And we'd also have to determine the best hours to open the gallery — before school, after school, lunchtime? We wouldn't have it open all day because there are some periods when no one would be looking at the exhibit and it'd be a waste.

"But we'd hate to give up the gallery because of theft," he said. "This thing has been going on for over ten years and I'd hate to see it stop now; I'd like to have the wall put up as soon as possible. The galleries contained many valuable things from top professional artists, painters, sculptors and craftsmen from all over the Chicago area, and now the opportunity to view these things is gone. Another sad thing is that some artists have given freely of their time and talent to come to HPHS and talk or give demonstrations. Now they no longer come because they are no longer part of an exhibit."

Problem Not Unique

He paused. "You know," he continued, "this is not a unique problem to Highland Park. Almost without exception, all schools on the North Shore have had damage or theft in relation to their artwork. The only beautiful thing — if you can call it that — is that, at least in our case, the stealing wasn't done by students.

"But even though the artists whose works were stolen received insurance checks," he smiled a little bitterly, "it's not quite the same thing as having something sold."

Shoreline

Vol. 50a, No. 25 — Highland Park High School, Highland Park, Illinois — April 1, 1971

National Merit Scores Validated, Corporation To Take No Action

After nearly a month of deliberation, National Merit Scholarship Corporation has decided it need not disqualify any of the Highland Park National Merit Scholarship Qualifying Tests interrupted by a fire alarm last Feb. 16.

Miss Roberta Shine, guidance counselor and administrator of the yearly exam, was contacted by an official of NMS last week, who informed her that the scholarship corporation had decided to "let it go" since Miss Shine felt that the five-minute break had not affected the thinking of students taking the test.

The 203 students who took the battery of tests were four minutes away from completing the final segment of the test, a vocabulary section, when the alarm in the mezzanine of the main auditorium was pulled by an unknown person. Those taking the test were outside the building for less than ten minutes before resuming work on their tests, far beyond the normal time limit in which students are allowed to be outside the testing area.

Those who took the test will receive their scores later this month, with the list of semi-finalists to be released next September. Highland Park had 21 semi-finalists in the 1971 competition, all of whom remain in the running for the National Merit Scholarships to be announced in May.

'It's Academic' To Be Broadcast This Saturday

Highland Park's appearance on the WMAQ-TV "It's Academic" series will be broadcast Saturday afternoon at 5 p.m. on channel five. The show was taped Sunday, Jan. 17, at the station's studios in Chicago's Merchandise Mart.

The Parker team of seniors Matt Rock, John Preskill and Jeremy Rosenblum held the lead going into the final round of the competition on the question-and-answer show, but were outscored in the concluding round to finish second, 70 points behind York Community High School and 50 ahead of St. Viator High School.

Year-Round Classes Approved by Board!

By Linda Packer and John Wilheim

In a landmark decision, the District 113 Board of Education last week gave its tentative approval to a revolutionary proposal which would see year-round classes for all sutdents at Highland Park and Deerfield High Schools. SHORELINE learned of the plan last weekend through a source in the administration who asked not to be identified.

The decision came about after the principals of the two schools first proposed opening their buildings on a twelve-month schedule with students attending the three quarters of their choice. A similar plan has been used elsewhere, most notably in the Valley View elementary school district, and was recently proposed for all of Chicago by Superintendent James Redmond.

Accelerates Process

In the ensuing study made by the Board, it was discovered that a more feasible method would be to accelerate the entire high school educational process, thereby making maximum use of both student time and the building maintenance, and allowing students to graduate, if they so desired, in as few as two and one-half years.

"Of course, this is all very tentative," said Mr. Theodor Repsholdt, special assistant to District Superintendent Dr. Karl Plath, when told that SHORELINE had learned of the policy switch. "We may decide to stick with what we've got now. Then again, it's possible that such a system could be instituted by next fall if everything goes as planned."

Mr. Arthur Gosling, principal, said that he had no immediate comment on how soon the system would be implemented, but cautioned that, "We're not married to the idea. This is going to take time to study, as we never expected the board to make a decision of this magnitude so quickly."

In making its decision, members of the school board pointed out the costs which would be saved by having the two facilities in full operation throughout the year. In years past, some summer school classes have been scheduled during June and July, but the schools have been almost completely deserted throughout the month of August. Considering the present financial straits of the district, it was felt that the year-round plan would provide an alternative to once again raising area tax assessments.

Furthermore, the board made reference to the statement found in the North Central Association evaluation team report to the effect that, "Students should be permitted to learn at their own rates without the interference of deadlines or the barrier of class limitations."

Hidden Benefits Told

"I don't see any reason why a student could not be enrolled in calculus within a year or so of reaching high school," opined Mr. Repsholdt while enumerating some of the hidden benefits of the year-round attendance format. "True, there'd be some problems in summer because of the lack of air conditioning at first, but I'm certain that that could be dealt with before too long without much difficulty."

A target date for instituting the proposal will be determined at the next regularly-scheduled meeting of the board. "Regardless of what action takes place at the meeting," Mr. Repsholdt hastened to add, "I hope those students who fail to see this proposal for what it really is will take a quick look at today's date before complaining too loudly about its enactment."

Junior Fourth in State Forensics, Debate Pair Eliminated Early

Junior Pam Carlton placed fourth in the state in oratorical declamation to capture Highland Park's only trophy at the statewide forensics contest held last Friday and Saturday at Illinois State University in Normal. The state debate meet was held at the same time, also on the SIU campus.

Pam was one of seven Parker speakers who made the trip downstate. Karen and Derin Altay, competing in the duet acting competition, and Jeff Segal, comedy reading, were the only other Highland Park representatives to make the finals in their categories.

Also participating were Mace Rosenstein, original oration; Gordon Horwitz, after dinner speaking; and Kathy Borowitz, serious reading.

The debate entry of seniors Jim Schuster and Marvin Bloom meanwhile finished with a 3-3 record in the six qualifying rounds of the debate tournament, but were unable to reach the semifinal round due to a lack of speaker points.

The duo had placed fifth at their sectional tourney last month to advance to the state level.

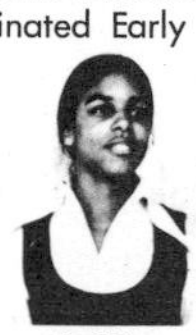

Pam Carlton

John Preskill Wins Award in Science

Senior John Preskill has been selected by vote of the science department as Highland Park's recipient of the annual Bausch and Lomb Science Award, sponsored by one of the nation's most prominent makers of scientific instruments.

John, who was recently honored for his project in the Westinghouse Talent Search, received the award as the senior maintaining the highest scholastic average in science courses. In recognition of his selection, he was given a bronze medal.

As Highland Park's winner, John is eligible to compete for a four-year scholarship at the University of Rochester. The official presentation of the award will be made later in the year at the spring awards night.

What's Ahead

FRIDAY, APRIL 2
End of Third Nine Weeks Grading Period.
Spring Vacation Begins, 3:40 P.M. (Continuing through April 11)

MONDAY, APRIL 12
Student Senate, MW212, 7:55 A.M.

WEDNESDAY, APRIL 14
Student Affairs Council, Counseling Department, 3:50 P.M.

FRIDAY, APRIL 16
Star Series, Main Auditorium, Third Period
SHORELINE Distribution, Homerooms, 8:40 A.M.

SATURDAY, APRIL 17
Scholastic Aptitude Testing, Cafeterias, Student Auditorium, 8 A.M.

Illustration #1—Two major stories are displayed prominently on this front page, one in a block across the top of the page and the other under the title plate. Subheads break up gray areas of body type since both are long stories. The contemporary geometric pattern is apparent here. Corners are anchored, no headlines bump one another. Slugs of space are used for greater readability. Note the half box for "What's Ahead" and the effectiveness of boldface caps for contrast.

Shoreline, Highland Park High School, Highland Park, Illinois—Simplicity of basic design and consistency in careful planning of each page are the secrets of success in this paper, as in many others. Note the effect of contrast in the boldface and lightface headline type. These pages consistently have an unornamented appearance. Spacing around the headlines rather than large size draws attention to various items on the page.

Fine, Applied Arts Among Combinations

Department Consolidation Proposal Forwarded to Board of Education

As part of a long-range plan that would later include the implementation of flexible scheduling, a consolidation of a number of the school's departments has been proposed to the Board of Education. A similar proposal involving its departments has been made by Deerfield High School.

"A couple of the combinations are obvious," said Mr. Arthur Gosling, principal. Among these are the merger of music, art, humanities, drama and stage into a fine arts department; the grouping of business education, industral arts, home economics and traffic safety under applied arts; the consolidation of the two physical education departments and health education into one unit; and the establishment of a catch-all special services department which would include counseling, health services and special education.

Programs not included in the proposed structure thus far are LARC, the Learning Project, the EMH program, the reading program and Wingspread, among others.

"Some very legitimate problems have been identified associated with this kind of consolidation," notes Mr. Gosling "some very good arguments pro and con. Some faculty members are upset and understandably so. I feel that the reasons are basically valid, but it's not a black and white thing."

The realignment wheels have been in motion for well over a year, with teachers notified last fall. The school board was apprised of the situation and a program report is due at the next regular meeting of that body Monday night.

Five reasons have been given as rationale for the move. As listed in the memo sent to the District 113 certified staff, these are a need for program changes, the recommendation by the North Central evaluaorst for more flexibility throughout the program, the economic pressure being felt by the district, the need to continue long-term development in the efficiency of the district's professional staff and an immediate need to give consideration to the structure in which instruction, supervision and administration is carried out.

The decision to consolidate certain departments was made at an administrative level by the district's administrative committee, which numbers both Mr. Gosling and Mr. Robert Benson, principal of Deerfield, among its members. According to Mr. Gosling, chances are good that the board will accept the concept when it is presented at Monday's meeting.

There are currently eighteen departments at Highland Park plus the health course. Emphasizing that it was his personal opinion, Mr. Gosling stated that, "my judgment is, there are too many." Under the revised set-up, there would be only nine.

As part of the same plan, the role of the department chairman is also being re-defined, something which Mr. Gosling considers "just as important as the consolidation."

The goal of the study is to focus on making teachers better at their work, and the creation of assistant department chairmen may result from the evaluation.

Affairs Council Picks Committee To Develop Open Campus Format

By a near-unanimous vote of the ten members in attendance, the Student Affairs Council last week approved the concept of open campus and appointed a committee to return with a specific plan by Wednesday, Feb. 24.

Following an unsuccessful motion to accept the open campus proposal (detailed in last week's SHORELINE) as written, discussion centered on the matter of hall traffic and disturbances. "What we must do," said faculty representative Mr. William Schildgen, "is insulate the abused majority from the minority and assure them of the best education possible. We don't know the cause, so all we can do is treat the symptom."

Committee member Mr. John Scornavacco, faculty member, sought to remove the specifics from the proposal, explaining that he felt the proposal was "too definite for what we have reached at this time." He failed to receive a second on the motion, after which an amended motion, calling for a detailed proposal to be forwarded to the appropriate parties by mid-March, was unanimously approved.

Mr. Richard Edwards, faculty member, and Stan Krauss, senior, were chosen as co-chairmen of the open campus study committee and instructed to appoint to the committee any student or faculty member they sought for the group.

On other matters, the council decided that it would review the student handbook and agreed that it would meet on a weekly, rather than a bi-weekly basis. The report on the rules committee, also on the agenda, was held until this week's meeting.

Those on hand for the meeting, in addition to the teachers and students earlier mentioned, were Harold Flegleman, Jeremy Rosenblum, Ted Sonnenschein, Patsy Jacobs, Mrs. Norma Hammerberg, faculty member, and Mr. Arthur Gosling, principal.

Seniors Asked To Pay Fees for Caps, Gowns

Seniors who have not yet paid their cap and gown fees or brought a note signed by a parent to the effect that they will not participate in the June graduation ceremony are asked to contact Mrs. Cardinal, senior class sponsor, as soon as possible. To date, 92 students have yet to pay or indicate that they will not appear when the class is graduated June 9.

Students who paid their fees but were not measured are advised to contact Mrs. Cardinal any morning before school to be measured.

Shoreline

Vol. 50a, No. 20 — Highland Park High School, Highland Park, Illinois — February 19, 1971

Twenty-one Seniors Reach National Merit Finals

All twenty-one of Highland Park's National Merit semi-finalists have advanced to finalist standing in the nationwide competition for college scholarships.

Named finalists were Phillip Berger, Richard Bernstein, David Birnbaum, Michael Dudnick, Cathy Felix, Mathew Hoffman, Kim Hogrefe, Nancy Jacqmin, Stanton Krauss, Deborah Krupp, Walter Lemann III, Cynthia Liebow, Jeffrey Melvoin, Robert Natkin, John Preskill, Jeremy Rosenblum, Diana Rosenstein, Mace Rosenstein, James Schuster, Laurence Segil and John Wilheim.

About ninety-six per cent of those named semi-finalists later become finalists, remaining in the running for the 1,000 one-time National Merit $1000 scholarships and some 2,000 scholarships of varying worth sponsored by business and industry. Nationwide, 1,470 finalists were honored. Each received a certificate of merit and a letter from the National Merit Corporation in recognition of his accomplishment.

To become a finalist, a semifinalist must receive the endorsement of his high school principal, fill out an information form and confirm his score on the National Merit Scholarship Qualifying Test by those he receives on the Scholastic Aptitude Test.

Scholarship winners will be announced the NMS corporation in mid-May.

Father-Daughter Banquet To Be Out of This World

Fathers and daughters are once again preparing for the annual HGA Father-Daughter Banquet, "Apoppo '71," to be held Thursday, Feb. 25 in the north cafeteria and student auditorium.

The banquet features an outer space theme, which will be carried through in the decorations, programs and favors.

The banquet's entertainment will include the father-daughter skit, in which a girl from each class pairs up with her dad. It will also feature the song contest, which is entered by a representative from each class and judged by all fathers who have two or more daughters in HGA.

"The banquet is the biggest event of the year for the HGA girls and their fathers," explained senior Linda Lauer, HGA president. "It's a good chance for the entire club to get involved in something."

The committees formed to prepare for one banquet provide a great opportunity for this. The committee in charge of the dinner is headed by Susie Liss and Leslie Dean, sophomores; programs are handled by Jan Isaacs, junior, and Cathy Nachman and Sandie Eisenstein, sophomores; the Senior Pole, which involves listing what college all the HGA seniors plan to attend on the pole in the cafeteria, is comprised of Margaret Klein and Pam Holmes, seniors; tags are made by juniors Janet Brusslan, Nancy Crane and sophomore Linda Davis; and the publicity chairmen are sophomores Nancy Lieberstein, Leslie Nathan, Debbie Sabol, and Debbie Freehling.

Linda Lauer and Jan Bauldauf, seniors, are in charge of supervising the banquet preparations. Decorations are painted by members who volunteer to come in and work during their free time.

The banquet will begin at 6:30 p.m. and only HGA members may attend.

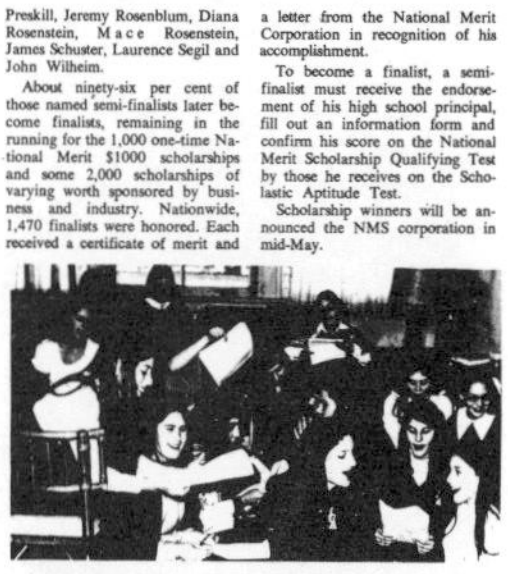

IN TRUE, ORGANIZED HGA fashion, these sophomore girls rehearse what they hope will be the winning song of "Apoppo '71," this year's Father-Daughter banquet, to be held next Thursday night.

Senior Chosen Scholarship Finalist In National Merit Negro Program

Debra Carlton, HPHS senior, has been named a finalist in the 1971 National Achievement Scholarship Program for Outstanding Negro Students conducted by the National Merit Scholarship Corporation.

Debbie, a senior, was among 950 finalists listed by NMS for some 225 one-time, $1000 National Achievement Scholarships and 100 additional sponsored scholarships awarded in March.

To become a finalist in the program, a student must be endorsed by his school, confirm his National Mert Scholarship Qualifying Test (NMSQT) score by placing high on the Scholastic Aptitude Test (SAT) and maintain an academic record which backs up his test performances.

In recognition of her status, Debra received a certificate of achievement signed by both the director of the National Achievement Scholarship Program and the president of the National Merit Scholarship Corporation.

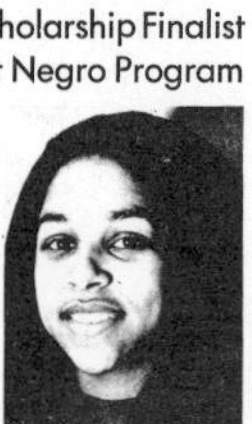

Debra Carlton

Changes Announced in Commencement

Several major changes in the procedure to be followed during the June graduation ceremony have been announced folowing discussion by administrators both here and at the administration building. The changes were revealed last week by Mrs. Loraine Cardinal, science teacher and senior class sponsor.

Beginning this year, only the valedictorian and salutatorian will be personally introduced at the ceremony, with the top ten per cent to be recognized as a group. Previously, the top six or eight students had been introduced in addition to the other two.

The top decile will now be determined on the basis of grade point average as figured at the end of the first semester rather than at the end of the year.

Furthermore, the "Class of 1971" will now include three groups, those who graduated at the end of summer school in August, 1970; those who were graduated in January, 1971; and those graduating in June.

The changes came about as the culmination of a study of the graduation situation by Dr. John Swanson, assistant superintendent, and apply to Deerfield as well.

Student Assembly Officers Elected; 1971 Prom Sanctioned

Ted Sonnenschein, junior, was elected president of the Student Assembly in the all-school election held on Tuesday, Feb. 9.

The election, which was marred by a small student vote turnout of just under a quarter of the school, found all of the offices being won by juniors.

Kathy Borowitz was elected to the post of vice-president, while Bob Kohn won his bid for treasurer. Tracy Page takes over the duties of secretary.

In a side ballot, members of the junior class voted to hold the Prom again this year, with the pro-Prom students carrying the issue by the scant margin of four votes.

Illustration #2—Again a major story is placed at the top of the page, with three secondary stories of about equal importance blocked in and supported by four lesser items. The multicolumn headlines give the long stories the appearance of being shorter and easier to read. Slugs of space in the body type and spacing around the heads make for a bright, airy look. Note the script in the title plate reflected in the kicker at the top of the page.

Illustration #3—This front page is characterized by extensive use of two-column headlines. With no arrangement of copy in blocks, columns are tied together somewhere to preserve the horizontal look somewhat and keep the page from breaking apart, or looking "too vertical." Capitalized lead-ins for cutlines afford contrast.

Illustrations #4 and #5—Variation on the editorial page is related to the copy to be displayed, as indicated here. In general, the format of the editorial page is fairly consistent from issue to issue. Note the attractiveness of the "Student Forum" overprint on the gray bar. The three-column italics is an unusual device, as is the "open campus" editorial framed generously with white space. Although a staff box is not usually carried at the top of a page, here it is designed for typographical effect and affords a prominent display for the editorial beneath it, which may be type or art. Advertising is not generally carried on the editorial page. A large amount of copy set wider than one column draws attention to all parts of the page.

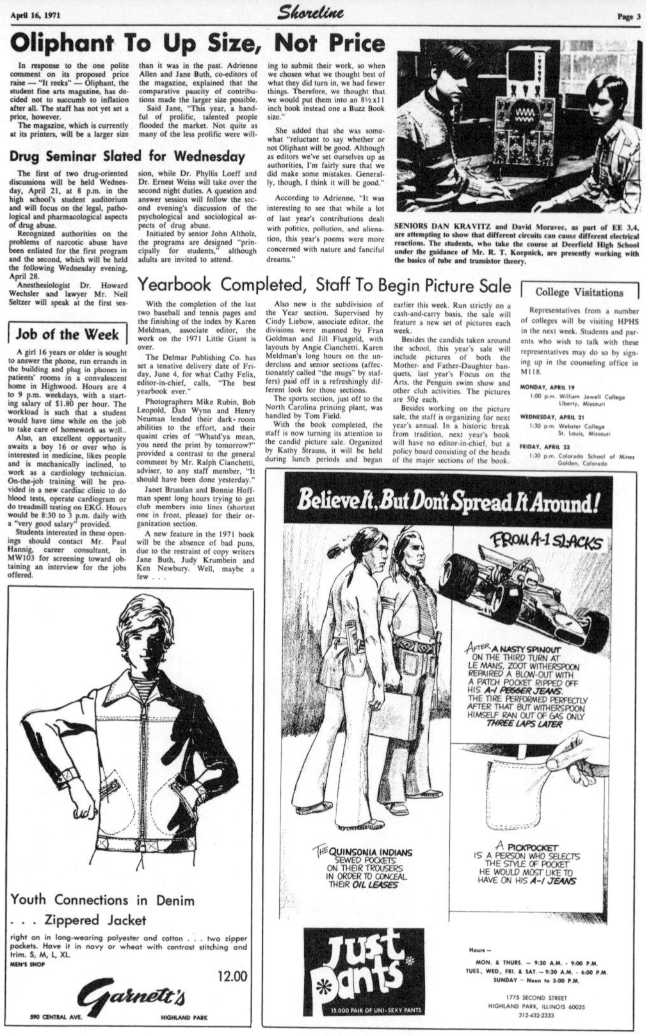

April 16, 1971 — Shoreline — Page 3

Oliphant To Up Size, Not Price

In response to the one polite comment on its proposed price raise — "It reeks" — Oliphant, the student fine arts magazine, has decided not to succumb to inflation after all. The staff has not yet set a price, however.

The magazine, which is currently at its printers, will be a larger size than it was in the past. Adrienne Allen and Jane Buth, co-editors of the magazine, explained that the comparative paucity of contributions made the larger size possible.

Said Jane, "This year, a handful of prolific, talented people flooded the market. Not quite as many of the less prolific were willing to submit their work, so when we chosen what we thought best of what they did turn in, we had fewer things. Therefore, we thought that we would put them into an 8½x11 inch book instead one a Buzz Book size."

She added that she was somewhat "reluctant to say whether or not Oliphant will be good. Although as editors we've set ourselves up as authorities, I'm fairly sure that we did make some mistakes. Generally, though, I think it will be good."

According to Adrienne, "It was interesting to see that while a lot of last year's contributions dealt with politics, pollution, and alienation, this year's poems were more concerned with nature and fanciful dreams."

SENIORS DAN KRAVITZ and David Moravec, as part of EE 3,4, are attempting to show that different circuits can cause different electrical reactions. The students, who take the course at Deerfield High School under the guidance of Mr. R. T. Koepnick, are presently working with the basics of tube and transistor theory.

Drug Seminar Slated for Wednesday

The first of two drug-oriented discussions will be held Wednesday, April 21, at 8 p.m. in the high school's student auditorium and will focus on the legal, pathological and pharmacological aspects of drug abuse.

Recognized authorities on the problems of narcotic abuse have been enlisted for the first program and the second, which will be held the following Wednesday evening, April 28.

Anesthesiologist Dr. Howard Wechsler and lawyer Mr. Neil Seltzer will speak at the first session, while Dr. Phyllis Loeff and Dr. Ernest Weiss will take over the second night duties. A question and answer session will follow the second evening's discussion of the psychological and sociological aspects of drug abuse.

Initiated by senior John Altholz, the programs are designed "principally for students," although adults are invited to attend.

Job of the Week

A girl 16 years or older is sought to answer the phone, run errands in the building and plug in phones in patients' rooms in a convalescent home in Highwood. Hours are 4 to 9 p.m. weekdays, with a starting salary of $1.80 per hour. The workload is such that a student would have time while on the job to take care of homework as well..

Also, an excellent opportunity awaits a boy 16 or over who is interested in medicine, likes people and is mechanically inclined, to work as a cardiology technician. On-the-job training will be provided in a new cardiac clinic to do blood tests, operate cardiogram or do treadmill testing on EKG. Hours would be 8:30 to 3 p.m. daily with a "very good salary" provided.

Students interested in these openings should contact Mr. Paul Hannig, career consultant, in MW103 for screening toward obtaining an interview for the jobs offered.

Yearbook Completed, Staff To Begin Picture Sale

With the completion of the last two baseball and tennis pages and the finishing of the index by Karen Meldman, associate editor, the work on the 1971 Little Giant is over.

The Delmar Publishing Co. has set a tenative delivery date of Friday, June 4, for what Cathy Felix, editor-in-chief, calls, "The best yearbook ever."

Photographers Mike Rubin, Bob Leopold, Dan Wynn and Henry Neuman lended their dark-room abilities to the effort, and their quaint cries of "Whatd'ya mean, you need the print by tomorrow?" provided a contrast to the general comment by Mr. Ralph Cianchetti, adviser, to any staff member, "It should have been done yesterday."

Janet Brusslan and Bonnie Hoffman spent long hours trying to get club members into lines (shortest one in front, please) for their organization section.

A new feature in the 1971 book will be the absence of bad puns, due to the restraint of copy writers Jane Buth, Judy Krumbein and Ken Newbury. Well, maybe a few . . .

Also new is the subdivision of the Year section. Supervised by Cindy Liebow, associate editor, the divisions were manned by Fran Goldman and Jill Fluxgold, with layouts by Angie Cianchetti. Karen Meldman's long hours on the underclass and senior sections (affectionately called "the mugs" by staffers) paid off in a refreshingly different look for those sections.

The sports section, just off to the North Carolina printing plant, was handled by Tom Field.

With the book completed, the staff is now turning its attention to the candid picture sale. Organized by Kathy Strauss, it will be held during lunch periods and began earlier this week. Run strictly on a cash-and-carry basis, the sale will feature a new set of pictures each week.

Besides the candids taken around the school, this year's sale will include pictures of both the Mother- and Father-Daughter banquets, last year's Focus on the Arts, the Penguin swim show and other club activities. The pictures are 50¢ each.

Besides working on the picture sale, the staff is organizing for next year's annual. In a historic break from tradition, next year's book will have no editor-in-chief, but a policy board consisting of the heads of the major sections of the book.

College Visitations

Representatives from a number of colleges will be visiting HPHS in the next week. Students and parents who wish to talk with these representatives may do so by signing up in the counseling office in M118.

MONDAY, APRIL 19
1:00 p.m. William Jewell College, Liberty, Missouri

WEDNESDAY, APRIL 21
1:30 p.m. Webster College, St. Louis, Missouri

FRIDAY, APRIL 23
1:30 p.m. Colorado School of Mines, Golden, Colorado

Youth Connections in Denim
. . . Zippered Jacket
right on in long-wearing polyester and cotton . . . two zipper pockets. Have it in navy or wheat with contrast stitching and trim. S, M, L, XL.
MEN'S SHOP
12.00
Garnett's
590 CENTRAL AVE. HIGHLAND PARK

Believe It, But Don't Spread It Around!
FROM A-1 SLACKS
THE QUINSONIA INDIANS SEWED POCKETS ON THEIR TROUSERS IN ORDER TO CONCEAL THEIR OIL LEASES
AFTER A NASTY SPINOUT ON THE THIRD TURN AT LE MANS, ZOOT WITHERSPOON REPAIRED A BLOW-OUT WITH A PATCH POCKET RIPPED OFF HIS A-1 PEGGER JEANS. THE TIRE PERFORMED PERFECTLY AFTER THAT BUT WITHERSPOON HIMSELF RAN OUT OF GAS ONLY THREE LAPS LATER
A PICKPOCKET IS A PERSON WHO SELECTS THE STYLE OF POCKET HE WOULD MOST LIKE TO HAVE ON HIS A-1 JEANS
Just Pants
15,000 PAIR OF UNI-SEXY PANTS
Hours —
MON. & THURS. — 9:30 A.M. - 9:00 P.M.
TUES., WED., FRI. & SAT. — 9:30 A.M. - 6:00 P.M.
SUNDAY — Noon to 5:00 P.M.
1775 SECOND STREET
HIGHLAND PARK, ILLINOIS 60035
312-432-2333

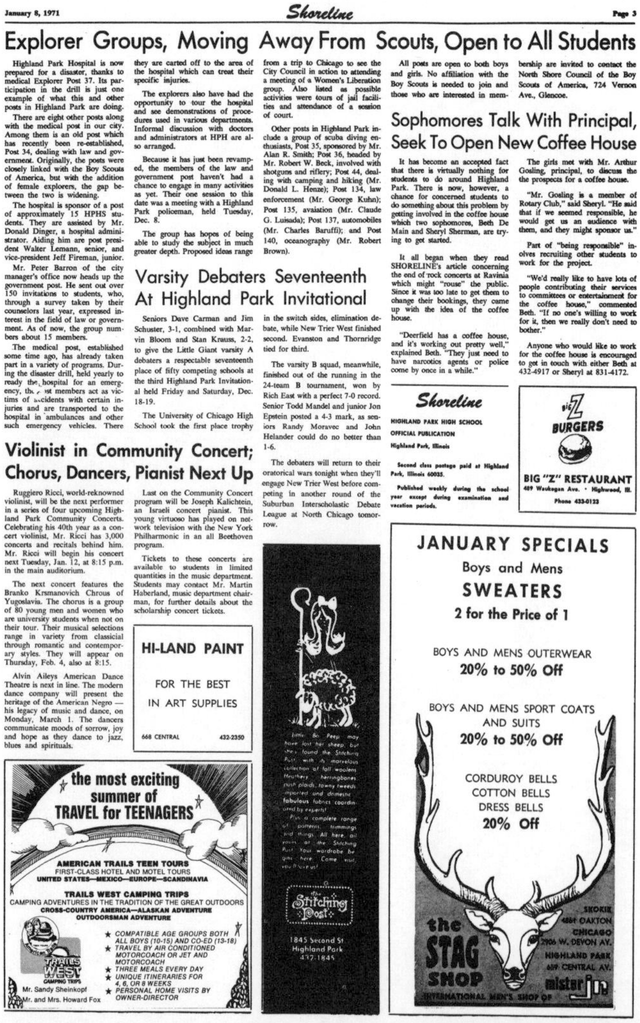

January 8, 1971 — Shoreline — Page 3

Explorer Groups, Moving Away From Scouts, Open to All Students

Highland Park Hospital is now prepared for a disaster, thanks to medical Explorer Post 37. Its participation in the drill is just one example of what this and other posts in Highland Park are doing.

There are eight other posts along with the medical post in our city. Among them is an old post which has recently been re-established, Post 34, dealing with law and government. Originally, the posts were closely linked with the Boy Scouts of America, but with the addition of female explorers, the gap between the two is widening.

The hospital is sponsor of a post of approximately 15 HPHS students. They are assisted by Mr. Donald Dinger, a hospital administrator. Aiding him are post president Walter Lemann, senior, and vice-president Jeff Fireman, junior.

Mr. Peter Barron of the city manager's office now heads up the government post. He sent out over 150 invitations to students, who, through a survey taken by their counselors last year, expressed interest in the field of law or government. As of now, the group numbers about 15 members.

The medical post, established some time ago, has already taken part in a variety of programs. During the disaster drill, held yearly to ready the hospital for an emergency, the post members act as victims of accidents with certain injuries and are transported to the hospital in ambulances and other such emergency vehicles. There they are carted off to the area of the hospital which can treat their specific injuries.

The explorers also have had the opportunity to tour the hospital and see demonstrations of procedures used in various departments. Informal discussion with doctors and administrators at HPH are also arranged.

Because it has just been revamped, the members of the law and government post haven't had a chance to engage in many activities as yet. Their one session to this date was a meeting with a Highland Park policeman, held Tuesday, Dec. 8.

The group has hopes of being able to study the subject in much greater depth. Proposed ideas range from a trip to Chicago to see the City Council in action to attending a meeting of a Women's Liberation group. Also listed as possible activities were tours of jail facilities and attendance of a session of court.

Other posts in Highland Park include a group of scuba diving enthusiasts, Post 35, sponsored by Mr. Alan R. Smith; Post 36, headed by Mr. Robert W. Beck, involved with shotguns and riflery; Post 44, dealing with camping and hiking (Mr. Donald L. Henze); Post 134, law enforcement (Mr. George Kuhn); Post 135, avaiation (Mr. Claude G. Luisada); Post 137, automobiles (Mr. Charles Baruffi); and Post 140, oceanography (Mr. Robert Brown).

All posts are open to both boys and girls. No affiliation with the Boy Scouts is needed to join and those who are interested in membership are invited to contact the North Shore Council of the Boy Scouts of America, 724 Vernon Ave., Glencoe.

Varsity Debaters Seventeenth At Highland Park Invitational

Seniors Dave Carman and Jim Schuster, 3-1, combined with Marvin Bloom and Stan Krauss, 2-2, to give the Little Giant varsity A debaters a respectable seventeenth place of fifty competing schools at the third Highland Park Invitational held Friday and Saturday, Dec. 18-19.

The University of Chicago High School took the first place trophy in the switch sides, elimination debate, while New Trier West finished second. Evanston and Thornridge tied for third.

The varsity B squad, meanwhile, finished out of the running in the 24-team B tournament, won by Rich East with a perfect 7-0 record. Senior Todd Mandel and junior Jon Epstein posted a 4-3 mark, as seniors Randy Moravec and John Helander could do no better than 1-6.

The debaters will return to their oratorical wars tonight when they'll engage New Trier West before competing in another round of the Suburban Interscholastic Debate League at North Chicago tomorrow.

Sophomores Talk With Principal, Seek To Open New Coffee House

It has become an accepted fact that there is virtually nothing for students to do around Highland Park. There is now, however, a chance for concerned students to do something about this problem by getting involved in the coffee house which two sophomores, Beth De Main and Sheryl Sherman, are trying to get started.

It all began when they read SHORELINE's article concerning the end of rock concerts at Ravinia which might "rouse" the public. Since it was too late to get them to change their bookings, they came up with the idea of the coffee house.

"Deerfield has a coffee house, and it's working out pretty well," explained Beth. "They just need to have narcotics agents or police come by once in a while."

The girls met with Mr. Arthur Gosling, principal, to discuss the the prospects for a coffee house.

"Mr. Gosling is a member of Rotary Club," said Sheryl. "He said that if we seemed responsible, he would get us an audience with them, and they might sponsor us."

Part of "being responsible" inolves recruiting other students to work for the project.

"We'd really like to have lots of people contributing their services to committees or entertainment for the coffee house," commented Beth. "If no one's willing to work for it, then we really don't need to bother."

Anyone who would like to work for the coffee house is encouraged to get in touch with either Beth at 432-4917 or Sheryl at 831-4172.

Violinist in Community Concert; Chorus, Dancers, Pianist Next Up

Ruggiero Ricci, world-reknowned violinist, will be the next performer in a series of four upcoming Highland Park Community Concerts. Celebrating his 40th year as a concert violinist, Mr. Ricci has 3,000 concerts and recitals behind him. Mr. Ricci will begin his concert next Tuesday, Jan. 12, at 8:15 p.m. in the main auditorium.

The next concert features the Branko Krsmanovich Chrous of Yugoslavia. The chorus is a group of 80 young men and women who are university students when not on their tour. Their musical selections range in variety from classicial through romantic and contemporary styles. They will appear on Thursday, Feb. 4, also at 8:15.

Alvin Aileys American Dance Theatre is next in line. The modern dance company will present the heritage of the American Negro — his legacy of music and dance, on Monday, March 1. The dancers communicate moods of sorrow, joy and hope as they dance to jazz, blues and spirituals.

Last on the Community Concert program will be Joseph Kalichtein, an Israeli concert pianist. This young virtuoso has played on network television with the New York Philharmonic in an all Beethoven program.

Tickets to these concerts are available to students in limited quantities in the music department. Students may contact Mr. Martin Haberland, music department chairman, for further details about the scholarship concert tickets.

Shoreline
HIGHLAND PARK HIGH SCHOOL
OFFICIAL PUBLICATION
Highland Park, Illinois
Second class postage paid at Highland Park, Illinois 60035.
Published weekly during the school year except during examination and vacation periods.

Big Z BURGERS
BIG "Z" RESTAURANT
489 Waukegan Ave. • Highwood, Ill.
Phone 433-0123

HI-LAND PAINT
FOR THE BEST IN ART SUPPLIES
668 CENTRAL 432-2350

the most exciting summer of TRAVEL for TEENAGERS
AMERICAN TRAILS TEEN TOURS
FIRST-CLASS HOTEL AND MOTEL TOURS
UNITED STATES—MEXICO—EUROPE—SCANDINAVIA
TRAILS WEST CAMPING TRIPS
CAMPING ADVENTURES IN THE TRADITION OF THE GREAT OUTDOORS
CROSS-COUNTRY AMERICA—ALASKAN ADVENTURE
OUTDOORSMAN ADVENTURE
★ COMPATIBLE AGE GROUPS BOTH ALL BOYS (10-15) AND CO-ED (13-18)
★ TRAVEL BY AIR CONDITIONED MOTORCOACH OR JET AND MOTORCOACH
★ THREE MEALS EVERY DAY
★ UNIQUE ITINERARIES FOR 4, 6, OR 8 WEEKS
★ PERSONAL HOME VISITS BY OWNER-DIRECTOR
TRAILS WEST CAMPING TRIPS
Mr. Sandy Sheinkopf
Mr. and Mrs. Howard Fox

The Stitching Post
1845 Second St
Highland Park
432-1845

JANUARY SPECIALS
Boys and Mens
SWEATERS
2 for the Price of 1
BOYS AND MENS OUTERWEAR
20% to 50% Off
BOYS AND MENS SPORT COATS AND SUITS
20% to 50% Off
CORDUROY BELLS
COTTON BELLS
DRESS BELLS
20% Off
the STAG SHOP
SKOKIE 4864 OAKTON
CHICAGO 2906 W. DEVON AV.
HIGHLAND PARK 659 CENTRAL AV.
INTERNATIONAL MEN'S SHOP OF mister jim

Illustrations #6 and #7—Makeup of inside pages is usually determined by advertising if ads are carried. The three-column headline and picture balance the ad copy. Also, the strong geometric effect of the ads dictates the arrangement of stories in blocks of copy with multicolumn headlines. The half box heads add variety, the two-line, two-column headlines pyramid to the right to follow the ad pyramid. Note the light, airy look of the *Shoreline* box, with no side rules. Slugs of space give these pages an easy-to-read appearance.

Illustration #1—This typical front page indicates the personality of the paper—heavier-than-usual headlines contrasted with fairly light body type in a compact package. Note that the boxes have rules at only the top and bottom. Subheads and boldface afford variety. The three major headlines define the reading diagonal boldly.

The *Muskogee High Scout,* Muskogee High School, Muskogee, Oklahoma—Pages from this paper illustrate the increasingly popular use of similarity in headline style. The simplicity of *Scout* headlines and the careful arrangement of stories give each page a trim, neat look. Note that occasional devices for ornamentation are included.

Illustration #2—Rather light in comparison with other pages, this inside page is characterized by use of space, variety in type with caps and boldface, asterisks for brightness, ornamental half box around the column heading, boxes and advertisements that demand attention. Major headlines are similar. Note that the dominant story and picture form a block at upper left, balanced by the ad at the lower right. Since the column falls into a block that creates a block effect for the lower left, the page has a neat, orderly appearance.

1971 Seniors Plan Final Activities

MUSKOGEE HIGH SCOUT

Our 51st Year—No. 27   Muskogee High School, Muskogee, Oklahoma, Friday, May 7, 1971   Price Five Cents

DECA Plans Club Dinner On Monday

Pat Cuccaro, David Barnes Win Student Body Offices For '71-72

NEW PRESIDENT—Pat Cuccaro, newly elected student body president, is shown as he makes his campaign speech before the general election. Candidates addressed the junior and sophomore members of the student body in a dual assembly in the Fine Arts Auditorium.

Juniors Receive Aid

OU Selects Warren

'The Sound' Sweeps Tri-State Contest

MHS Delegation Gets Recognition

SCOUT Receives Awards In Press Day Competition

TROPHIES—Dr. Charles Adams, MHS principal, is admiring the trophies won by the SCOUT staff at the Northeastern State College Press Day. Looking on are SCOUT editors Sherry Phillips, Bunson, Judy Warren, Vickie Morgan and Gretchen Bebb.

Attention Students

MUSKOGEE HIGH SCOUT—Friday, January 15, 1971—Page 5

Study, Practice . . .

Students Construct Cabinets

Robert Thompson, Chris Taylor, and Roger Davis are patiently and carefully adding finishing touches to a chest constructed by Rodney Johnson. The students are all members of the sixth hour cabinet making class.

Choir Goes To Weatherford; Presents Concert Program

Attention Juniors

Support Our Advertisers

Bill's & Coye Generator Service
—All Work Guaranteed—
Ph. 682-1255
36th & Shawnee

Scouting Through The Years

FIFTY YEARS AGO
January 1921

FORTY YEARS AGO
January 1931

THIRTY YEARS AGO
January 1941

TWENTY YEARS AGO
January 1951

TEN YEARS AGO
January 1961

JCL Holds Contest

Page 4—MUSKOGEE HIGH SCOUT—Friday, March 12, 1971

Rougher Nine Start Year; Battle Tahlequah Tigers

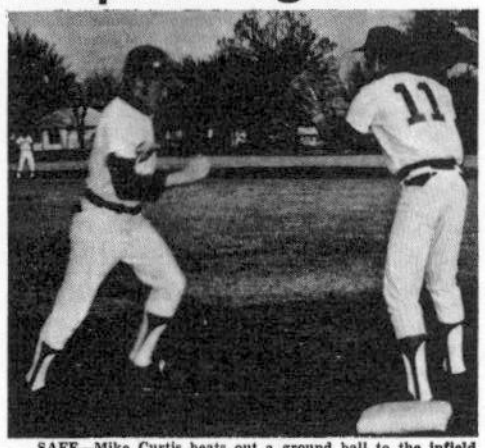

SAFE—Mike Curtis beats out a ground ball to the infield during a Rougher practice. Bob Miller awaits the throw. Both baseballers are seniors.

Rougher baseballers begin their busy season today by playing Tahlequah. The game will be played at Legion Park at 3:45. Saturday, Muskogee will host Tulsa Hale at Legion Park in a 1 p.m. game. First conference game will be against Booker T. Washington March 16.

Coach Expects Improvement

"I expect them to be a greatly-improved ball club," commented John Leafer, baseball coach, about Tahlequah. "This is the third year most of them have played together, in some cases, four."

Hale Remains Tough

Coach Leafer listed Hale as being "tough, a perennial favorite that is always powerful. They've been in the top two for the last four years." The coach explained that their strong point is pitching.

MHS Meets Washington

First conference opponent for the Roughers will be Tulsa Washington. This is the first meeting between these schools in baseball. "Last year was their best season in ten years," recalled the coach. "They beat Tulsa McClain and East Central, who went on to the state championship."

Starting line-up for the Rougher nine will be either Greg Webb or John Greer, catching, and either Ray Steely or Kenny Lehman on the mound. First base will be held down by Bob Miller, with Kevin Backes on second, Rick Olzawski on third and Ron Cowan on shortstop. Mike Gugello will start in left field, Mike Curtis in center and either Ray Steely or Roger McClain in right.

"Our defense and hitting is strong," explained Leafer. "I think we have an outstanding chance for winning conference. We have the type of team that would go all the way if they continue to play with the attitude they've shown so far."

Big Green Cindermen Roar Past Hornets

The "Green and White" swept the field events and six of the running events in the process of putting down Tulsa Washington 97 to 30. This was the first outing for the Muskogee High cindermen and set them in the right direction to another conference championship.

Outstanding performances were handled out by Jimmy Littrell, John Barnett, and James Williams. Each of these superstars won two events. Littrell swept the field in both the low and high hurdles, and was a member on the winning 440 relay team. Williams won in both the shot put and the discus. Barnett won the 880 run and the mile.

Other winners and their events were Randy Tibbles and Mike Ford, tieing in the two mile run; and Littrell, Mike Smith, Reuben Givens and Vernon Givens, winning the 440 relay. The field events were dominated by the Roughers with first place wins in every event and complete sweeps in the shot put, discus and the pole vault. Kevin Grober jumped 5-8 for first in the high jump, Tyrone Clemmons vaulted 11 feet 3 inches for the top score in the pole vault, and Holton Harris placed first in the broad jump with a distance of 19 feet 4 inches.

In the mile relay Muskogee had the best time but fouled on the final leg and the nod went to Washington. This was the first conference match for the Rougher thinclad of the 1971 season.

Lassies Play In Tourney

Muskogee High School girls tennis team participated in the Lawton Invitational Tournament on March 5 and 6. Coach Nancy Harrold directs the Rougherette squad.

In the "A" singles, Becky Reese played Susan Rhodes of Lawton and was beaten 6-3, 1-6, 0-6. Melony Martin played Kathy Savage of Wichita Falls, Texas. She won 7-5,5-7,6-4 for the only MHS victory in the tourney. Melony then met Kathy Belie of Lawton and lost 1-6, 2-6.

Toni Ranallo and Jody Robinson battled Higgins and Duke of Amarillo, Texas in the "A" doubles. Higgins and Duke won the contest 6-0, 6-1. Terrye Jefferson and Denise Bitting played Elkouri and Cook of Chickasha and dropped that match 1-6, 4-6. Rougherettes will see action against in McAlester on March 16.

Spirit Leaders

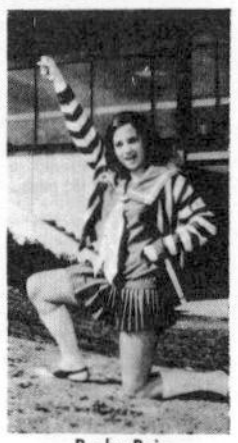

Becky Bois

Becky Bois, cheerleader of Muskogee High, works hard to keep spirit on high terms. Becky said that making new friends and being able to travel with the players to out of town games is what she likes best about being a cheerleader.

This 5'7", green-eyed, brunette resides at 429 N. 12th with her parents, Mr. and Mrs. Bill Bois. She has one younger brother, Wesley, who attends West High. Andrea, her sister, goes to Franklin Grade School. Becky and her family attend First Baptist Church.

Besides being a cheerleader, Becky is in the choral club, J.C.L., French club, and Teens for Christ. Becky was a Sophomore, Junior, and All-School Queen candidate. Sailing, horsebacking riding, canoeing, traveling, and playing the piano are favorite hobbies of Becky. She also likes seafood and strawberry shortcake.

Becky's ambition in life is to give something of herself instead of trying to gain everything for herself. Her most exciting moment was when she was able to go to the Bahamas.

"I think the students need to take more pride in their school and this would improve the school a lot," stated Becky.

GRA Members Sponsor Event

The Girls Recreation Association will be hosting a basketball sports day on Saturday, March 27. Any girl wishing to join a team or create one, should contact Owana Wilbourn, club president, Mrs. Nancy Harrold or Mrs. Linda White, club sponsors.

This event will proceed all day in the Muskogee High School gym, and trophies will be given to the first and second place teams.

It is hoped that there will be many teams entered. There will be a one dollar entry fee per team. Each team should have at least eight members. The deadline for entering a team is March 15.

Darrell's Beauty College
Special for High School Students
Night Classes
212 West Broadway or 682-1451
Cash or Term Tuition

KRAKER'S
Muskogee's House of Fashion
415 W. Broadway

Patricia's
AT THE PLAZA
CUTEST CLOTHES in Town

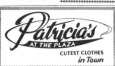

Arla Jean Campbell's
School Of Dance
Phones 682-7369 – 682-4778

SMITTY'S
TEXACO
Is The Place
For Roughers
To Get Flats Fixed,
Oil Changes
York & Gibson
Ph. 687-4412
Bill Smith, Manager

If it has anything to do with insurance: We do it better.
M-F-A INSURANCE
LARRY CASEY
707 North Main
Ph. 683-3001 Ph. 682-9852

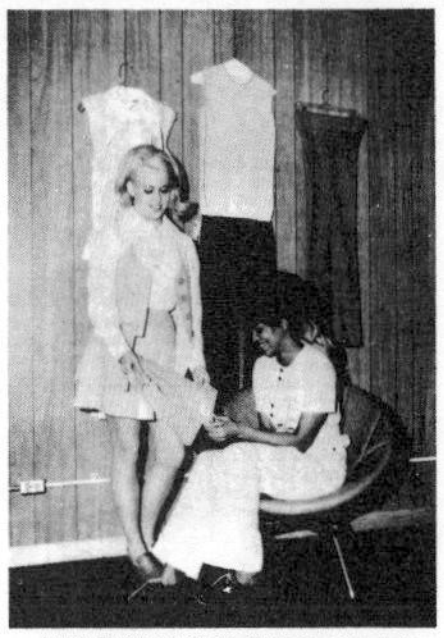

Aretas Davis and Sandy Christmas seem to have found a hidden treasure of Spring clothes in one of Muskogee's out-of-the-way clothing stores, Gordon's Ready To Wear. The treasure and savings are worth the search at a price worth looking for.

Gordon's
Ready To Wear
610 South 15th

Illustration #3—Here the basic page design is adapted for sports coverage. The vertical advertisement offers pleasing balance for the three-column headline at the upper left. Pictures in ads improve page layout. Since every advertiser wants his ad copy read, careful editors plan so that type touches every ad at some point. For this reason, the "well" arrangement is often used.

Page 2—MUSKOGEE HIGH SCOUT—Friday, March 12, 1971

SCOUT Editorials

Red Cross Sends Plea

No matter how we feel about the war in Vietnam, the fate of the American prisoners is an important matter to their wives and children, to their parents, to the signatories of the Geneva Convention, and to all the rational people of the world.

Following is a plea from the American Red Cross to show our concern and the concern of millions for our boys and men in Vietnam.

"We are not asking you to take a stand on the war itself but to observe the humanitatian provisions of the Geneva Convention.

"Ask Hanoi to release the names of the men they hold prisoner, to allow their prisoners to communicate regularly with their families, to repatriare seriously ill and wounded prisoners, and to allow a neutral intermediary to inspect places of detention. These are serious problems that we as Americans need to face; even we as students need to realize this.

"We need to ask Hanoi these things and the more letters of interest they receive the more results they will give us. We need everyone's help."

It only costs 25 cents to send our letters airmail; send them to: the Office of the President, Democratic Republic of Vietnam, Hanoi, North Vietnam. Become involved in this humanitarian issue.

• • • • •

People Need Education

Some high school students say they are not going to college after graduation. They say they cannot afford it. In a recent survey conducted by Dr. Charles G. Cole, a leading educator, it was found that three out of ten high school students who do not enter college have the capacities to "rival our most intelligent professors and the best productive inventors."

Any graduate with the grade average of "C" or higher should plan to attend the college of his choice. College can be attended by anyone with a desire for learning. There are scholarships for students with talent in special fields. Most colleges have a work-study program to help the student pay his college expense.

With a college degree, the average person will make an increase in their salary, according to what field they select. The payoff, a college degree, is worth the money, time, and work it will cost.

SENIOR HORIZONS

"Learning is a continous process in which the student, motivated by interest, need, and defined purpose, actively participates in purposeful and meaningful experiences." This is the acknowledged philosophy of Saint John's School of Nursing. Located in Tulsa Oklahoma, at Saint John's Hospital, this school was built in 1926 to all fields of service.

Admission requirements are that the student should be a high school graduate, ranked in the upper 3rd per cent of his class or signs of progressing, and have a "C" average in English, mathematics, and physical and biological science.

The applicant is required to take a pre-entrance examination, either the Scholastic Aptitude Test or the American Testing Program examination. There are numbers of aids and loans available to those who are in need of financial assistance towards their education.

Educational program of Saint John's Hospital School of Nursing is conducted by the Sisters of the Sorrowful Mother. The school is accredited by the Oklahoma Board of Nurse Registration and Nursing Education and the National League for Nursing.

Main objective for graduates of Saint John's is to use fundamental concepts of social and scientific disciplines in planning, implementing and evaluating nursing care plans. Request application forms may be obtained from Registrar, St. John's Hospital School of Nursing, 1802 East 19th Street, Tulsa.

Novelist Orwell Desribes 1984

The clock struck thirteen o'clock, the year is 1984, in Anywhere, U.S.A., and "big brother" can watch every move that we can possibly make. "Big brother" represents the government at this time. It has control of just about everything and everyone. It could control our thinking and keep sharp tabs on our behavior.

In "1984," George Orwell takes the life of one man, and shows how it is run, and how all the people have changed. It explains different phases of his life, and different moods that he is in. The main point of the book is to show how the government has completely taken over.

At the end of the book, this particular man is tortured with what he hates most: rats. Everyone has their own personal opinion of this book, some like it, and others have felt as though they are doomed and that their destiny is already set.

If this sort of book appeals to you, it is an excellent book to read. The story combines one man's view of the future with things of reality.

Melony, Robbie . . .

Couple Participate In Council

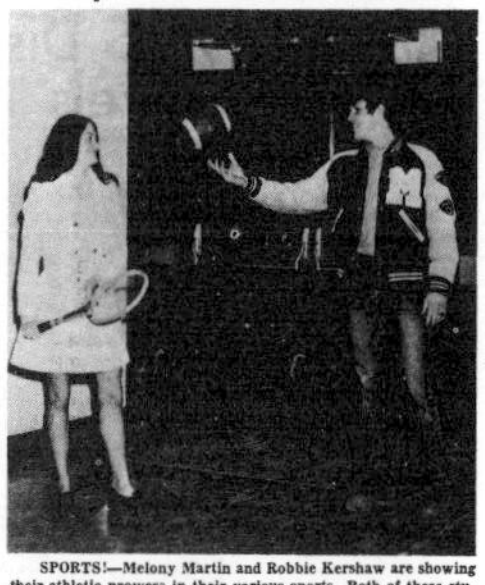

SPORTS!—Melony Martin and Robbie Kershaw are showing their athletic prowess in their various sports. Both of these students are MHS seniors.

The senior spotlight this week lands on Melony Martin and Robbie Kershaw. They both are active in the Student and Advisory Councils.

Melony is also an active participant on the senior board. She is Junior Classical League ristorian, and a mem- of the tennis team. The broad horizons of curriculum the sohool offers is what Melony likes about MHS.

This senior's philosophy of life is to "receive the highest amount of education that one can obtain in a life time.„ In her spare time, Melony likes to read books, write poetry, and paint pictures. Her two most exciting moments were winning Elks Leadership Contest and being made guest artist by Tom Rodgers, art instructor at MHS.

Melony plans to attend Oklahoma University and main in Latin and minor in archaeology. Robbie is still uncertain of what college to attend but plans to major in law and minor in political science.

Besides being active in the councils, Robbie also participates in football and Letterman's Club. His favorite sport is football. He likes the hardworking dedication of all athletes in all of the sports at MHS.

"Observe the golden rule; mind your own business; and be yourself" is Robbie's philosophy of life. His most exciting moment was the night the Roughers won the conference title over Tulsa Washington.

Robbie's pastimes are hunting, fishing, and listening to music. The strangest thing that happened to him in his life was breaking both of his wrists on Friday the 13th last year.

Melony lives with her parents, Mr. and Mrs. Bob L. Martin, at 320 South 15th. She has two sisters, Karen, a sophomore at MHS, and De Ann, a five-year old.

Robbie resides on Country Club Road with his parents, Mr. and Mrs. R.E. Kershaw. He has four sisters, Peggy, 19; Jane, 16, a junior at MHS; Anne, 11, attending Harris Jobe Elementary School; and Joan, a four-year old.

Frenchman Produces Stories; Writes Tragedy, 'November'

"November" is either the 202nd or 203rd novel written by George Simenon under his own name. The story concerns a crisis in life; in this case the lives of a whole family trapped together in a grossly unhappy hermetic situation. "November" is translated from French by Jean Steward.

The denouement, where the daughter declines to voice her suspicions that her alcoholic mother has murdered the seductive maid, is not so much a turning point as a fact that something was there all along. Writing with directness, the author seems to have an understanding of every character's behavior. One of the main characters in the book is Inspector Malgretia, a pipe-smoking psycholgist, who falls somewhere between Sherlock Holmes and Father Brown.

The author, Simenon, seems to collect people the way some people collect portage stamps. He is the creator of at least 2,000 characters. He has slowed down with age. He now writes a novel in eight days. His record is 25 hours.

One seems to grab for Simenon's books with the fear of not being able to take hold of it, but it is all but impossible to run out of them. "November" is as perfect an example of the Simenon "hard" or non-detective novel as any that has been published in this country recently.

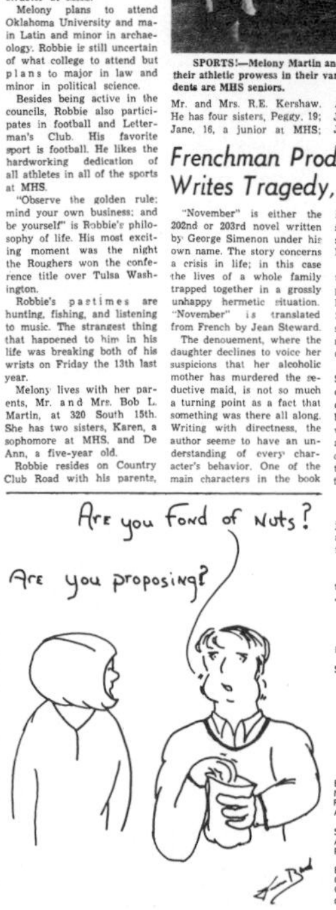

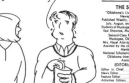

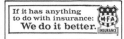

Are you Fond of Nuts?
Are you proposing?

• • •

Optimist, someone who jumps off a 14 story building and when he gets to the 13th floor says' "so far so good."

• • •

Shopper, someone who likes to go buy-buy.

THE SCOUT
"Oklahoma's Livest High School Newspaper"
Published Weekly, Except During June, July, August, and September, by Students of Muskogee High School, 3200 East Shawnee, Muskogee, Oklahoma
Second-Class Postage Paid at Muskogee, Oklahoma 74401
Mrs. Hazel Aldridge, Faculty Adviser
Assisted by the classes in Journalism
Member of
National Scholastic Press Association
Oklahoma Interscholastic Press Association

EDITORIAL STAFF
Editor in Chief .... Judy Warren
News Editor .... Susan Witt
Feature Editor .... Vickie Morgan
Activities Editors .... Sherry Phillips, Gretchen Bebb
Sports Editor .... Billy Duzan
Advertising Editor .... Linda Doty
Photographers .... David Waters, John Lehman
Exchange Editor .... Debbie Hambrick
Circulation Manager .... Mark Hughes
Cartoonist .... Ken Blood
Offset Printed By Muskogee High Press

Illustration #4—The same basic design used for inside pages is obvious here, adapted for the editorial page. In the prime optical area, editorials set boldface attract reader attention. The ornamental half box "senior horizons" is repeated elsewhere in the paper from time to time. The lower right corner is attractively anchored by the masthead. Cartoons now generally do not have lines to define the borders.

Illustration #1—This front page is a good example of prominent display of a very important story. No devices except a few slugs of space are used to attract reader attention, because the excitement of the subject itself is enough to gain and keep interest. Note the contrast in the adjoining heads on the "Indian Club" and "royalty" stories and the use of small but bold heads to anchor the corners.

Spontaneous combustion blamed

MHS fire stuns community

White Buffalo

Vol. XXV, No. 10 MADRAS HIGH SCHOOL, MADRAS, OREGON February 26, 1971

Only the skeleton remains of what was once the choral music room, after fire destroyed the contents and greatly damaged the structure. The blaze is believed to have started in the robe closet at the rear of the room.

Indian Club approved By student council

Royalty of Hearts to be crowned At Sweetheart Ball, Feb. 27

Phone installed in student lounge

Deadline extended

Sophomores choose Class ring design

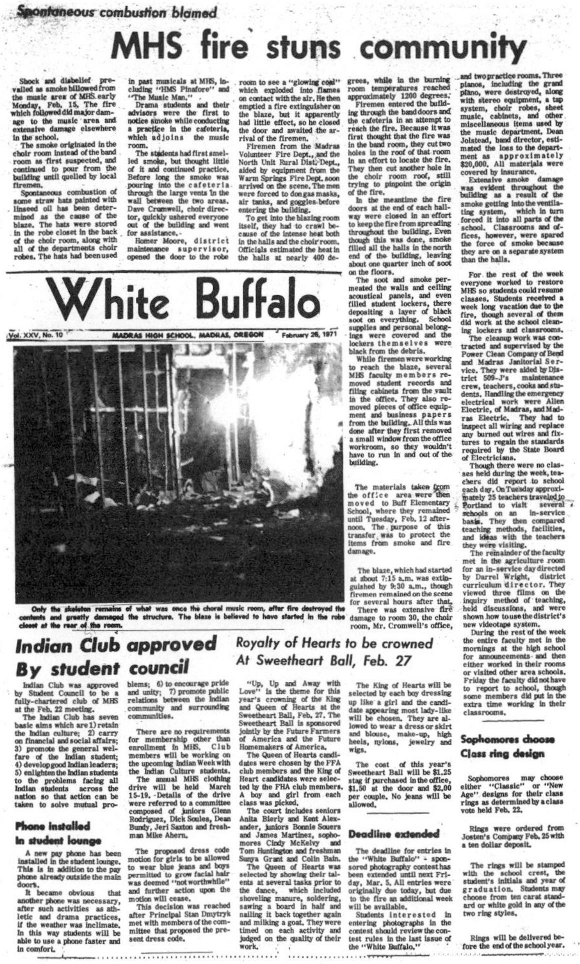

The *White Buffalo,* Madras High School, Madras, Oregon—A quick look at several issues of the *White Buffalo* shows that the personality of this paper is characterized by extreme simplicity. The pages have a rather tight, compact look, with heavy but fairly small headlines of bold type used to gain contrast.

Page 6 January 22, 1971 White Buffalo

Bill Cram invited to run In Oregon Indoor meet

Buffalo Splatter

By Dick Soules

Poor sports criticized

OUCH! Was the feeling of junior Jim Kollen as his heavyweight opponent put the pressure on. The head and shoulders hold proved to be the right choice as Kollen was pinned.

Cagers upset Lakeview With a single point edge

JV's capture Past 3 bouts

Are You Building? Visit MILLER LUMBER for Supplies

A & W DRIVE IN Your Patronage is Appreciated Snack or a Meal "First Come, First Served" Mr. & Mrs. Lester Bennett Madras

Teen of the Moment Candy Amlin

AHERN'S STOP 'N SHOP Open 7 to 11 • All Kinds of Groceries • Fast Service • Ice Cold Beverages Across From Old Ericksons Phone 475-3106

NINE PEAKS GOLF COURSE Stay in the Swing of Things Madras, Oregon

IHC FARM MACHINERY GASOLINE DIESEL FUEL STOVE OIL Deliveries with Automatic Meter-Stamped Receipts Jefferson County Co-op Complete Line Hardware Madras, Oregon Phone 475-2254

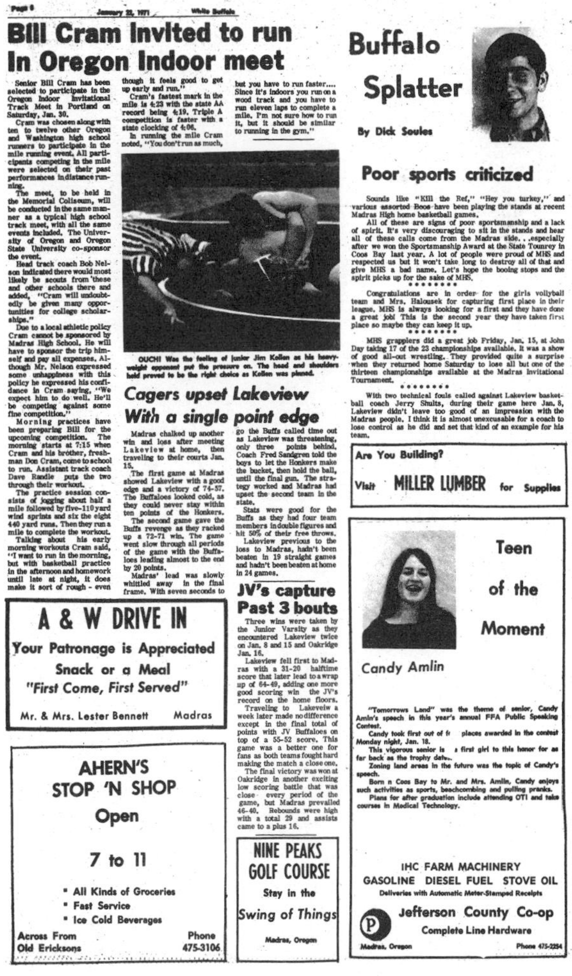

Illustration #2—A bold look for the sports page is achieved by the two-line, three-column head with picture in the upper left and the heading with picture for the sports column in the upper right. Special effect is gained by the "poor sports" headline, double-column type and asterisks for ornament. Note how the vertical advertisement with picture balances the major story. Note also that the major story and cagers story form a block. The "well" arrangement for ads makes it possible for type to touch all ads.

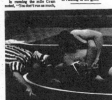

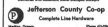

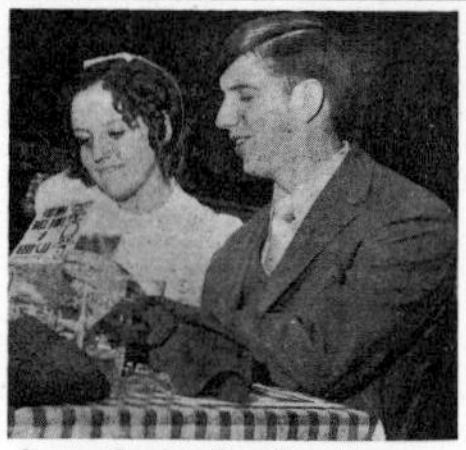

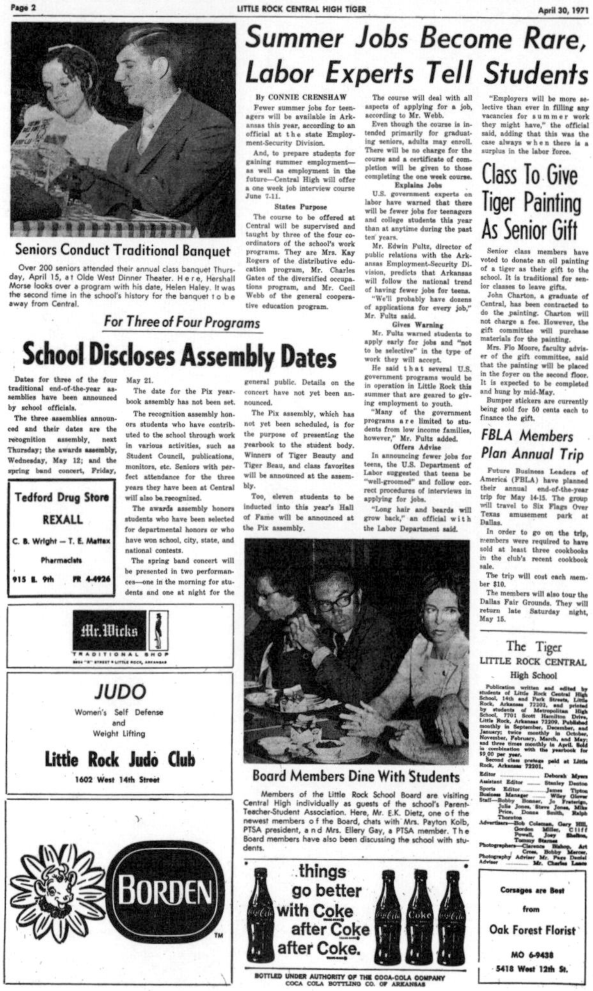

Seniors Conduct Traditional Banquet

Over 200 seniors attended their annual class banquet Thursday, April 15, at Olde West Dinner Theater. Here, Hershall Morse looks over a program with his date, Helen Haley. It was the second time in the school's history for the banquet to be away from Central.

Summer Jobs Become Rare, Labor Experts Tell Students

By CONNIE CRENSHAW

Fewer summer jobs for teenagers will be available in Arkansas this year, according to an official at the state Employment-Security Division.

And, to prepare students for gaining summer employment—as well as employment in the future—Central High will offer a one week job interview course June 7-11.

States Purpose

The course to be offered at Central will be supervised and taught by three of the four coordinators of the school's work programs. They are Mrs. Kay Rogers of the distributive education program, Mr. Charles Gates of the diversified occupations program, and Mr. Cecil Webb of the general cooperative education program.

The course will deal with all aspects of applying for a job, according to Mr. Webb.

Even though the course is intended primarily for graduating seniors, adults may enroll. There will be no charge for the course and a certificate of completion will be given to those completing the one week course.

Explains Jobs

U.S. government experts on labor have warned that there will be fewer jobs for teenagers and college students this year than at anytime during the past ten years.

Mr. Edwin Fultz, director of public relations with the Arkansas Employment-Security Division, predicts that Arkansas will follow the national trend of having fewer jobs for teens.

"We'll probably have dozens of applications for every job," Mr. Fultz said.

Gives Warning

Mr. Fultz warned students to apply early for jobs and "not to be selective" in the type of work they will accept.

He said that several U.S. government programs would be in operation in Little Rock this summer that are geared to giving employment to youth.

"Many of the government programs are limited to students from low income families, however," Mr. Fultz added.

Offers Advise

In announcing fewer jobs for teens, the U.S. Department of Labor suggested that teens be "well-groomed" and follow correct procedures of interviews in applying for jobs.

"Long hair and beards will grow back," an official with the Labor Department said.

"Employers will be more selective than ever in filling any vacancies for summer work they might have," the official said, adding that this was the case always when there is a surplus in the labor force.

Class To Give Tiger Painting As Senior Gift

Senior class members have voted to donate an oil painting of a tiger as their gift to the school. It is traditional for senior classes to leave gifts.

John Charton, a graduate of Central, has been contracted to do the painting. Charton will not charge a fee. However, the gift committee will purchase materials for the painting.

Mrs. Flo Moore, faculty adviser of the gift committee, said that the painting will be placed in the foyer on the second floor. It is expected to be completed and hung by mid-May.

Bumper stickers are currently being sold for 50 cents each to finance the gift.

FBLA Members Plan Annual Trip

Future Business Leaders of America (FBLA) have planned their annual end-of-the-year trip for May 14-15. The group will travel to Six Flags Over Texas amusement park at Dallas.

In order to go on the trip, members were required to have sold at least three cookbooks in the club's recent cookbook sale.

The trip will cost each member $10.

The members will also tour the Dallas Fair Grounds. They will return late Saturday night, May 15.

For Three of Four Programs

School Discloses Assembly Dates

Dates for three of the four traditional end-of-the-year assemblies have been announced by school officials.

The three assemblies announced and their dates are the recognition assembly, next Thursday; the awards assembly, Wednesday, May 12; and the spring band concert, Friday, May 21.

The date for the Pix yearbook assembly has not been set.

The recognition assembly honors students who have contributed to the school through work in various activities, such as Student Council, publications, monitors, etc. Seniors with perfect attendance for the three years they have been at Central will also be recognized.

The awards assembly honors students who have been selected for departmental honors or who have won school, city, state, and national contests.

The spring band concert will be presented in two performances—one in the morning for students and one at night for the general public. Details on the concert have not yet been announced.

The Pix assembly, which has not yet been scheduled, is for the purpose of presenting the yearbook to the student body. Winners of Tiger Beauty and Tiger Beau, and class favorites will be announced at the assembly.

Too, eleven students to be inducted into this year's Hall of Fame will be announced at the Pix assembly.

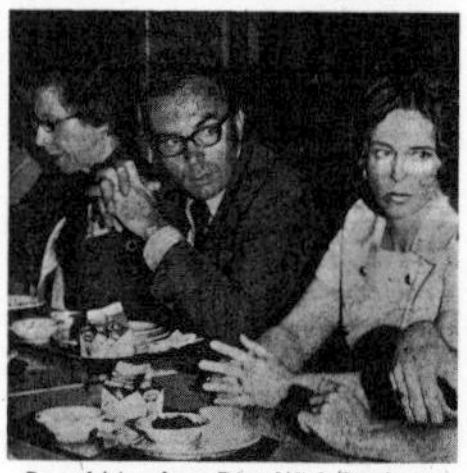

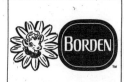

Board Members Dine With Students

Members of the Little Rock School Board are visiting Central High individually as guests of the school's Parent-Teacher-Student Association. Here, Mr. E.K. Dietz, one of the newest members of the Board, chats with Mrs. Payton Kolb, PTSA president, and Mrs. Ellery Gay, a PTSA member. The Board members have also been discussing the school with students.

The Tiger
LITTLE ROCK CENTRAL
High School

Publication written and edited by students of Little Rock Central High School, 14th and Park Streets, Little Rock, Arkansas 72202, and printed by students of Metropolitan High School, 7701 Scott Hamilton Drive, Little Rock, Arkansas 72209. Published monthly in September, December, and January; twice monthly in October, November, February, March, and May; and three times monthly in April. Sold in combination with the yearbook for $9.00 per year.
Second class postage paid at Little Rock, Arkansas 72201.

Editor .... Deborah Myers
Assistant Editor .... Stanley Denton
Sports Editor .... James Tipton
Business Manager .... Wiley Glover
Staff—Bobby Bonner, Jo Freterigo, Julie Jones, Steve Jones, Mike Price, Donna Smith, Ralph Thornton
Advertisers—Bob Coleman, Gary Hill, Gordon Miller, Cliff Powell, Joey Shelton, Tommy Starnes
Photographers—Clarence Bishop, Art Cross, Bobby Mercer,
Photography Adviser Mr. Page Daniel
Adviser .... Mr. Charles Lance

Illustration #1—Headlines on this page follow the time-accepted procedure of descending importance from top of the page down. The two-line head is a quick way to add dominance to the top of the page copy. Note that the picture in the upper left is balanced by one lower on the page. The *Tiger* pyramids ads to the left on the left page of a double page spread, thus creating a "well" effect on the spread. The smaller type in the masthead affords contrast. Note the centered kicker for the three-column story.

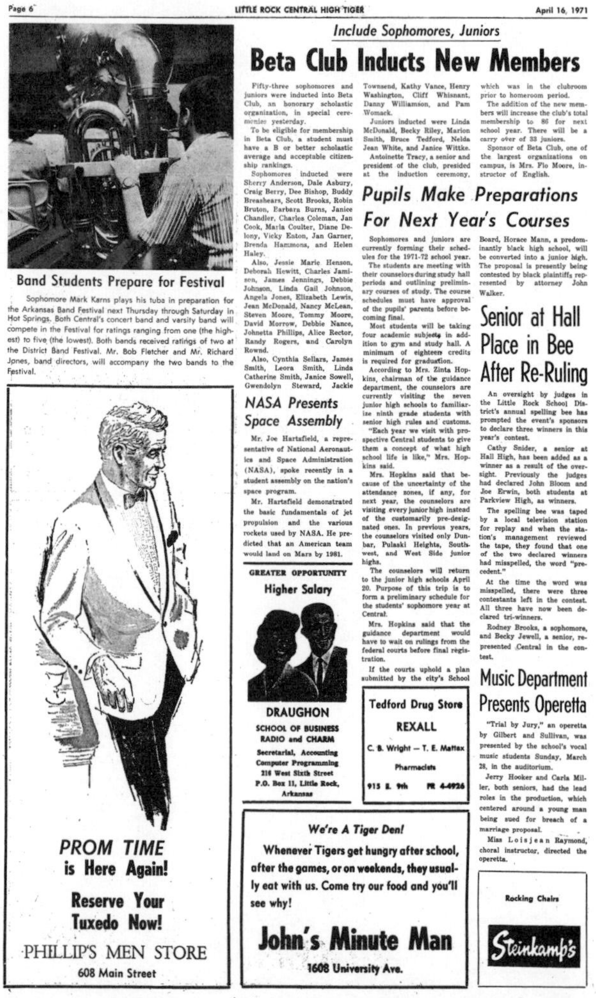

The *Tiger,* Central High School, Little Rock, Arkansas—In the following sheets from the *Tiger,* note the variety in treatment at the top of inside pages. This is achieved, however, with minimum variety in headline type. Imaginative use of variation in the length of headline, depth of headline, and kickers in several sizes of the same type affords unity not only on the page but from page to page in the issue. Note that pictures are run in various sizes and shapes.

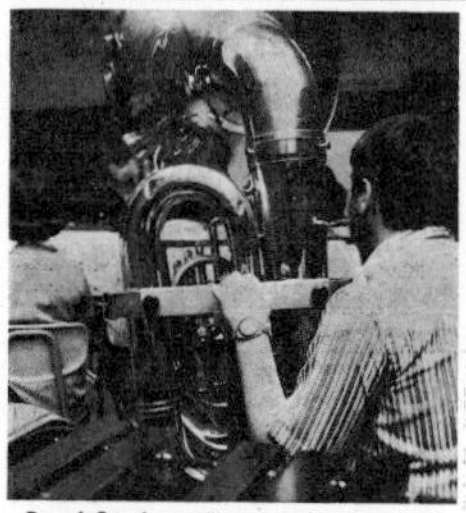

Band Students Prepare for Festival

Sophomore Mark Karns plays his tuba in preparation for the Arkansas Band Festival next Thursday through Saturday in Hot Springs. Both Central's concert band and varsity band will compete in the Festival for ratings ranging from one (the highest) to five (the lowest). Both bands received ratings of two at the District Band Festival. Mr. Bob Fletcher and Mr. Richard Jones, band directors, will accompany the two bands to the Festival.

Include Sophomores, Juniors

Beta Club Inducts New Members

Fifty-three sophomores and juniors were inducted into Beta Club, an honorary scholastic organization, in special ceremonies yesterday.

To be eligible for membership in Beta Club, a student must have a B or better scholastic average and acceptable citizenship rankings.

Sophomores inducted were Sherry Anderson, Dale Asbury, Craig Berry, Dee Bishop, Buddy Breashears, Scott Brooks, Robin Bruton, Barbara Burns, Janice Chandler, Charles Coleman, Jan Cook, Marla Coulter, Diane Delony, Vicky Eaton, Jan Garner, Brenda Hammons, and Helen Haley.

Also, Jessie Marie Henson, Deborah Hewitt, Charles Jamison, James Jennings, Debbie Johnson, Linda Gail Johnson, Angela Jones, Elizabeth Lewis, Jean McDonald, Nancy McLean, Steven Moore, Tommy Moore, David Morrow, Debbie Nance, Johnetta Phillips, Alice Rector, Randy Rogers, and Carolyn Rownd.

Also, Cynthia Sellars, James Smith, Leora Smith, Linda Catherine Smith, Janice Sowell, Gwendolyn Steward, Jackie Townsend, Kathy Vance, Henry Washington, Cliff Whisnant, Danny Williamson, and Pam Womack.

Juniors inducted were Linda McDonald, Becky Riley, Marion Smith, Bruce Tedford, Nelda Jean White, and Janice Wittke.

Antoinette Tracy, a senior and president of the club, presided at the induction ceremony, which was in the clubroom prior to homeroom period.

The addition of the new members will increase the club's total membership to 86 for next school year. There will be a carry over of 33 juniors.

Sponsor of Beta Club, one of the largest organizations on campus, is Mrs. Flo Moore, instructor of English.

NASA Presents Space Assembly

Mr. Joe Hartsfield, a representative of National Aeronautics and Space Administration (NASA), spoke recently in a student assembly on the nation's space program.

Mr. Hartsfield demonstrated the basic fundamentals of jet propulsion and the various rockets used by NASA. He predicted that an American team would land on Mars by 1981.

Pupils Make Preparations For Next Year's Courses

Sophomores and juniors are currently forming their schedules for the 1971-72 school year.

The students are meeting with their counselors during study hall periods and outlining preliminary courses of study. The course schedules must have approval of the pupils' parents before becoming final.

Most students will be taking four academic subjects in addition to gym and study hall. A minimum of eighteen credits is required for graduation.

According to Mrs. Zinta Hopkins, chairman of the guidance department, the counselors are currently visiting the seven junior high schools to familiarize ninth grade students with senior high rules and customs.

"Each year we visit with prospective Central students to give them a concept of what high school life is like," Mrs. Hopkins said.

Mrs. Hopkins said that because of the uncertainty of the attendance zones, if any, for next year, the counselors are visiting every junior high instead of the customarily pre-designated ones. In previous years, the counselors visited only Dunbar, Pulaski Heights, Southwest, and West Side junior highs.

The counselors will return to the junior high schools April 20. Purpose of this trip is to form a preliminary schedule for the students' sophomore year at Central.

Mrs. Hopkins said that the guidance department would have to wait on rulings from the federal courts before final registration.

If the courts uphold a plan submitted by the city's School Board, Horace Mann, a predominantly black high school, will be converted into a junior high. The proposal is presently being contested by black plaintiffs represented by attorney John Walker.

Senior at Hall Place in Bee After Re-Ruling

An oversight by judges in the Little Rock School District's annual spelling bee has prompted the event's sponsors to declare three winners in this year's contest.

Cathy Snider, a senior at Hall High, has been added as a winner as a result of the oversight. Previously the judges had declared John Bloom and Joe Erwin, both students at Parkview High, as winners.

The spelling bee was taped by a local television station for replay and when the station's management reviewed the tape, they found that one of the two declared winners had misspelled, the word "precedent."

At the time the word was misspelled, there were three contestants left in the contest. All three have now been declared tri-winners.

Rodney Brooks, a sophomore, and Becky Jewell, a senior, represented Central in the contest.

Music Department Presents Operetta

"Trial by Jury," an operetta by Gilbert and Sullivan, was presented by the school's vocal music students Sunday, March 28, in the auditorium.

Jerry Hooker and Carla Miller, both seniors, had the lead roles in the production, which centered around a young man being sued for breach of a marriage proposal.

Miss Loisjean Raymond, choral instructor, directed the operetta.

Illustration #2—Although the upper left again carries a picture, a one-line headline with centered kicker provides variety. Note that the headlines on this page form what we call the "X" line to make certain that large areas of gray body copy do not occur. Gradation of headlines down the page is again important.

Illustration #3—Once more a picture in the upper left, but this time it is varied with a four-column headline. Although the page is dominated by the "nightscene" advertisement, every story on the page attracts the reader's eye. Use of subheads in the "Officials" story affords contrast. White space in the "Stenger" ad draws the reader there, too.

Illustration #4—This very bold treatment at the top of the page demands heavy headlines for other stories. Note that even the ad copy is bold here. The use of combined story and cutline copy for the pictures is becoming increasingly popular. Setting this copy wider than one column affords contrast, aided also by the wider spacing between the two columns.

Top-Rated Cadet

Chris Taylor, a sophomore, has been named the "outstanding cadet" in the school's Air Force Junior Reserve Training Corps (ROTC) for the third grading quarter.

He was selected for the honor on the basis of a composite score on tests given during the quarter. He has received a service ribbon for winning the honor.

Say He Should Listen to Members

Officials in AEA Assail Executive Secretary

Mr. James O'Cain, president of the Arkansas Association of Classroom Teachers and an instructor of history at Central High, has accused the executive secretary of the Arkansas Education Association, Mr. Forrest Rozzell, of "failing to listen to the AEA membership."

Mr. O'Cain became the second elected AEA official to criticize Mr. Rozzell in recent weeks.

Baker Attacks

The outgoing AEA president, Mr. C. Ray Baker of Fort Smith Southside High School, had earlier said that Mr. Rozzell "does not consult sufficiently with the AEA membership before making important decisions concerning the AEA."

Mr. Rozzell has refused to comment on the allegations of both Mr. O'Cain and Mr. Baker.

"I'll answer any charges at the AEA's board meeting," Mr. Rozzell said. The board will not meet until June unless a special meeting is called.

Cites Legislature

Mr. O'Cain said that the AEA program for the recent legislative session was an example of Mr. Rozzell's failure to consult the membership.

Mr. O'Cain, who heads the largest AEA department, said that the legislature program was apparently drawn up by Mr. Rozzell and the AEA professional staff, and that neither Mr. Baker nor the AEA legislative committee were consulted until after the program had been completed.

At a recent meeting of AEA officials, Mr. O'Cain and Mr. Rozzell disagreed sharply on several figures concerning the AEA's request to the legislative assembly for funding of school programs.

Figures Differ

Mr. Rozzell maintained that the AEA had received about 72 per cent of what they sought from the legislators but Mr. O'Cain said that the figure was "closer to 56 per cent."

Mr. O'Cain suggested that the figure might have been different if Mr. Rozzell had been "more cooperative" with the AEA membership and helped to supply the membership with more efficient leadership in gaining passage in the legislature for the AEA program.

Mr. O'Cain said that in the past Mr. Rozzell had done "a great job" for AEA but that he thinks Mr. Rozzell should listen more closely to what the AEA membership has to say.

Declines Comment

Asked by the Tiger if Mr. Rozzell should resign from his position, Mr. O'Cain declined comment.

There are 21,000 members in the AEA which represents both teachers and administrators.

Central Gets Sweepstakes Prize At High School Journalism Day

Central High journalism students won sweepstakes honors in the 33rd annual Journalism Day contests at Arkansas State University Thursday, April 15.

It was the fifth year in the past six that Central had won sweepstakes.

In the printed newspaper contest, the Tiger was named first place winner.

The El Dorado Hi Gusher was second.

Nine individual writing contests were conducted at Journalism Day.

Individual winners from Central were Deborah Myers, first in news writing, second in editorial writing, and second in feature writing; Stanley Denton, first in headline writing, second in radio-TV commercials, and honorable mention in feature writing; and Mike Price, honorable mention in news writing.

Also, Julie Smith, second in radio-TV news writing; Ronnie Collar, honorable mention in copy reading; and Greg Bryant, honorable mention in radio-TV announcing.

First runner-up to Central for sweepstakes was Little Rock McClellan, second runner-up was Wynne, and third runner-up was DeWitt.

Approximately 275 students from 22 Arkansas high schools attended this year's Journalism Day activities, which were supervised by Mr. Roy Ockert, instructor of journalism at ASU.

Twenty students from Central attended, accompanied by Mr. Charles Lance, instructor of journalism.

Assembly, Afro-Dress, Display Highlight Negro History Week

For the second consecutive year, Central observed National Negro History Week February 7-12. The week was observed with an all-student assembly, black students wearing Afro-dress, and bulletin board displays.

In the picture at left, Ursula Holmes, Veronica Halliburton, and Sandra Myers sing during an assembly. The assembly's featured speaker, Dr. Lawrence Davis failed to show up for the assembly. He had car trouble on the way from Pine Bluff, where he is president of Arkansas AM&N College.

In the center, Glenda Knox, a senior, wears a dashiki to school.

At right, student librarians Joyce Jenkins and Renee Costley decorate a bulletin board in the school's library, honoring black history-makers.

Students for Black Culture will present an assembly February 26 with a theme of "Peace, Pride, and Power," which will be a continuing part of National Negro History Week.

Circuit Court of Appeals Removes Injunction; Construction Resumes on Junior High School

Work has resumed on construction of an addition to Henderson Junior High after the U.S. Eighth Circuit Court of Appeals in St. Louis lifted an injunction that had barred work on the project.

The court issued the injunction in early January and gave the plaintiffs, represented by Little Rock civil rights attorney John Walker, one month to post the injunction.

Efforts Fail

However, the black plaintiffs let the month expire without posting the bond.

As soon as the month's injunction expired, "The School Board authorized John E. Stowers, Inc., contractor for the project, to commence work and ordered the Board's attorney, Herschel Friday, to investigate the possibility of suing to recover $8,735.93 in additional expense caused by the delay.

The suit would be filed against the black plaintiffs, Mr. Walker, and the National Association for the Advancement of Colored People's Legal Defense Fund, which financed the action by the plaintiffs.

Explains Costs

The month's delay resulted in additional costs because of price increases for equipment and labor.

Too, the contractor has informed the Board that the addition will not be completed by the opening of the 1970-71 school year as had been scheduled. Henderson Junior High has been termed over-crowded by school authorities.

A $25,000 bond to cover any possible damages resulting from the injunction.

The injunction had been issued when Mr. Walker asked that all construction at schools be halted until the Appeals Court rules on whether the present school desegregation plan employed by the District is constitutional.

Too, Mr. Walker contends that junior highs are constructed in locations for "the primary purpose of maintaining predominantly white and all-black junior highs." Henderson is predominantly white.

The present school desegregation plan was approved in federal court in early September and was immediately appealed by Mr. Walker. The appeal has not been decided.

Board President Attacks Dress Of Some High School Students; Committee To Draft Regulations

At the request of its president, Mr. Daniel Woods, the School Board has ordered school administrators to select a committee of students, principals, and parents for drafting a dress code for high school students.

At its February meeting, the Board heard Mr. Woods explain visits that he made to the District's high schools.

"I was appalled at the appearance of some students," he said, indicating that he observed girls in jeans and loosely knit shirts and boys wearing T-shirts with the sleeves cut away.

There was some discussion by Board members as to whether enforcement of a dress code would be constitutional in view of recent federal court rulings. However, the Board passed the proposal.

The committee will represent a group from each school that will include the student body president, the student body vice president, two other students selected by the Student Council, the principal, a female teacher (since all principals are males), the PTA president, the PTA vice president, and two other parents selected by the PTA's executive committee.

The Board, according to Mr. Woods, will not instruct the committee to make any specific requirements but will leave it "entirely up to the committee."

The code would not be put into effect until next school year.

Pupils Give $63 In 'Dimes' Drive

Students contributed $63.27 in this year's March of Dimes drive conducted recently in homerooms.

The $63.27 was the smallest amount ever collected in a March of Dimes drive at Central. Last year students gave $76, which was the previous low.

Several homerooms failed to participate in the drive.

Mr. Douglas Green   **Mr. Gary Cheetam**

School Gains Two Instructors; Three Classes Change Format

Two new instructors — Mr. Gary Cheetam and Mr. Douglas Green — joined the faculty at semester.

Mr. Cheetam was hired as a replacement for Mrs. Carol Harvey, who was granted a leave-of-absence for the remainder of the school year because of illness. He will teach social studies.

Mr. Green was hired as an addition to the faculty because of over-crowding in the special education classes. His addition increases the faculty to 88.

The two teachers were the only changes made in the faculty at semester, according to Mr. Harry W. Carter, principal.

Several changes were also made in the curriculum at semester.

Students enrolled in business law, economics, and sociology—which are one-half year courses —changed classes. Consumer education replaced business law, world geography replaced economics, and problems of democracy replaced sociology.

The new semester began Monday, February 1, and will continue through Thursday, June 3. One holiday—a day at Easter—is scheduled for second semester.

Teachers Protest

(Continued from Page 1)

with the Legislature, which was in session.

However, when the teachers arrived at the State Capitol, most of the legislators refused to come out and talk with the teachers. Some went out the back doors of their chambers to avoid confronting the teachers.

Governor Unimpressed

Governor Bumpers said that he was unimpressed by the visit of the teachers and that he would maintain a belief that the tax program he has proposed to the best program. (The tax program allows for a $900 raise for teachers.)

Teachers advocate higher taxes to provide money for the raises they want.

Group Announces Contest Planning

Members of the Future Business Leaders of America are selecting contestants for contests to be conducted at the group's county convention, which will be next Saturday, Feburary 27.

Ten individual contests, ranging from spelling to typewriting, will be conducted at the convention. Each school may enter three contestants in each contest.

A scrapbook and chapter exhibit contest will also be conducted.

Students Learn Future Roles Through Adult Living Course

By DEBORAH MYERS

Twenty years ago senior girls began taking a course called "home management." Purpose of the course was to help the girls become acquainted with the aspects of adult life.

Four years ago senior boys enrolled in the course. The one unit course changed its name to "adult living," which it is still called.

Explains Units

Taught by Mrs. Teresa Austin, Mrs. Margaret Blalock, and Mrs. Kathy Venable (who is also the kindergarten instructor), adult living includes such special assignments and projects as units on housing, money management, foods, sex, and clothes—all essential remnants of the old home management course.

Mrs. Blalock defines the purpose of the adult living course as an offer "to try to help young people understand themselves, understand what it means to be a good mother or father, and to get along with other people."

Although it may seem that boys would lack interest in learning the necessities of fatherhood and husbandhood, the young men tend to disagree with the outsider's assumption.

Pupils Comment

Bernard Bogard, who is enrolled in Mrs. Blalock's third hour class, said, "Adult living just helps you accept yourself as you are with maybe a few changes. Every high school student should take adult living before he graduates; he can understand himself better."

According to Mrs. Blalock, her students' responses indicate that they enjoy the class activities, which usually involve discussions. "I really can't tell any difference in the responses of the boys and girls in class," she said. "Some of my best students are each. But, last time I counted, there were more boys than girls."

Some students generalized their ideas of what the course involves. Rosalyn Grant and Glen Nowlin, who both are enrolled in adult living, agree that the course is a "preview" to adult life.

"To me adult living involves what should be instinctive," Rosalyn said.

Nowlin believes that the course "gives you a taste of what it would be like to be an adult. I think it's good preparation."

ADULTHOOD TRAINING—Mrs. Margaret Blalock, instructor of adult living, discusses a topic with Nona Turley (left) and William Norwood. The course in adult living is enjoying popularity among students.

Knight Withdraws From Board Race

One of the four candidates who filed for position 2 on the Little Rock School Board has asked that his name be withdrawn from the race.

Mr. Hubert Knight has received permission from county election officials to have his name removed, leaving three candidates in the race for the position being vacated by Mr. Daniel H. Woods, presently the Board president.

The three remaining candidates are Joe Anderson, 39, owner of a construction company; Jim P. Spradley, 39, vice president of an insurance agency; and Howard Watson, 40 a former broadcaster currently enrolled in law school.

Mr. Knight said that he was withdrawing in favor of Mr. Spradley.

The election will be conducted March 9.

Mr. E. Kearney Dietz, 58, an advertising executive, is unopposed for Position 1.

The Tiger

LITTLE ROCK CENTRAL High School

Publication written and edited by students of Little Rock Central High School, 14th and Park Streets, Little Rock, Arkansas 72202, and printed by students of Little Rock Central High School, 7701 Scott Hamilton Drive, Little Rock, Arkansas 72209. Published monthly in September, December, January; twice monthly in October, November, February, March, and May; and three times monthly in April. Subscription price is in combination with the yearbook for $9.00 per year.

Second class postage paid at Little Rock, Arkansas 72201.

Editor .... Deborah Myers
Assistant Editor .... Stanley Denton
Sports Editor ...... James Tipton
Business Manager ... Wiley Gleese
Staff—Bobby Bonner, Jo Franquiz, Julie Johns, Steve Jones, Mike Price, Donna Smith, Ralph Thornton
Advertisers—Bob Coleman, Gary Hill, Gordon Miller, Cliff French, Jeep Sheldon, Tommy Stanton
Photographers—Clarence Hulbert, Art Gordon, Bobby Malone
Photography Adviser Mr. Page English
Adviser .... Mr. Charles Bennett

Yearbook Staff Nears Final Dedline

The 1971 Pix yearbook is nearing completion. The staff is scheduled to mail 96 pages to the book's publisher on Monday with the last 32 pages of the book to be sent prior to March 15. Here Greg Bryant (standing) discusses the final pages with staffers Donna Joyner (center) and Clai Morehead. The book will arrive in mid-May.

Illustration #5—Here portraits in the upper left afford a change of pace in pictures, and the upper right picture is a variation of the frequently used base design for this inside page. The two-line headline is needed to balance the picture lower on the page. The very bold type for the "teachers" jump story provides excellent contrast. Note that cutlines are double column, are larger type than the body copy, and are sans serif. Headlines are used with cutlines when no story accompanies the picture. Boldface caps and a dash open cutlines for pictures used with a story.

Sportscope

Two-Session Track Meets Would Better Cinder Sport

by James Tipton

Track at all levels is heartily thriving in Arkansas. More fans, admittedly including many college scouts, are coming out to view track at places which several years ago gave only token interest to the sport.

Arkansas has gained national attention in track and manages yearly to produce several top-ten rankings in track categories. As evidence to the sport's growing interest, state funds have been appropriated for a modern grass-tex track at Scott Stadium.

Yet regardless of the continued improvement in performances that accompanies increased competition, interest in track for the fan has reached its apex in the state.

Most meets have become so drawn out and the running of events so tiresome that few fans can bear to sit through the full length of them.

Most meets incorporate all divisions—junior high, high school, and college—into one complicated extravaganza, hoping to increase attendance. But the AIC schools which make up the bulk of colleges invited to the high school meets have no real fans in this area, and the extra events tend to bore the high school fans.

The result is that the most meets become less and less inviting to the track fans.

Perhaps a solution to the time problem would be to spread the meet over two days, preferably Friday and Saturday. Not only would this cut out the cumbersomeness of the one night meets, it would also allow athletes rest in between nights.

Preliminaries would be run Friday morning or afternoon. That might four or five races and all the field events could be finished. Saturday the remainder of the events would conclude. Tickets would be good for either or both.

A two-day meet would lessen confusion by lessening the athletes running up, give athletes added rest, thus giving them better times; and lastly fans could see an hour of exciting, well-organized track.

Too, a two day meet would improve attendance.

Wins State AAAA Title

Pine Bluff Dominates Relays

The Pine Bluff Zebras climaxed a perfect season by winning the AAAA state championship Friday, May 7, at Scott Field in Little Rock.

The Zebras were undefeated, winning every meet they entered this year.

"We never really doubted that they (Pine Bluff) had the personnel to win the state," Central's head track coach Clyde Horton said, "but I think our boys did a great job considering their inexperience."

The Tigers finished third in class AAAA track. Little Rock Hall finished second.

Pine Bluff set a new record in the 440-yard relay. Their quarter-relay team, anchored by speedy Clarence Willis, broke the old record of 42.0 set by Central in 1968, with a time of 41.7.

Central's husky field-man, Ed Horvath, won first place in the discuss throw. Horvath bettered his season record with a throw of 162 feet, 6 inches.

Sophomore Will Robinson rated a new season best in the 180 yard low hurdles, with a timing of 19.1 Robinson, however, was edged at the wire in the 120-yard high hurdles. Robinson was previously undefeated in both events.

VAULTING—Senior Mike Comer goes over the bar in the pole vault in the state AAAA track meeting, which was won by Pine Bluff. Central was the defending state champion.

Zebras Sweep Relays; Dominate 4A Regional

Pine Bluff continued its winning ways in Class AAAA track by virtually dominating the AAAA regional meet at Scott Stadium April 30.

The Zebras took first place in seven events, placed in ten, and set new regional meet records in three events. The new records were set in the 440 and 880-yard relays and the 880-yard run. (The broken records had been set by Central thinclads in all three events.)

Central and Hall were the distant contenders in the meet. The Bengals won two events and placed in 13.

Will Robertson bettered his times in both hurdle events. By winning both contests, he remained undefeated.

All three of the Tigers' relay teams, 440, 880, and mile, placed second.

Both Robinson and Horvath are picked to win the Meet of Champions in their events tonight. The meet begins at 7:30 tonight at Scott Field.

Tiger Baseballers Win First Games From Mann, Cab

Making its debut as a powerful offensive team, Central's baseball squad defeated Horace Mann 25-5 and Checker Cab 4-8 last week.

The Tigers faced Mann at the Southend Boys Club Field Wednesday afternoon. Sophomore Pete Campbell directed the pitching as the Tigers powered 32 hits and scored 23 runs. Senior Bobby Bonner led the Tigers in batting with four hits, including a triple and a double.

Thursday afternoon the Tigers met Checker Cab at Curran Conway American Legion Field. Gary Hill pitched and hit a triple in the fifth inning to lead the Bengals to a 4-3 victory.

Girls' Net Team Claims 3rd Place

El Dorado claimed the title in the singles and Pine Bluff won the doubles competition in the Girls' State Tennis Tournament at Walker Tennis Courts in Fair Park April 30.

Central finished third in the doubles division.

A WHOPPER!—Fishing is proving to be a popular sport with Central's male population. Here, Gordon Miller pulls in a bream as James Tipton and David Heffington watch.

Dating Back to Medieval England, Game Fishing Still Thrives Today

By JAMES TIPTON

"There's something about a good secluded fishing trip that brings out the natural qualities in a man. There's nothing like it for making a man think clear."

The quote originates with Teddy Roosevelt, but the recognition of fishing as a natural sporting pastime goes back much further.

In fact it goes back to sixteenth century England when Wynkyn de Worde published his "Treatyse of Fishing With An Angle."

So, as fishing ceased to be a means of supporting life and became a sport, man gradually chose the most pleasurable means of catching fish. Now, in the 20th century, sport fishing, or angling, has come to mean fishing with a rod, reel, line, and hook. It is still a growing sport, especially in Arkansas.

Unlike several states, Arkansas has no seasons for sport fishing. The season for game fish is open to the public all year.

Arkansas has more than 50 lakes owned by the Game and Fish Commission that are open to the public. These state's game fish range from rainbow trout in the northern section of the state to bass, bream, and crappie in the warmer waters of the central and southern areas.

The only requirement is the purchase of a fishing license by all state residents 16 years of age and older. The license are sold for $3.50 each.

Illustration #6—On this sports page in the prime space at the upper left, attention is drawn by the double-column copy with the boldface indented paragraphs. Note the column heading and by-line framing the headline with lines. This page breaks into neat geometric patterns. It once more illustrates the importance of a three-column head in avoiding a stacked effect of too many double-column headlines.

Page 8 LITTLE ROCK CENTRAL HIGH TIGER May 14, 1971

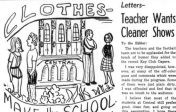

Board Should Reject Code

We would imagine that the Little Rock School Board will refuse to adopt a proposed dress code written by a committee of students, parents, teachers, and administrators appointed by the Board to study possible dress regulations. And, it would be a wise move on the part of the Board to refuse to accept the code.

The dress code proposed by the committee has a major flaw that would create havoc in the School District and would possibly cause the Board to end up in court. That flaw is that the proposed code gives the individual secondary schools the right to set their own clothing regulations.

Of course, the code says that "suggestive or indecent clothing, any clothing posing a health or safety hazard, and any clothing causing a disturbance or interfering in the instructional program" will be banned; but, views on what is decent or indecent, safe or hazardous, etc., vary with individuals.

If the code is adopted by the Board, we predict that students in one school will be permitted to wear certain fashions that will be banned in other schools. That, my friend, is going to cause many, many complaints from both students and parents.

Just this week, male students and faculty members at Central gained the right to wear "bermuda or walking shorts" to classes. We don't know if other secondary schools have extended this privilege to males, but we know that School District administrators and Board members will hear from students at those schools where the privilege has not been given.

It is only fair to all students in Little Rock that each student has the same rights and privileges in dress.

We know the work done by the dress code committee took many hours and we commend them for providing their services, but we are unable to support their proposed code. In fact, on behalf of the student body, we ask the Board to reject the code as being "ineffective."

Help Central Stay Beautiful

We are pleased that Central High has been selected to receive the J. M. Cook Memorial Trophy, awarded by the Little Rock City Beautiful Commission to the secondary school in the city showing the "greatest improvement" in beauty and cleanliness.

The student body, teachers, and administrators have done a commendable job this year in keeping Central clean. We hope that this "job" will continue in the years to come.

Just one year ago, the Tiger was reporting on Board members speaking at Central on the "dirty" condition of the school. The school has come a long way in that year.

We especially offer our thanks to Mrs. G. D. Gleason and other members of the Parent-Teacher-Student Association who have worked long hours this year at Central in helping to provide a more beautiful, cleaner atmosphere for students.

Central has long been recognized by many as "America's Most Beautiful School." Hopefully, the day will come when it will also be known as "America's Cleanest High School."

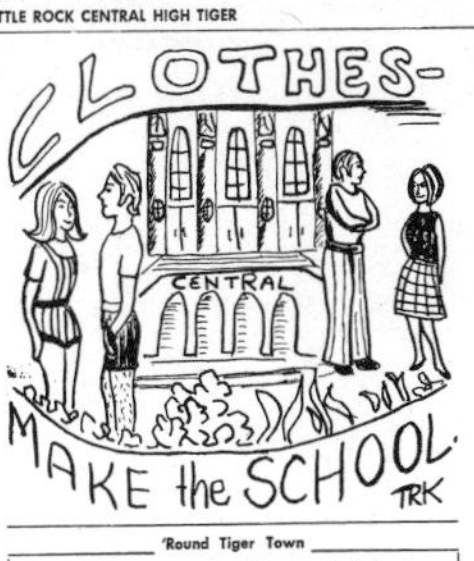

'Round Tiger Town

Rock Concert, Art Festival, Movies Comprise City's Top Entertainment

By DONNA SMITH

Highlighting entertainment in Tiger Town during the next few weeks is a rock concert next Friday night, May 21, at Barton Coliseum.

The rock concert features two nationally-acclaimed groups, "Steppenwolf" and "Bloodrock." Both have had songs recently on the top ten chart.

Tickets for the concert are on sale now throughout Little Rock for $4.50. They will be $5 at the door.

Winning paintings from the Arkansas Art Festival contests will be shown May 18-31 at the Arkansas Arts Center.

Also remaining on display at the Arts Center is the Arkansas Young Artists exhibit, which features works by school students from throughout the state. Several Central students have works in the exhibit.

"New Leaf" has opened at the Arkansas Theater. The movie, which stars Walter Matthau and Elaine May, has been hailed by reviewers as "the funniest of the season."

The movie centers around Matthau, a free-spending bachelor with a love for fine automobiles, who finally spends himself broke and must look for a rich woman to wed.

The Olde West Dinner Theater has changed its style for productions with the opening of "The Green Apple Nasties," which will be at the theater for the remainder of the month.

"The Green Apple Nasties" consists of a young off-Broadway group of performers who play musical instruments and sing.

Showtime during the week is 8:30 p.m. with dinner served at 7. Admission during the week is $5.40 per person. Weekend performances and prices of admission may be secured by calling the theater.

An exhibit of old clocks and watches is the current main attraction at the Museum of Science and Natural History in MacArthur Park.

Letters–

Teacher Wants Cleaner Shows

To the Editor:

The teachers and the football team are to be applauded for the touch of humor they added to the recent Key Club Capers.

I was very disappointed, however, at many of the off-color puns and comments which were made during the program. Some of them were just plain dirty. I was offended and feel that it was an insult to the audience.

I believe that most of the students at Central still prefer good, clean fun; and going on this assumption, I hope there is a more careful control of the material presented in future assemblies of this type.

—Mrs. Sherrie Culbertson
Instructor, Business

• • •

To the Editor:

The family of Chris Thomas would like to express their heartfelt appreciation for the thoughtfulness of all the students and faculty of Central High, Hall High, and Parkview High.

You will never know how much your presence and words of encouragement strengthened us during this time of bereavement. May the good Lord bless you all.

—The Family
of Chris Thomas

High Court Rules Jury Has Powers To Declare Death

Even though the U.S. Supreme Court has ruled that it is not unconstitutional to execute criminals sentenced to death by juries, it is apparent that Arkansas will not execute criminals—at least for two yeras.

Three Arkansans were on death row at the time the Supreme Court decision was rendered. Immediately, Governor Dale Bumpers commuted the sentences of two of the prisoners to life.

He indicated that he would have commuted the other sentence but that it remained on appeal in the courts.

As of last week, 644 men and seven women in 33 states were awaiting execution.

The last execution in the nation was in June of 1967 in California.

In early January, out-going Governor Winthrop Rockefeller commuted the sentences of 15 of the 18 inmates on death row in the Arkansas Prison. It was one of his last acts of office.

The Supreme Court voted 6-3 for upholding the death sentences by juries.

City Manager Speaks to Democracy Students; Answers Questions About Ward Representation

By MIKE PRICE

Several members of Mrs. Diane Wahlquist's problems of democracy classes recently decided that perhaps it would be better if School Board representatives could be elected by each of the city's five wards instead of by a vote at large.

Thinking that he had jurisdiction in such matters, the students wrote letters to the city manager, Mr. Jack Merriwether, seeking his opinion and advice on how to initiate such a change.

Instead of merely "passing the buck" and just telling the students that he had no control over the situation, Mr. Merriwether offered to speak to the students on how to contact "the right agency" when there is a problem. He did so Tuesday, April 27.

Though Mr. Merriwether offered no solution to the students' specific problem, he did discuss the origination of the city's wards and their use in city government.

"As far as city government is concerned, the city's wards have little or no meaning, "Mr. Merriwether said, explaining that the wards were established under another type of city government in which each ward elected a representative to the City Council.

Mr. Merriwether told the students that this practice had been abandoned in 1958 because each Councilman had a tendency to be more interested in the welfare of his own ward than that of the city.

"Nowadays, wards are merely used to designate certain areas and do not necessarily associate with a particular political idea," he added.

In discussing popular allegations that the fourth and fifth wards controlled most city elections, the city manager reminded the students that these two wards had the greatest number of people and if these voters happened to want the same things, they could probably get it. He also revealed that Little Rock and several other cities in Arkansas are currently being sued in federal courts, with the plaintiffs claiming that the present use of representation at-large was "unconstitutional."

"Both ward representation and at-large representation have their advantages as well as their disadvantages," Mr. Merriwether observed. "Personally, I'd like to see a set up in which each ward is represented along with three members elected at-large because this would use the best of both systems."

I Fly

I fly through my mind
until the dark and solid parts
close in to crush the
key to the supernal essence that
yearns to be the
overwhelming messenger of the
utopia of my soul.

—Rube Warren III

In Behind-the-Scene Action

Stage Crew Controls Every Assembly

By DEBORAH MYERS

Though it may be a hidden fact, there is a dictatorship behind the scenes at Central.

The stage crew, which includes eight juniors and seniors, has control of every production that goes on stage.

If the lighting is bad or the sound is not right, then no speaker, actor, singer, dancer, model or otherwise can clearly convey a message. So, the fact remains that the stage crew "runs the whole show."

The members of the crew includes Charles Frost (president), Sandy Mill (vice-president), Fred Heggs, Vincent Dunlap, Daniel Pritchett, Woody Black, and Skip Jones. Cynthia Dismuke complements the crew with a spark of Women's Liberation. The hard-hitting, hard-driving boss man is Mr. Page Daniel, an instructor of science.

Very seldom (if ever) is due credit given to stage crew members. According to Daniel Pritchett, "It take hours of work before and after school for one hour of production." Pritchett added that the most difficult thing to learn was co-ordinating the lights with the sound while the performer is doing his act.

Since the great percentage of school-wide communications is via assemblies, the stage crew is the most vital part of the production. If the crew is upset, they need only lower a lever and the steel curtain seals the performer off from the scrutinizing public.

It normally takes one full school year to learn the basic operations of all the gadgets that comprise the world of "stage crewism."

Illustrations #7 and #8—These two examples of *Tiger* editorial pages indicate the possible variations within a pattern. Most layout designers would use a bolder headline in the upper left because of the heavier headlines down the page. The four-column and the five-column headline offer many possibilities for variety in page design. Note the use of the half box around the headline under the cartoon with the column heading centered. The *Tiger* runs the editorial page as the last page of each issue.

Page 8 LITTLE ROCK CENTRAL HIGH TIGER April 16, 1971

Does Prom Fulfill Need?

The most extravagant and most expensive event of Central's year is approaching. That event is the senior class prom, which is scheduled for Friday, April 30, in the fieldhouse.

We don't know what percentage of this year's senior class will attend the prom; however, we imagine that it will be much less than 50 per cent—probably in the neighborhood of 30 per cent. For the past several years attendance at the prom has been declining.

We would imagine that parents spend an average of $50 for each son or daughter attending the event. Males are expected (but not required) to wear formal attire, which means renting a tuxedo for around $17.50 from one of the clothing rental outlets in the city. Males must also purchase the tickets ($6.00 per couple), buy a corsage (around $5), and of course pay for the gas used in the car and for the refreshments.

Females are also expected (but again not required) to wear formal attire, which in most cases will mean that mom and dad will have to purchase a formal for the daughter. Then, there is that trip to the beauty parlor and those other incidental expenses involved in seeing that "true beauty" is displayed on prom night.

Central High has few dances each year. In fact, we can think of only two dances scheduled during this entire school year. This compares to around ten dances just ten years ago, including the Turkey Trot dance at Thanksgiving and a Valentine's Ball, both of which exceeded the senior prom in attendance.

We don't know why the senior prom has endured this long at Central when so much expense and time is involved in the event and when so few students take an active part in it. Many schools across the nation no longer have senior proms for the reasons just named.

We believe that dances are important to the curriculum of the school. They are important in providing relaxation and a break in school routine and they are important in teaching social graces and encouraging students to lead a well-rounded social life. However, no part of a curriculum should be so expensive as to exclude many students, which the present cost of the prom does.

Congratulations To Mathes

We offer our congratulations to Mike Mathes on his recent election to the student body presidency, the most important student position at Central.

Mathes has the ability to provide the positive leadership that students need. We sincerely hope that he will exert this leadership—and we are sure that he will—in making the 1971-72 school year one of the best ever for Central High.

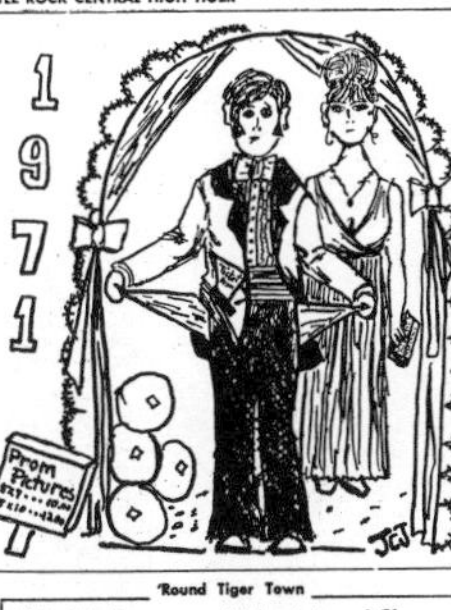

'Round Tiger Town

World-Renowned Magicians' Show To Appear Here Saturday Night

By DONNA SMITH

Magic wil be prevalent in Little Rock tomorrow night when some of the world's best known magicians make an 8 o'clock appearance in the Hall of Industry at the Arkansas State Fair Grounds.

A few of the magicians scheduled to appear are Lee Grable of California, billed as "America's No. 1 Magician"; Geoffrey Buckingham of London, billed as the "world's greatest sleight-of-hand artist"; and Don Tawton of California, named "California Magician of the Year" in 1970.

The show will feature the sawing of a woman in half, disappearing rabbit acts, removing chains locked around the body, etc.

Admission to the magic show will range from $2 to $5 with tickets available at the door.

Kenny Rogers and the First Edition will play in concert at Barton Coliseum next Saturday, April 24. Ticket prices and performance time had not been set at press time.

Looking ahead, three well-known musical groups will make appearances at the Coliseum. These are James Brown on May 2, the Temptations on May 13, and Steppenwolf on May 21.

Burns Park in North Little Rock has opened for its 1971 season. The Park, featuring numerous rides, will be open daily from 1 to 10 p.m.

Wrestling continues each Tuesday night at Robinson Auditorium with the first match beginning at 8. Admission to the matches, featuring some of the top names in the sport, is $1.50 with ringside seats costing an extra 75 cents.

"Love Is a Time of Day" continues to show at the Olde West Dinner Theatre located in the K-Mart Center. Admission prices and times of performances may be obtained by calling Olde West.

'Long' Session Of Legislature Closes Monday

By RONNIE COLLAR

The Arkansas Legislature recessed April 2 after being in session for 82 days, one of the longest sessions in modern times.

The Legislature is scheduled to report back to Little Rock Monday to make any necessary corrections in bills that were passed containing typographical errors or incorrect phrasing.

If there are no errors found in the bills, a skeleton session is expected to be on hand to vote final adjournment for the session.

The state's press as well as veteran politicans has praised this session of the Legislature as being "both productive and harmonious." The criticisms given the legislators have been mainly for allegedly interfering in the operations of the state prisons by witholding funds for the prisons until the Board of Corrections dismissed the prisons' director, Robert Sarver, and for not providing enough funds for the state's public schools and colleges.

Major accomplishments of the Legislature, as cited by the state press, are the reorganization of state government as proposed by Governor Dale Bumpers, the increasing of taxes to provide "better services" for the state, and the passage of a consumer protection law.

Actions of the Legislature just prior to the recess included the ratification of a proposed amendment to the U. S. Constitution that will lower the voting age to 18 in all elections, a refusal to vote money for a state kindergarten program, and the merger of Arkansas AM&N at Pine Bluff with the University of Arkansas.

Governor Bumpers said he "is pleased" with the Legislature.

State Will Switch To Savings Time

Daylight Savings Time will officially begin Sunday morning, April 25, at 1 a.m.

The U.S. Weather Bureau has suggested that all clocks be set back one hour before retiring on Saturday night, April 24.

Daylight Savings Time will end the last Sunday in October when clocks will be set up one hour, according to the Weather Bureau.

After Assigning Book After Book for Students, Instructors of English Disclose 'Favorite' Novels

By BETH LACEY

Throughout the school year English teachers assign hundreds of books for their students to read and report on.

Students often wonder about their teachers' favorite novels and recently the English teachers at Central were questioned about this subject.

Mrs. Hazel Bullock said, "My favorite novel is 'The Man' by Irving Wallace. I particulary liked this book because of the true attitudes displayed concerning Negroes."

Mr. Sam Blair listed "Nicholas and Alexandra" as his favorite novel, saying, "It was a stunning and exciting book about the final days of the last Russian Czar."

Mr. Barry Hardin said that "Steppenwolf" by Herman Hesse was his favorite novel, and that he "was intrigued by the way Hesse probed deep into man's mind and exposed a terrible but accurate psychological trip."

Mr. Marvin Zimmerman said, "My favorite novel is 'Dr. Zhivago'. It is very interesting the way the author reflects man's basic humanistic conflicts and presents the passionate nature of man."

Miss Cynthia Crain said her favorite novel was "Atlas Shrugged" by Ayn Rand. She said the the novel "beautifully illustrated objectivism, the superiority of the individual, and the evaluation of one's self."

Mrs. Wanda Hill named "To Kill a Mockingbird" as her favorite novel, saying, "I love the characterization of Scout and the tracing of her education through realizing why it is a sin to kill a mockingbird."

Cover of Agenda Features Cartoon

The editorial cartoon that appeared in the last issue of the Tiger is being used on the cover of the April agenda for the Little Rock School Board.

The cartoon was drawn by Julie Jones and portrays a perplexed student wondering where he will attend high school next school year.

It Aids Suspended Students

Gateway School Proves 'Prosperous'

By RONNIE COLLAR

Now entering its seventh month of operation, the Gateway School, located in the School Board Building Annex in downtown Little Rock, is having a "successful program," according to Miss Reba Stone, adjustment counselor for the school.

Gateway School was created in the fall by order of the School Board to handle students who have been suspended from their regular schools.

"Our main purpose is to keep suspended students from falling hopelessly behind in their regular school work and in getting them back into their regular schools as soon as possible," Miss Stone said.

"In other words, we are a dropout prevention center," she added.

Miss Stone said that in past years many of the students who drew suspensions from school never returned to classes or that they returned to find they were hopelessly behind and then dropped out.

Approximately 1400 students were suspended during the 1969-70 school year from schools in the District.

Thus far in the school year, according to Miss Stone, there have been 450 students suspended from schools.

Miss Stone said that it was now District policy to require any student suspended from a regular school to attend Gateway, which, she said, "probably aided in better behavior in schools."

Has Two Sessions

Gateway has two daily sessions—one in the morning from 8:45 to 11:15 and one in the afternoon from 1 to 3:30. There is an average daily attendance of 55 to 60 students at the sessions.

In addition to Miss Stone, the school—headed by Dr. Don Roberts, director of pupil personnel—has three other employees. They are Mrs. Jean Fleming and Mr. Odell Waller, instructors, and Mr. Richard Maple, case worker.

A progress sheet is kept on each student in attendance at Gateway, which is made available to the student's regular principal when the student returns to his regular school.

Defines 'Length'

The length of a student's stay at Gateway is the length of his suspension from a regular school. The student is not permitted to return to his regular school, however, until he attends Gateway.

Too, Gateway has developed a student behavior guideline and students must follow the guideline if they are to be readmitted to their regular schools.

Although Gateway is a new school and its too early to provide a comprehensive evaluation, Miss Stone and others associated with the school believe that Gateway has become an important part of the School District and will continue to play an important part in the future.

The *Shield*, Northwest Classen High School, Oklahoma City, Oklahoma—Whereas most high school newspapers are now using sans serif headlines, the *Shield* has chosen a serif type for general use, set off by sans serif in kickers and elsewhere occasionally for contrast. This immediately gives this paper a personality that is further defined by various means of ornamentation, plus greater use of white space for effect than in most papers. It has style, is easy to read.

(next page)→

JAVA MAN ... Skull replica is examined by Brenda Bartlett, junior, and Mr. Terry Montgomery, who will instruct the new anthropology course being offered next fall.

New mode of enrollment to speed up procedures

Curriculum revisions figure prominently in modified pre-enrollment procedures scheduled for February 2-12.

Activities, centering in advisories this year, feature special assemblies and discussion periods. A faculty meeting after school February 2 will prepare advisers in guiding their students in course selection.

Advisory discussions concerning enrollment will both precede and follow three class assemblies during blocks one and two, February 4. Underclassmen will be dismissed by Central Sound to attend their grade's meeting.

"We have planned the assemblies to give students an in depth look at the curriculum," explains Mr. Jim Tomlinson, assistant principal.

Students will be given an information letter for their parents and enrollment sheets in advisory February 5. The modified "green sheet" forms are a new system for reporting course selections which first came into use last year.

At the same time, juniors will receive a copy of their transcript.

February 8 and 9 teachers will work with individual students on their special enrollment problems. Prerequisites and content of the various courses will also be explained.

Students will receive a list of teachers designated to approve certain advanced course selections. Required signatures may be acquired from 8:00-9:40 a.m. February 10.

Such courses as Intermediate Math, College Algebra-Analytics, Great Books, World Literature, Religions of Mankind, Cry-Slur, Advanced Journalism, Drama, Debate and all advanced business classes require approval of teachers.

Block six classes and students at the vocational-technical center may obtain approval that afternoon during block ten.

Green sheets will be collected

and checked during advisory February 11. Thursday advisees may return their enrollment sheets February 12.

Many proposed revisions are tentatively scheduled for next year.

"We will not know until the forms are tabulated whether the changes will materialize or not. Final determination of course offerings are measured by student response during pre-enrollment," pointed out Miss Bernice Webster, coordinator of counselors.

Up With People cast attending NW

"Up, up with people ..."

This is the sound which has been filling the halls of Northwest during the past week.

The Up With People Company, nationally-known singing group, performed for two assemblies Tuesday to begin an action-filled week at the school and in Oklahoma City.

Group B of the six group company attended classes this past week during their Oklahoma City engagement.

The group will conclude their Oklahoma City stay with the final performance tomorrow night at the Oklahoma City Civic Center.

shield

Volume 16, No. 7   Northwest Classen High School   Friday, January 22, 1971

Bard's answer to women's lib

Drama department casts play

Women's Lib in Shakespeare's time?

It seems a bit incongruous, but "Taming of the Shrew" is a "battle between the sexes" and will be presented as such by the Northwest drama department Wednesday and Thursday, February 10-11, in the auditorium.

Cost is 50 cents for the Block 10 performance at 1:15 Wednesday and $1 for the 8 p.m. show the following day.

"The play, viewed in the light of a sort of 'women's lib' movement, is very relevant to today," said Mrs. Betty Hall Allred, director.

The entire play deals with a man's efforts to tame Katherina, the shrew he has acquired for his wife.

The cast includes Kay Long in the leading role as Katherina, with Mike Kyle playing her unlucky husband, Petruchio. Kate's sister and father, Bianca and Baptista, are portrayed by Pam Lemmon and Phil Farley, while Bianca's fiance Lucentio is depicted by Rex Humphrey.

The Hostess, Hortensio and Tranio are played, respectively, by Harriet Hall, Rick Bayless and Terry Meek, while Beverly Farmer is the Widow. The two servants are Candy Foster and Lynn French.

Co-student directors for the production are Julie Jacobs and Sue Salmon.

The art department is designing multicolored posters and working on sets for the performance.

Technical adviser for the production is Mr. James Morehead. David Turnipseed will act as stage manager.

News briefs

Biology lab claims more space

Another first for Northwest has been marked.

Miss Hazel Smiley, biology teacher, said that with the conversion of the old chemistry room to a biology lab, her classes are the first in the city to have two separate facilities for students.

When it was learned that advanced science courses, formerly offered at Northwest, would be moved to Northeast under the new cluster plan, equipment was disconnected from room 203 and moved to Northeast.

This move made possible the changes which have provided the extra space.

* * *

Art for fun and profit could be the catch words for the Art Boutique, a fund raising project of National Art Honor Society.

The art display case exhibits the paintings, boutiques, jewelry and other art work that the members of the club are selling.

One member, senior Debbie James, created all the tree trunk paintings.

* * *

Two Seniors have been nominated for appointment to two U.S. Military Academies, by Senator Fred R. Harris.

Mike Ostrander has been nominated to the Merchant Marine Academy in New York and Bob Tropper is a candidate for the U.S. Air Force Academy located in Colorado.

Mike and Bob passed their nomination through a preliminary examination conducted by the U.S. Civil Service Commission in Oklahoma and will have further examinations to determine final selections.

* * *

Paul Rahe, '67 grad, was selected as a Rhodes Scholar recently in the New Orleans school-arship competition.

In the six-state Gulf District, the Yale University senior competed with 12 other finalists for a full year's scholarship to Oxford University in England.

* * *

Editor of Northwest's literary-art magazine, Questings, was announced recently by Mrs. Maxine Houstolder, adviser, who teaches creative writing.

Tom Harrison was chosen literary editor.

The fourth edition of the magazine, which hasn't been published at Northwest since 1968, will appear in the spring.

PROBING ... into the little world is sophomore Bobby Fleet as he experiments with the new lab in room 201.

Principal joins celebrities at Super Bowl spectacular

Northwest's principal and head football coach were the envy of all those remaining in Knightland last week.

Dr. June Dawkins was the guest of his brother-in-law, NBC sports announcer Curt Gowdy, at the fifth annual Super Bowl game in Miami, Florida, last weekend.

Dr. Dawkins participated in pre-game activities and sat in the press box during what is probably the most spectacular event in the sports world.

Curt Gowdy, termed by a commentator before the game as a sportscaster "who has reached the pinnacle of success," got his start in Oklahoma City.

While Dr. Dawkins was basking in the Florida sun, Coach Dean Choate also traveled south to Houston, Texas, to attend the forty-eighth annual American Coaches Association convention.

Highlight of the session was the awarding of Coach of the Year honors to Darrell Royal, football coach at the University of Texas.

what's inside

Page 2, 'Love Story' rates raves

Page 3, La Mingos whip up spirit

Page 4, Smoking — in depth report

Page 5, Tankers prep for tourney

Page 6, B-ballers vie for title

La Mingos' routines spice pep rallies, sports events

Take 20 assorted girls, mix with two smart sponsors, add a dash of twirling and marching, line up in four rows and set to a speed of a 35 rpm record for five minutes.

This is the recipe that has produced a piping hot drill team, the La Mingos.

This newest of the spirit organizations made its debut last year. The 16 regulars and two alternate lend color to pep rallies, parades and sports events

twirling in their gold and purple uniforms. Caryl Young is drill master.

Twirlers must master four basic drills before they are accepted into the group-the flag, the figure eight, flat-hand spin and two-hand spin.

"The two-hand spin is the hardest of all," said Miss Judy Lorton, sponsor.

Tryouts are held periodically to expand the organization. Judy Colerick, a freshman, has

been nicknamed "Little Bit" because she is the smallest girl and somewhat of a pet.

The girls originate their own routines, but are aided by their sponsors, Miss Lorton and Mrs. Elgerine Roberts. Mrs. Roberts was a twirler at Douglas during her high school days and studied Modern Dance for two years in college.

"My closest association was water ballet. I was a swimmer in college," said Miss Lorton.

PRACTICE MAKES PERFECT ... reason La Mingo drill team members Karen Johnson, Judy Colerick and Caryl Young, head twirler.

Mummers get help

Stage-struck Thespians usher

"Unlike the girls who worked the coat room during opening night, I haven't gotten to try on any very expensive furs!"

Such was the comment made by senior Mary Ann Craig, who has joined other Northwest students in volunteer work for the new Mummers Theater.

Community participation has been the promotional key of the professional acting troupe and the success of their efforts is evident in the large number of Oklahoma City high school students that have volunteered for ushering duties.

Members of Northwest's National Thespians and the Great Books Clubs have been contributing their time as ushers and coat check attendants.

Kay Boyles and Mary Craig Humphries, Susie Cornielson, Vicki Tebow, Linda Sanders, Judy Wilmoth, Julie Ogden, Cyndee Parks and Tina Warren, sergeants-at-arms.

dents receive free admission to a regular performance.

Meyer, one of the first Northwest students to become involved in the program, thinks the enthusiastic participation is a good example of the increased interest in the Arts.

"Also, the people who work there are afforded new experiences and contacts that could result in later employment or career opportunities," he explained.

Ann Gillespie, another senior usher, just "likes to meet all the people who attend the performances, especially the kids from other schools."

Club column

Barn dance, concert on agenda

"Sound Crusade" music will fill the Uptown Kiwanis Club, N.W. 35 and Western, Saturday, January 30, from 8 to 11 p.m., at the annual Courtesy Club Barn Dance.

Bids will be sold until January 29 for $1.50, members; and $2, non-members.

Chairmen for the dance are Patty Cunningham and Sharon Browning, decorations; Shari Matthews, bids; Jan and Jill Brown, publicity; Julie Jacobs, refreshments; and Pam Lindley and Karen Blackburn, entertainment.

* * *

Reorganized after an inactive period of three years, the Band and Orchestra Girls have elected officers.

They are Barbara Bradney, president; Vicki Thomas, vice president; Patty Sinclair, secretary-treasurer; Karen McAnulty, parliamentarian-historian; and

Jean Griffith and Patti Stoolz, sergeants-at-arms.

* * *

The group was organized to help the band and orchestra with all activities, such as the cleaning and mending of uniforms.

* * *

Members of Future Teachers of America will observe classrooms at Taft junior high and Cleveland elementary schools February 3.

They will visit classes at the schools to obtain ideas about the teaching profession.

* * *

Oklahoma legislature members will be entertained by the Cry-Slur's small group tomorrow at 12 p.m. at the Oklahoma Press Association.

Beginning March 1 the Cry-Slur choir will compete in the annual spring contests.

* * *

Coronets and Cygnets recently elected second semester officers.

Coronets chose Debi Green, president; Jan Overby, vice president; Joanne Booth, recording secretary; Vicki Thomas, attendance secretary; Kathy Mott, treasurer; Wilma Johnson, assistant treasurer; Cindy Miller, parliamentarian; Jill Brown, reporter; and Becky Coggins, Leslie Hawkins, Kathy Hicks, Tina Love, JoAnn McDonald and Nancy Robertson, sergeants-at-arms.

Cygnet officers are Kathy Jackson, president; Jeneece Towe, vice president; Shari Matthews, recording secretary; Dianne House, attendance secretary; Kay Boyles and Mary Craig, treasurers; Brenda Bartlett, parliamentarian; Paula Fullerton, historian; and Kathy May, Sheryl

---

PRACTICING HIS BACKSTROKE is Junior tankman Henry Bockus in preparation for the All-City swim meet.

Tankers set to try for city tourney

Looking forward to a tough upcoming match with John Marshall, swimmers captured their dual meet with Putnam City West 60-35 to boost their record to 3-2.

Coach Kamil Shanbour's squad has beaten Grant, Classen and Putnam West while falling to Bartlesville and Putnam City.

Individual winners for the Putnam West meet were Henry Bockus, 200 free style; Bruce Bockus, individual medley; Mike Weiss and Don Rogivue, first and second in the 50 yard event.

Bob Trosper and Harold Robinson placed first and second in diving; Weiss, 100 yard butterfly; Henry Bockus, 100 free style; Bruce Bockus and Rogivue, 400 free style.

Also the two took a first place berth in the 400 free-style team of the Bockus brothers, Weiss and Rogivue.

With two meets left before city competition, Northwest must swim against Marshall and Capitol Hill.

"We're hoping to upset the favored Marshall team, and if we do, we should take it easy," said Coach Shanbour.

Traveling to Mid-state and State competition February 5 and 26 will be Bob Trosper, who placed third in state last year in diving.

Henry and Bruce Bockus also have qualifying times for state.

"Mike Weiss and Ron Rogivue might also be traveling if they improve their times," commented Coach Shanbour.

With a stronger squad this year, Coach Shanbour has really improved last year's record of 0-6 and has hopes of placing in state competition.

C-squad post four victories

Set for the Northwest Invitational Tournament tomorrow, Coach Fred Holloway's C-squad wrestlers have posted a 4-2 dual match record.

The Little Knights travel to Capitol Hill January 29 and to Classen February 5-6 for the 16-team Classen tournament to close the season.

Recent matches included victories over Millwood 34-15 and Roosevelt 43-20.

Team captains are Gary Martin and Mike Lukehar. Other top wrestlers are David Fleet, Steve Robertson, Rick Tatum and Mark Yeats.

Northwest is host for the 10-team junior high tournament.

Basketball schedule set

Sportswomen view new season

Trading volleyballs for basketballs, the girls' sports teams finished their pre-winter season with a 7-1, 5-2 volleyball record for A and B squads and will now turn their attention to basketball play.

A-squad posted victories over Edmond, Northeast, Putnam City, Southeast, John Marshall, Putnam City West and Capitol Hill high schools. They fell only to Douglas.

B-squadders posted wins over all their opponents except Putnam City and Putnam West.

Snapping a seven year losing streak to Douglas, the B-team defeated the Trojan Bees, while Northwest A-squad was beaten two of three games with Douglas.

Senior Rose Street and soph-

omore Cheryl Randol tallied 15 points the first game to lead the B-team to 15-9, 15-3 wins over Douglas' B-team. The A-team lost to the Trojans 15-9, 15-7.

Both the A and B teams caught the Edmond Bulldogs off guard by 16-14, 15-4 and 15-4 triumphs.

Both A and B team outpointed Northeast and Southeast with lopsided scoring. A-team toppled the John Marshall Bears with a 15-2, 13-15, 15-12, upset and B-team overwhelmed their

opponents 15-1, 15-2.

Putnam West lost to the A-team but redeemed themselves with the Bees. To wind up the season, both teams defeated Capitol Hill.

The season's star players for the A-team were Nora Gerred, Libby Tabor and Cheryl Randol with the Bees.

After a month of practice the girls' sports teams will concentrate on basketball competition with neighboring schools in early February.

Editorial commentary (right column)

Illustration #1—Page one establishes the personality of the paper as bright and airy. The rather light but large headlines, some with kickers, require space, which is further gained by use of downstyle in capitalization. The downstyle is introduced in the title plate and repeated in such standing heads as "what's inside." The "open look" is also achieved by slugs of space in the body type, the use of asterisks to separate items in the news briefs block and the boldface capitalized lead-ins for cutlines set with suspension points and indention of next line. Stories with accompanying pictures are arranged in neat blocks, supported by smaller items, to achieve a trim geometric appearance. Corners are anchored. All items on the page attract attention. This page is a good example of the reading diagonal and of what we call the "X" line.

Illustrations #2 and #3—These inside pages show how a basic design can be adapted for various needs. Both pages depend on the multicolumn headline and the arrangement of pictures and related copy as a block. One of the important principles to remember in this kind of design is what is called the "buddy system"—that is, "Line something up with something." With ads pyramided to the right, it is natural to display your most prominent elements in the upper left. Note how headlines are "alike but different" and show gradation. Boldface lead-ins for some paragraphs and asterisks in the club items break up gray areas. Again, correct space makes for easy reading.

never get it to the reader unless the actual presentation of the copy causes him to stop and read the words. That puts a great responsibility on you as the layout man, because so many things distract the reader's attention these days—some inviting in themselves, others designed to entice his interest. It is your responsibility as the person in charge to arrange the most attractive possible layout with the copy and pictures you have for your pages of white space.

White space has become such an important element of layout now that even advertising agencies are selling white space. Advertisers now seldom want a crowded space, since they are aware that today's reader is visual-minded and simply will not struggle through any collection of words that look uninteresting. *Techniques that help sell products for advertisers also help sell copy to readers.*

The Seventy Look

You could hardly be aware of general changes occurring from day to day, but if you find examples of newspapers from the late 1950's to the early 1970's, you will discern a marked difference.

It is obvious in such a comparison that the 1960's saw a number of changes in visual presentation. Or take one of the popular new books that are collections of front pages of newspapers over the years and compare the older pages with the latest ones—or better yet, with one of today's forward-looking professional dailies. Here, too, you observe trends directed toward attracting reader attention. You will even find yourself skipping over most of the older sheets, simply because they are not interesting in appearance.

Briefly, the new look is light, bright, airy, open.

The slogan of the times is "See that everything is easier to read." That means:

(1) Large expanses of gray body copy are gone.
(2) There is no crowding of heads and copy.
(3) Headlines are not in such large or heavy type as heretofore.

(4) Single-column headlines and headlines with decks are less frequently used.
(5) Column rules and cutoff rules are disappearing.
(6) Narrow columns are on the way out.
(7) Pictures are as large as possible.

In speaking of heavy headlines and crowding, one professional consultant describes the seventy look this way: "Pages don't scream at you any more."

The changes have been brought about thus:
(1) An increase in column width where possible. Many professional papers have changed from eight columns of 11 or 12 picas to six of 14 or 15 picas.
(2) The practice of keeping headlines apart so that they do not compete for reader attention.
(3) Keeping headlines simple, framing them dramatically in white space.
(4) Selection of only one or two type faces for headlines instead of the variety formerly used.
(5) Headlines run downstyle. (Meaning that words are capitalized as in sentences.)
(6) Headlines set flush left.
(7) Larger and better pictures and closer cropping for special effect.
(8) Variety in the way cutlines are run.
(9) Ideas borrowed from magazines for a fresh look where suitable.

In such new procedures, many of the old "rules" have been set aside. Now editors and layout men are questioning practices that have long been accepted, always searching for a better way to gain reader interest. A contributing factor in some instances is the cost of the printed word. All of those changes are being reflected in the school press.

Geometric Layout

One aspect of the contemporary trend in the professional newspaper is being only slowly

#1—The front page from *The Southerner* (Wichita High School South, Wichita, Kansas) shows the contemporary trend in several ways. The page is laid out in rectangles, with space added around the headlines and between paragraphs in the stories. The "Mid-term grads" story illustrates the variety gained by running four columns of type in five columns of space, especially effective with increased spacing between the columns. This page lacks an "anchor" in each of the lower corners to direct the reader to the bottom of the page. Boldface caps lead-ins for some paragraphs add contrast.

The following group of pages from high school papers illustrate the "new look" that is described by professional newsmen as "light, bright, airy, open." Note that headlines are arranged to gain reader attention—no tombstoning, no bumping of heads—and consequently no expanses of gray body type. Heads are planned for "built-in air"—that is, with space around them. Note the use of downstyle in capitalization in headlines. Note, also, that none of these pages have column rules. Corners are generally well "anchored" to direct the reader to all parts of the page.

#2—A large picture and accompanying story dominate this inside page from *The Southerner* (Wichita High School South, Wichita, Kansas). Note the balance afforded by a vertical advertisement of approximately the same weight. Other stories are arranged in neat rectangles. "Senior girl" headline is a little high but effectively breaks up the gray expanse. Names in the "Honor roll" story are run in smaller type to gain contrast and save space.

#3—A number of devices are used on this front page of *The Riparian* (Broad Ripple High School, Indianapolis, Indiana) to gain the "new look"—including the light title plate, pictures planned for special effect, variety in the way cutlines are run, boldface box for contrast with copy indented on left, boldface lead-ins for contrast in stories, asterisks to separate news briefs, the News Briefs overline for emphasis, and a definitely horizontal appearance to the page.

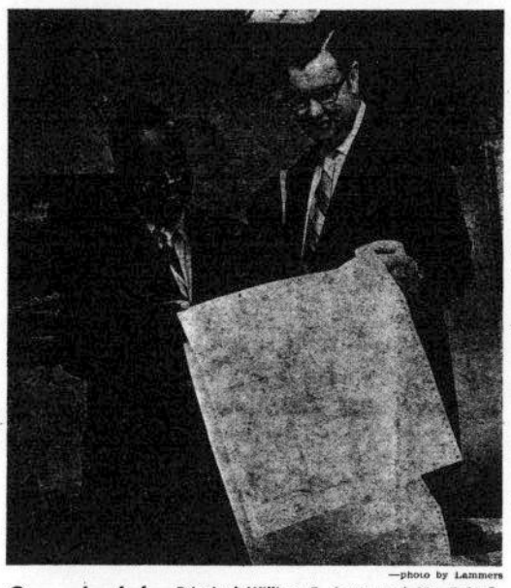

—photo by Lammers

On schedule—Principal William E. Jones and Mr. Bob G. Carnal, vice principal in charge of student personnel, check the computer print-out of student schedules.

THE *Riparian*

42nd Year, No. 1——Broad Ripple High School, Indianapolis, Indiana——September 17, 1970

Curriculum, personnel groups formed

A Curriculum Council, Student Personnel Council, and a Human Relations Committee have been established to "improve communications among the student body, faculty, and administration," said Mr. William E. Jones, principal.

Mr. Bob G. Carnal, vice principal, is chairman of the Student Personnel Council. The Council is composed of the deans, counselors, social workers, school nurse, athletic director, and three students. Senior Jay Cohen, Student Council president, will be a permanent member while two other students will be selected on a rotating basis.

"I see the Student Personnel Council as being both a highly trained professional group to deal with student problems and a means of involving students in a policy-making group which will make recommendations to the administration," said Mr. Carnal.

The Curriculum Council, headed by Vice Principal Albert R. Mahin, is set up to evaluate and improve high school instruction at Broad Ripple.

Other members of the council are Mr. Jones, Mr. Carnal, all department heads, Mr. Thomas Potter, social science teacher; Mr. James Davis, math teacher; Mrs. Carolynne Bobbitt, librarian; Mrs. Mary Hogg, social worker; and Mrs. Ruth Marie Griggs, director of publications.

"The first order of business of the Curriculum Council will be to study the North Central Evaluation and recommend which suggestions can be implemented, deferred for a later date, or deemed impossible to fulfill," said Mr. Mahin.

The Human Relations Committee, chaired by Mr. Thomas Potter, social science teacher, will "attempt to improve relations among the staff, student body, community, and administration. We hope that the school atmosphere will be conducive to success," said Mr. Potter.

Faculty representatives are Mr. Robert Casey, social science department head; Mrs. Jan Ellis, English teacher; Mr. William Fisher, Latin teacher; Mr. William Fletcher, science teacher; and Mr. Carl Sams, assistant dean of boys. Mrs. Carolynne Bobbitt, librarian, is the faculty alternate.

Mrs. Laura Snyder, cafeteria manager; Mrs. Elizabeth Pillow, registrar; and Mr. Bob Summers, custodian complete the list.

Enrollment highest since '61

With the addition of three new feeder schools, Broad Ripple's total enrollment rocketed toward the 2,000 mark, the highest figure since 1961.

New feeder schools, Schools 11, 69, and 43, boost the enrollment figure to 119 more than last year.

The number includes 419 seniors, 430 juniors, 507 sophomores, and 603 freshmen, for a total of 1,959 pupils.

"Despite the fact that we have made a considerable number of innovations, including the use of data processing, the opening of school went smoothly," said Mr. William E. Jones, who was appointed principal last May.

"It took the processing computer only 18 minutes to prepare the schedules of all students," said Mr. Bob G. Carnal, new vice principal.

Mr. Jones earned BS and MS degrees from Butler University. Mr. Carnal received a BS degree from Evansville University and an MS degree from Indiana University.

New department heads are Mr. Ferd Brumblay, Art Department; Mr. James Hinshaw, Business Ed. Department; and Miss Hilda Ellis, Home Economics Department.

Miss Ellis has a BS degree from Butler University and an MS degree from Indiana University.

Joining the English Department are Mrs. Lois Kaylor, who has a BS degree from Ohio Northern University, and Mr. Joel Schopmeyer also teaches in the Art Department.

Mrs. Barbara Hawkins, who has a BS degree from the University of Cincinnati and an MS degree from Butler University teaches in the Business Ed. Department.

Mr. Richard Orban, new social science teacher, freshman football coach, and assistant wrestling coach, has BS and MA degrees from Ball State University.

Two administrative positions have been created: assistant dean of girls and assistant dean of boys.

Mrs. Shirley Loyd, with BS and MS degrees from Butler University, is assistant dean of girls.

Mr. Carl Sams is assistant dean of boys.

Extra!

Riparian Newspaper and Yearbook were awarded the highest possible ratings again this year.

The yearbook, edited by Dori Patterson, '70 grad, received an A+ rating from the National School Yearbook Association.

The newspaper, edited by Dave Johnson, '70 grad, won the George H. Gallup Award for the seventeenth consecutive year.

Presented to "newspapers of superior achievements, the Gallup Award is sponsored by Quill & Scroll, an international honorary society for high school journalists.

Six seniors semi-finalists on NMS test

Six Ripple seniors have been named semi-finalists in the National Merit Scholarship program.

Jane Donnella, Bill Hogan, Holly Hughes, Sue Matchette, Betsy Morris, and Jim Shaw are among the top two percent of all high school students who took the qualifying test last spring as juniors.

In Indiana 431 high schools participated in the program. Of the 17,848 students who took the qualifying test, 374 are semi- finalists.

In order to encourage high school students to perform to the maximum of their abilities, the NMS Program recognizes those who show academic talent on the National Merit Scholarship Test.

The test is basically a screening device to determine the recipients of the scholarships; but by measuring a pupil's educational development, the test can aid in determining future plans as far as education and careers are concerned.

Subscription sales begin; Riparian says 'good buy'

Hear ye, hear ye! Read "all about it" in the upcoming issues of the Riparian Newspaper and Yearbook.

From today until October 5, any Ripplite can purchase the package deal from staff members for the price of $7. The staff members can be contacted in the Cafeteria during lunch periods, as well as in the Riparian office and throughout the building during the school day.

Students unable to raise $7 on short notice may subscribe on the installment plan, paying $4 down and making an additional $4 payment in February.

Two or more Ripplites from the same family qualify for the Brother and Sister Special. If one of the students buys the entire package at the regular price, his brothers or sisters may subscribe to receive the yearbook alone for only $5.

"Subscribers are getting a real bargain," said senior John Mohr, circulation manager. "If each student were to pay the actual cost of the newspaper and yearbook, excluding income from advertising, he would pay $14."

Rumor Clinic dispels Ripple misconceptions

"Have you heard about the Rumor Clinic? Is there really a Rumor Clinic?"

Well yes, Virginia, there is a Rumor Clinic at Broad Ripple.

What is a Rumor Clinic?

It's a new program instituted to 'squelch' rumors about the school as the year progresses. The clinic, a joint effort of the school administration and parents, consists of a representative from each feeder school area whom parents and students may call to check out any rumor.

"Students will also be included in the clinic since, as one girl indicated to me in a letter, 'students are the closest thing to the student body I know of'," said Principal William E. Jones.

"The idea of a rumor clinic was conceived in my first meeting with Mr. Jones," said Mrs. Harold H. Austin, Association of Parents and Teachers president.

"The list of members participating will be included in the first APT mailer, which will be sent to all parents," said Mrs. Austin.

Mrs. Austin said that anyone should feel free to contact the representatives to clarify any questions or rumors that arise.

"This is our way of guaranteeinf that parents have a good feeling when they send their children to Broad Ripple," she said.

News Briefs

Dave Johnson reaches finals in contest

ONCE AGAIN . . . Former Riparian Newspaper editor Dave Johnson, '70 grad, was one of five finalists in the journalism division of the American Academy of Achievement.

As the Indiana state winner, Dave competed with state winners from all over the country at the national finals in Houston last June.

• • •

500 MILES . . . David B. Lockton, '54 grad and president of the Ontario Motor Speedway, has taken the Indy 500 to Ontario, California. The second 500 will be an annual Labor Day event.

• • •

PRINCIPALLY . . Mr. William E. Jones, principal, attended a conference of junior and senior high school principals at Indiana University in July.

The state-wide conference was sponsored by the Association of Junior and Senior High School Principals, the North Central Association, and the IU College of Education.

Drug problems at the high school level, student unrest, and student responsibility were discussed.

• • •

ROAMIN' . . . Mr. William Fisher, Latin teacher, travelled to Rome and Naples for an eight-week Fulbright Seminar last summer. As the only teacher from Indiana participating in the program, Mr. Fisher accompanied 18 teachers of Greek and Latin from various states.

While in Rome, the group studied at the American Academy.

#4—Headlines in *The Grizzly* (Northside High School, Fort Smith, Arkansas) illustrate the many ways to gain variety with one type face. Slugs of space are used on the page as subheads would be used to help create a light look. The geometric approach here begins with a vertical column of pictures arranged for contrast with horizontal headlines and blocks of copy.

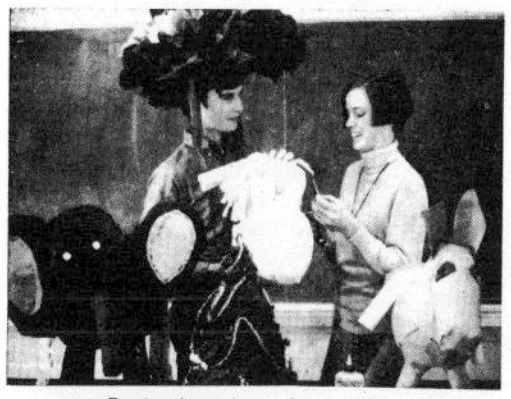

Latin American decorations

To add to the festive holiday atmosphere, Robert Klock and Jenny Bourne, Spanish students, create pinatas, traditional Spanish Christmas decorations.

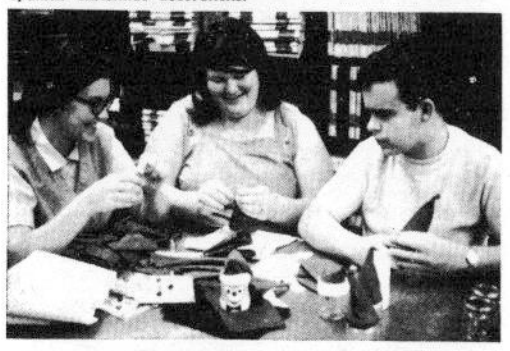

Christmas party favors

With red felt and a dash of glue, small jars are turned into tiny Santas by library workers Phyllis McFarland, Maria Brown and Darrell Meadows for the Roger Bost School.

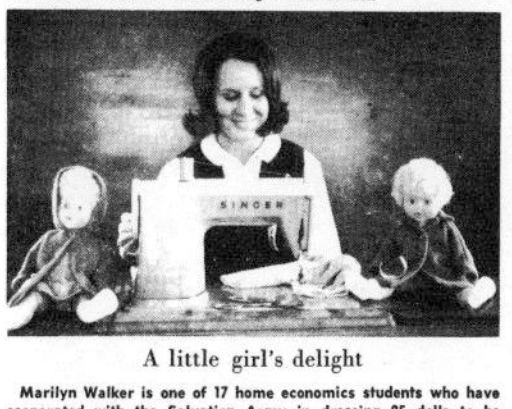

A little girl's delight

Marilyn Walker is one of 17 home economics students who have cooperated with the Salvation Army in dressing 25 dolls to be given to underprivileged children.

Photos by Martin

Assembly tomorrow

Gala festivities to climax

The fragance of burning candles and pine will prevail as strains of "Joy to the World" climax the yuletide season at Northside tomorrow in the annual Christmas assembly.

Led by Russell Brammer, the program is centered around both the religious and light aspects of the holiday season. A pantomime of the holy nativity and a light reading by Kacey DeNoi will be featured.

Mixed Chorus numbers include "Christmas Is," "Carol of the Bells," "There Shall A Star from Jacob," "Mary's Lullaby" and "While Angles Sing." The massed choruses will present "O Come, All Ye Faithful." The Northside Men of Song will sing Christmas carols.

Clubs and councils have been preparing for the hoildays for several weeks.

Featuring carols and floats, the annual miniature Christmas parade, sponsored by the Senior Council was conducted this morning before school.

Winners of the float contest, which will be announced later today, will receive $5 for first, $3 for second and $2 for third place.

Off campus, the Senior Council is conducting a Christmas tree sale across from Peabody Annex. Mistletoe and wreaths are also available.

The Student Council post office which opened last Wednesday continues until the end of fourth period today. For two cents, council members deliver cards to students in their home rooms. Names may be stamped in gold for 10 cents.

To add to the holiday atmosphere, Hi-Y again is sponsoring the traditional door decoration contest. Entrants will be judged today. First place wins $25.

A Christmas card contest closed yesterday in the French department. In home economics classes have been making holiday cookies and gifts. Speech students have told yuletide tales to visiting children.

Teachers will be feted tomorrow morning in the annual Christmas tea to be given by the Columbians in the Columbian lounge.

THE GRIZZLY

Vol. 46 Northside High School, Fort Smith, Arkansas, December 18, 1969 No. 6

Sock and Buskin slates play

The honeymoon is over, now what? Paul and Corie, an exuberant young married couple return from a six-day honeymoon to live in a high-rent apartment in New York City. Then the troubles begin.

After the elated couple climb six, breezy flights of stairs to reach the new home that Corie has chosen for them, they discover that not only is their apartment completely bare of furniture but also the paint job is bad and the skylight leaks snow.

Paul, filled with thoughts of marital happiness, reaches his breaking point when Corie suggests that they walk barefoot in the snow in the park.

These comical situations occur in the play "Barefoot in the Park" to be staged January 9-10 in the Northside auditorium at 8 p. m. by Sock and Buskin, theatrical group. Mrs. Jeanie Tankersley, speech instructor, is director.

Ellis Collier as Paul Bratter, a young lawyer, and Jana Hawley as Corie Bratter, his wife, have the leading roles.

Rita Harvell is Mrs. Banks, Corie's mother; David Jeffers is Valsco Belasco, an international playboy; Larry Pickett is the telephone repairman; and Mike Moore is the delivery man. Shirley Culver and Jenny Dennis are alternates for Corie.

Committees for the play include Scott McKay and David Jeffers—backstage; Cindy Cheyne and Bobby Fletcher—props; Vicki Lyon—publicity; Monique Scott—wardrobe; Sharon Shelby—makeup; Richard Grimshaw—lights; and Fred Kelsey—sound.

Tickets cost $1 in advance and $1.25 at the door.

The cast is limited to Sock and Buskin members. Thespian points are awarded in proportion to the amount of work done.

Daily schedule announced for annual semester exams

New Year's resolutions will survive only two short weeks for many Northside students, because semester exams January 14-15 will prove whether promises of hard study will be kept.

Wednesday, January 14, students will report to their first, third and fifth period classes for tests. Thursday, tests will be given for second, fourth and sixth periods.

The schedule for both exam days is as follows: 8:25-10:10, first test; 10:25-12:00, second test; 12:00-12:50, lunch; 12:50-2:25, third test.

No school will be held the day after exams. However, all teachers will report to school to score tests, average grades and make out report cards.

Report cards, January 21, will carry the second nine weeks grade and the semester average.

All semester tests have at least one section of essay questions.

"This is done to give students experience in answering essay questions," says R. Earl Farnsworth, principal, "because in college, most examinations are the essay type."

No students are exempt from semester tests at Northside.

Work for the second semester will begin January 19. The only holiday remaining in the year is Easter, March 26-30. Classes end May 27, Senior Day, and students stay home May 28 while teachers make out report cards. Grade cards are to be issued May 29.

A rose is a rose

If at first you don't succeed, change the goal. This seemed to be the philosophy of senior Robert Klock, who when constructing a pinata for Spanish class, started out to make a basketball, but ended with a circular object loosely covered with orange strips of crepe paper. He called it an orange.

Nixon impresses spectators with his ordinary guy image

by Tom Halliburton

Razorback stadium's press box door opened at half time of the Arkansas-Texas game. To my surprise, a warm, friendly average type guy walked inside just like a typical football fan, saying "That was the quickest half I've ever seen."

It was President Richard Nixon, our nation's chief executive, but at that moment he was just a typical football fan.

Cordial and sociable, this man didn't seem to be aloof. He was too typical and unassuming to be a politician. He wasn't a big thumb in the crowd, about to make a big political speech.

He was better looking than he is in front of TV cameras and newspaper cartoons.

After the opening kickoff, his casual arrival from a nearby practice field had gone unnoticed by a majority of spectators and there wasn't any play stopped or any kickoff delayed. He was just another "John Q. Citizen."

Although he was something special in every way, President Nixon impressed me as an ordinary fan, enjoying a ball game and not asking a favor from anyone. When a secret service man asked a spectator to make room for his exit, Nixon replied to a cooperative lady, "Oh, never mind that!"

His versatility and charm were evident in the two dressing rooms after the game. He praised the victorious effort of the Texans with "You came back, you won and you deserve to be number one." He identified himself with the losers by reminding the Hogs that "I've lost a few political battles, too."

At Fayetteville he was gracious, understanding, appreciative and ordinary,. . .yet he's the President. How could a man of such great stature be so normal? He's got the world's power at his fingertips, but he's my next door neighbor in the White House.

When he said "Hi" and waved at me, I felt like he was another of my sportswriting buddies. He knew the game like one, too. In fact, at half time he called the shots in the second half almost exactly as they were.

This man knew he would attract the public eye, but he made it clear that he had come to enjoy a ball game. Over 40,000 spectators provided him this rare but joyful opportunity.

Ex-Grizzly honored

Razorback Terry Stewart, who earned nine letters in Bruin athletics, was named to the Academic All-American team at the NCAA Hall of Fame meeting December 9.

Tomorrow night

Rebels seek Texas method on how to slaughter Hogs

Southern Sidelines

Miler Brent Jones places first in Arkansas AAU Road Race

by Curtis Sawyer

The Locker Room Drama

And now, straight from Broadway...

by Danny Allen

Record now 6-4

Johnny Rebs break even in contests against two AAA-conference B-squads

The Anthem
701 Greenwood

The Chicken House
1624 Rogers

Mr. Vic's
MEN'S WEAR
908 Garrison
782-4139

"Your headquarters for all your pre-recorded music needs."

Elmore's Record Shop
715 Garrison

Hank's Record Bar
in Hunt's Grand Plaza

Newton's Jewelers

With one eye on the goal and the other on their opponents, Buzz Karsten, senior, aims for two, while juniors Kenny Jones and Max Roberts try their hands at moving the ball towards the basket.

#5—A sports page from *The Rebel* (Southside High School, Fort Smith, Arkansas) also illustrates the horizontal look, with one of the stories and cutlines set double column for contrast. The page gains an open, easy-to-read look with space around the headlines achieved by use of kickers and lines of asterisks in the column.

Roaring Tigers Seek Revenge After Comeback Upset Win

A bouquet of hands reach for a bounding basketball in the Heights-Home Fogg game. Unfortunately for Heights, not enough of the rebounds came into possession of the Tigers.

Sports Gems

Huskers On Top

By Greg Grimmer

Wrestlers Gain Experience

Wrestlers Top CMA For First Victory

Reeves Signs Grant With Memphis State

Swimmers Face Old Baylor Foes

Harris Gholson, offensive star of the stirring 58-47 victory over Battle Ground, prepares to make his move while Eddie Baird (12) and Scott Bennett (40) await their cue.

QUIK-STOP SUPERETTE
506 West Main
Phone 444-6006
OPEN 7 DAYS
7 a.m. to 11 p.m.

HENDERSON'S FLOWER SHOP

Mack and Jim's
OUTFITTERS FOR MEN AND BOYS
On The Square
Phone 444-5342

DICK'S FOOD MARKET
1010 West Main—444-3108
Open Nights
Until 9:00 P.M.
Sunday 7:00 to 7:00

CAPITOL Theatre   FRI - SAT
Barbra Streisand
Yves Montand
On A Clear Day You Can See Forever

#6—This sports page from *The Cavalier* (Castle Heights Military Academy, Lebanon, Tennessee) demonstrates possibilities in the use of pictures to gain readability. Also, variety in column widths is created by double column for "Sports Gems." This type of boxed head with name of column centered and by-line centered is an effective way to gain space around the headline. Note the use of smaller type in the sports summaries, with boldface for contrast. Also, slugs of space between summary blocks make the page more readable. Note that harmony and unity are gained by using the same type face for most of the headlines.

adopted by school editors. That is the geometric approach to page layout.

If you study the newspapers in any of the groups in which the contemporary look is being stressed, you will note a dominance of rectangular shapes.

That means body type and related pictures are squared off in neat rectangles, usually horizontal. On large pages the small rectangles are grouped into an arrangement of three large rectangles. (Seldom do the rectangles break at the fold, except with an exceedingly long story displayed thus prominently.) The layout man tries to blend vertical and horizontal elements in interesting patterns.

The geometric approach to newspaper layout is not difficult, but it does require care—care that must be exercised even as the initial sketch of the page is being made and as copy and heads are being written. The guideline is *Think in terms of page totality.*

It means learning to visualize the page in terms of blocks of type. It means avoiding zigzags across the page.

Editors Speak

Voicing their enthusiasm for the contemporary look, a number of editors of commercial dailies and weeklies have tried to summarize some of the features that are proving popular in their papers:

(1) "We are trying to get away from the black, heavy, busy newspapers."

(2) "What all of us are searching for in our layout: a clean, fresh, bright newspaper that is compact, convenient, better organized, more attractive, and easier to read."

(3) "Pains with minute details in white space reap dividends in readability."

(4) "Use white space in areas that make a telling difference:
(a) beneath the nameplate, above and below the top cutoff rule in the dateline and above and below the bottom cutoff rule in the dateline,
(b) between the lines of headlines,
(c) between headlines and leads,
(d) between paragraphs,
(e) above and below by-lines,
(f) at termination of stories."

(5) "Use big art. And for cutlines, write as you would a condensed story. Cutlines should tell the story the picture cannot. Use descriptive nouns and verbs."

(6) "Give your paper a new look with
(a) neat rectangles of body type and art,
(b) emphatic weight in each corner,
(c) dropping your cutoff rules,
(d) modernizing your nameplate if it is not easily readable—the today look is built around simplicity,
(e) using ample white space between all elements,
(f) running your headlines downstyle."

(7) "General weaknesses are
(a) faded-out bottoms of pages,
(b) lack of emphasis in focal points,
(c) lack of white space in minute but important areas, as around nameplate, between headline and lead, etc.,
(d) painful zigzags of body type,
(e) too many elements per page,
(f) mixture of headline faces that cause stories to lose their identity."

(8) "Four steps in simplicity as a key to functional, readable layout: (1) Harmonious placement of body type, heads, and art. (2) Abundant white space. (3) Emphasis in the 'hot spots.' (4) Elimination of ornaments."

(9) "Functional typography is the use of devices and patterns that enhance readability . . . Make typography work for

you. Employ some eye-catching device now and then . . . Use italics and kickers for typographical effects."

(10) "Subtle change of pace within the confines of the overall format is desirable . . . Invite the eye, make reading easy."

Closing note: "In layout and design, *minute detail is not minor detail*. Our purpose is to enhance readability."

CHAPTER VIII

MAKE YOUR PLANS

Since this is a book for beginners, it is assumed that you are new to the subject of layout—and being new, you might question why the first chapter in this section should be devoted to the late trends in newspaper design.

The answer is that while you are learning, it is better to be studying and following new patterns rather than old ones.

Layout is not easy, but it is interesting. Generally speaking, students enjoy layout more than any other aspect of the work on the school paper. Some people call it an art and some call it a craft. Perhaps it is both, since certainly a sense of design is a talent—and yet the techniques that make for success can be learned, as skills are learned.

Starting Point

Before any staff can get to work successfully on their school paper, they must have an understanding of their purposes and the way to achieve them. Therefore a staff meeting should be held before the first issue to cover areas of general concern. Among those is the format of the paper.

Suggestion: Acquire some copies of as many varied examples of school papers as possible. Scholastic magazines carry lists of school papers when announcing national contest ratings. Any of their editors or advisers would be happy to send you a copy for your study. You might want to exchange with a few of them during the year.

Also, acquire some copies of leading dailies and weeklies. Study them, comparing with them recent issues of your school paper. If you want to try something new, it would be wise for you to use one of the papers you like, either a school paper or a professional one, as a model so that you will have some kind of guide to help you make basic decisions.

If you prefer to continue with the format established in preceding issues of your school paper, then select as your guide those issues that seem to be the most suitable for your needs and the most pleasing to you. Bind them into a file to use for easy reference.

In order to have guidelines that all can follow and thus ensure consistency from issue to issue, as well as from page to page, compile a style sheet and manual of instructions. Have it duplicated so every staff member will have a copy available at all times.

Word of caution: The actual printing of a newspaper is an important factor here. Be sure that whatever you decide to do is practical. Much that you might want to do—and much that might look very simple to you—would be impossible in your printshop or by the printing process you employ.

Unless the staff members print their own paper, they must always be mindful of the shop or the office that does the printing. In some cases, that is severe regulation, in others not so severe—but it is always there, determined by such factors as the size of the shop or office, other jobs in progress at the same time, equipment available, personnel, even the distance from the staff room.

Cost is almost always a problem, sometimes a serious one.

Dummy Talk

There are two philosophies regarding the approach to putting a page together. One might be called the pre-dummy philosophy and the other the post-dummy philosophy.

The pre-dummy people think the news budget —the term used to cover the copy and pictures for a certain issue—should be studied in advance and a preliminary sketch of the page made, giving each item the approximate space to correspond with the importance, and assigning to it a certain kind of headline.

It is fairly easy to estimate the length of any one given story. Thus, the space necessary can be figured. Stories should always be written so that they can be cut from the bottom to aid the layout man.

Steps in knowing how to estimate the length of a story and the amount of space it will require:

(1) Study a copy of the paper you are using as a model—as to kind of type, size of type, spacing added if any, and the column width.

(2) Count the words in several columns by the inch so that you can arrive at an approximation and know how many words you average per column inch in this particular paper. Thus, if you average five words per line and there are eight lines per inch, you will average 40 words per column inch. Therefore if your story is likely to run about 200 words, you will need about five column inches of space.

(3) To make it easy to estimate the length of a story after it is typed, set up a standard typewriter margin for all to use. To arrive at the margin that will give you the best approximation, again study the paper you are using as a model.

(4) This time, type the copy in several of the printed columns, line for line. Then see what the average length of the lines is. Thus if your lines average 30 characters per line, set your typewriter margins at 10–40. Then every time you type a line of copy, you know that you have approximately one line of type one column wide. If you have come as near as possible to 30 characters in every line and are sure that you have an average of 30 characters per line for the entire story, then you know exactly how many lines to expect in type. For example, if the story as typewritten runs to 48 lines, and you get eight lines of type per column inch in your newspaper, then this story will require six inches of space one column wide.

Especially on school papers on which the staff usually has more time between the day the assignments are made and the day the layouts must be completed than between the layout deadline and press time, the preparing of the pre-dummy seems reasonable. It gives the layout editor time to plan carefully, perhaps even experiment a little if he likes. Also it gives editor, layout man, and adviser some control—a kind of emergency insurance.

Such pre-planning is not possible, nor necessary, for most layout men on professional papers. BUT the school paper is not the professional paper, and the student who is just venturing onto the journalistic scene is not the experienced and trained producer. The school paper is a training ground—not a business in which the miracle of the daily paper takes place under the expert direction of professionals.

In addition to affording the student layout editor an opportunity to prepare each layout to the best of his ability, the pre-dummy ensures a better finished product and fewer mistakes because there is no great time pressure. Also, the pre-dummy procedure ensures better copy for the paper.

When a reporter knows that his story must fit a certain space—and knows that that space is already allocated on a pre-dummy—he is more careful about writing to exact length than if he knows that the layout man will take a story of any length and fit it onto the page as best he can. The pre-dummy also ensures control over headlines, which figure more prominently in today's layout than formerly and so must be planned for size more carefully.

The post-dummy procedure seems to be based on the assumption that all stories will be written to approximate suitable length and that all will have paragraphs arranged so they can be cut as much as necessary at the end. Sometimes, also, the headlines are written in the size and style that seems appropriate for the story and are turned in with the story. That complicates things for the layout editor, who then has to use whatever comes in.

On a school paper that can be a serious problem, because class time runs out. Also, if there is too much copy, something goes—and if there is not enough copy, then there may be a crisis of a sort.

CHAPTER **IX**

FOLLOW YOUR FORMAT WITH FLAIR

"Readers react to readability."

That phrase used as the keynote of a recent newspaper layout editors workshop might well be posted over every layout editor's desk.

Readability is your business.

To achieve readability, you want to be constantly aware of your purposes in designing layout. Those, too, could well be posted over your desk as constant reminders—since without basic purposes no plan can succeed with much direction.

(1) *Attracting the reader's notice* comes first. You manage that by designing a page that has a pleasing effect. (That means care with regard to "total look.")

(2) *Gaining his attention* comes next. To accomplish that, you carefully plan headlines and pictures to arouse his interest—and here you realize again and again that *layout is secondary to message.* Since you must depend on *what the headline says* and on *what the picture shows* to gain his interest.

(3) *Keeping him interested* is your third purpose. You achieve that by so arranging your headlines and art that you break up gray—and dull-looking—areas of body type and thus entice him from one bit of interest to another before he can turn the page.

(4) *Helping him evaluate* what he has read is your fourth concern. Since the purpose of all layout is to aid in the process of communication, it is your responsibility as layout editor to indicate which stories are most important to him.

(Note: Some stories that are important to the reader do not have any built-in interest and, furthermore, it is hard to write these so that they are the bright, sparkly copy that "sells itself." In such cases, you must devise some way to entice—and keep—his attention.)

The importance of a story is indicated by the size of the headline written for it and the amount of space devoted to it. Pictures and other art also are a means of indicating importance.

Page Patterns Vary

When the members of a staff decide on their format, they make decisions regarding the overall appearance of the paper from page to page and from issue to issue. Every paper wants to have an identity. It should be possible for the reader to know upon glancing at a sheet that this is a paper he is familiar with. This is well illustrated on a national level, where each of many well-known papers has a personality of its own. For example, *The New York Times, The Christian Science Monitor, The National Observer,* and *The Wall Street Journal* have such individuality that no one would ever mistake one for the other.

As layout editor, you want to plan pages that will observe the total look and keep the personality of the paper always before the reader. And yet, each page must be so fresh and new that the reader will always see at a glance that this is something he has not seen before.

Within the total format of the paper, several contrasting pages are designed, each determined by the kind of copy included on that page. For school papers, they are the front page, editorial page, sports page, and other inside pages.

Most school paper staffs are organized so that as many students as possible can have experience in layout, along with the pleasure of putting a page together. Thus they use the page plan, with one person in charge of layout for the front page, one for the sports page, one for the editorial page, and one for each of the other inside pages. Other papers have a layout editor who oversees all pages.

In any one issue there is a difference in pages so the reader will know at a glance which page is which. In small papers that is not very important, but in large papers it helps the reader to find easily what he wants.

Since page one is really a kind of showcase for the entire issue, every effort is made to give special appeal to this page. The sports page is usually bolder and more lively because of the nature of sports news (and also the enthusiasm of sports reporters).

For contrast, the editorial page is generally light, airy, pleasant to sit with for a few minutes. Feature copy and editorials contain enough built-in interest that the reader does not have to be coaxed to look at the page. Other inside pages are made up to show as much variety and color as possible, determined by the news and picture budget.

Getting Started

Question: What do I do now?

Answer: First, get a list of all the stories assigned for the issue, with an estimate of length, and the pictures that have been requested.

Note: Because you will be working with a photographer, be sure that you always understand what is assigned, and always be sure that the photographer and you have the same idea about what picture he is to take. To ensure success here, see that the photographer has a photograph assignment card filled in for every picture order. It is imperative that he know exactly what is wanted in the picture and what shape it is to be. As lay-out editor, you are especially interested in shape —and in size, too, if you must have pictures the exact dimensions the layout shows.

Next, discuss the assignments with others concerned with layout to determine which stories are most important and therefore should be included on the front page, which could go elsewhere, and which could be held over or not used if space were limited.

Two points to remember: (1) Choose enough stories for your front page to be newsy. (2) Select those that will appeal to a cross section of readers.

When you know exactly what stories should definitely be run on page one, list them in what you consider the order of importance. Then list the additional stories you might use, also numbering them as to importance. For each, note the length of the story and the "cutting line."

Some stories would be ruined if cut too much. And sometimes a feature, especially a human interest story, is written with a punch line that must be included. Make a note of those so you won't have to depend on your memory when you get to arranging—and rearranging—the various stories on the page.

For rough sketching and initial "page thinking," you will need a medium-size note pad. You can easily pencil in column lines, or you can make yourself a pad of small ruled sheets for sketching.

The point is, you will save time if you make quick sketches and do some estimating instead of taking the time to draw carefully every story as you think about the page. When your sketch seems to be satisfactory, then you can transfer your idea to the page dummy and draw it exactly.

The Reading Diagonal

Because we read from the upper left of each page to the lower right, we know how to guide the reader across the page and then keep him reading from item to item before he finally arrives at the bottom corner and then turns the page.

Take a sheet of dummy paper and draw a line from the upper left corner to the lower right. (In fact, it might be helpful to do so on every dummy sheet, perhaps in color, in order to remember about this.) This is called the "reading diagonal."

The upper left-hand part of the page is called the "prime optical area"—which means that this is where you place what you want the reader to see first—because this is where he looks first. Therefore you place here something designed to capture his interest, such as a feature picture, and lead him on across the page to the right-hand corner.

On page one, if you attract the reader's attention in the upper left corner, you can then place your most important story in the upper right area. However, many editors and layout men feel that the most important story on page one should be put in the upper left. You can gain variety by running your main story sometimes upper left, other times upper right.

After drawing the reading diagonal across your dummy sheet, draw another diagonal, this time from the upper right to the lower left. Make this a dotted line, as it is lighter "in meaning" than the other. As you lay out a page, always see that you have headlines along the diagonals, attractively spaced. It is a way to check against having large areas of unbroken body type.

Note: Headlines should be surrounded by body type so that they do not compete with one another for reader attention. Be sure to have at least one heavy head—perhaps more, unless your page is small—below the fold, and a picture if possible.

With your *X line* sketched in, you are ready to define the corners of the page.

Anchor the Corners

To "anchor the corners" means to put something strong in each corner so that the reader will not overlook the total length of the reading diagonal and the dotted diagonal. This may be a headline, or a box, or a picture. And this should vary from issue to issue so your pages do not have a formula look.

In order to have plenty of variety for small boxes, you need to have everyone look for suitable material to box. Formerly boxes were actually rectangles defined by rules, with copy set in boldface and usually indented at each side. Now a much lighter version of the box is popular. It

may have a very thin rule above and below the copy, with no side rules. The type may be set boldface and indented on the left, or occasionally on both sides. The contemporary box sometimes has only a suggestion of line around it, as it is framed by space instead of by lines. If used in the lower right corner, all the indention is usually at the left side.

For page one variety, see that you have a nameplate suitable for floating. That means you will have one design to use when you want the nameplate the full width of your page. Then you need a smaller version to use with copy beside or above it. For a five-column paper you could use a five-column nameplate, a four-column, and a three-column. Anything as narrow as half the width of your page is too narrow.

The nameplate should always fall within the top third of the page if floated, for easy identification.

As you try to work your stories in with the X line, concentrate on thinking in terms of copy blocks. Remember: The copy blocks will be rectangular shapes made up of the headline, the body type, and any pictures that are related. As you work with them, make some of the rectangles very shallow, crossing several columns. Those shallow rectangles will give your page variety and will help you avoid many single column heads.

Balance on the Page

Once you begin to arrange copy blocks on your page, you sense the need for balancing one element against another. The chief guide here has to be your own sense of suitability. In order to train your eye, so that you can gain confidence in your judgment, study examples of pleasing design to see what makes each effective.

Two kinds of balance are used in layout: formal and informal.

The formal page is seldom practical, as the news budget does not usually afford enough similar elements to balance one another exactly. However, it can be very attractive for special effect when such copy is available.

Informal balance is much more popular than formal balance and much more easily achieved. You will hear a number of phrases coined to indicate how layout editors go about it. "Strive for balance off-balance," one says. Another puts it this way: "You balance something with something."

To gain experience and confidence here, dig into your clipping box and arrange the copy blocks, complete with headline and related art, on your planning board until you feel satisfied with the result. Generally a small dark area balances a larger light area.

(1) Begin with what might be an inside page. Balance your ad pyramid in the lower right with a picture and story with heavy headline in the upper left. Then follow the dotted X diagonal with headlines placed along at pleasing intervals. Generally they are heavier at the top of the page, growing lighter as you move down. Vary the procedure as many ways as you can.

(2) Find pages you like in other papers. Mark the elements that balance each other. Then design a page using similar balancing, using copy blocks from your clipping box. Note: Generally the top of the page is heavier than the bottom. Elements in the lower half are usually lighter than in the upper half.

Planning Boards

Can you imagine how imaginary blocks of copy are going to look with imaginary headlines on an imaginary page?

Since for most of us the answer is "no," the following suggestion is proposed as a guide to success while you are learning:

Acquire a sheet of corkboard or wallboard in which thumbtacks can be easily used. Cut it to your exact page size or draw off the exact page size with the columns indicated. At the same time begin to clip various stories, with headlines and pictures, from your paper or from other papers in which the typography is similar.

In considering your page design, simply try the copy blocks in one arrangement or another until you find the arrangement that seems most pleasing to you. Then hold the clippings in place with thumbtacks.

As you check your assignment sheet, you can visualize certain stories as similar to certain of your clipped copy blocks. That way you do not have to imagine how the story will look in place, since it is there to see.

If you have a variety of clippings with pictures of varying sizes and shapes, you will begin to see many combinations that are pleasing to you. It is much more satisfying to shift a story on the planning board by moving a thumbtack than to see it in print and then wish you had placed it differently.

Suggestion: Clip pages that you like from various papers and keep them as a reference file for ideas. Also, you may paste up pages of your own designing and file these as ideas for possible future use.

The one thing that can help you most is developing an awareness for attractive layout in any and all publications. Study techniques, clip examples, try them out as you can—all, of course, within the basic format of your page.

In a Nutshell: A Skit

Scene: The office of a flourishing country weekly.

Characters: The grizzled editor and his new layout man.

Synopsis: Editor is giving instructions to new man.

Editor speaks:

Hit 'em hard in the upper left-hand corner—bammmmmmmmmmmmmm!

"Everybody knows you start to read—and keep on reading—from left to right. This leads them on across the page to the upper right-hand corner. Then *anchor the corners*—so the reader is kept on the page.

"Then size it up for *balance off-balance*. Top of page is heavier than lower part. It all tends to taper off on weight. For variety you can reverse this. Also for variety you can invert this. But you don't do these reversals and inversions just for kicks. You do them because you know what you're doing.

"Just any old thing that is different is not effective. You've got to know the rules before you can depart from them or improvise on them. A good makeup man is like a good cook. He has a feeling for this and knows what to do for the page here and there by a sense of rhythm, by what seems right. A cook will add a dash of sugar—or season to taste.

"Larger pictures at bottom should be lighter— longer pieces at bottom should be lighter in tone, perhaps features, such as it's spring in the park.

"Feature picture takers should aim for the upper left-hand corner. Always shoot your faces so they look into the page from the upper left-hand corner.

"The purpose of makeup is to make the page look good on the newsstand and then entice the reader to pick it up and then keep on reading— and also know how important everything is by the way you place it.

"Break up the gray. Stay with the X. Go horizontal."

CHAPTER **X**

REFER TO GUIDELINES

General

● Blocks of body type handled as rectangular units can be very attractive. With the addition of a block-width headline to complete the rectangle, designing the page then becomes merely a game of arranging the blocks in a pleasing pattern.

● A rectangular block may also be made by squaring off a picture with captions, the accompanying headline, and body type. Be sure that it is precisely aligned.

● Run wide horizontal stories frequently, as lines of type arranged in a wide block make a story look shorter than the same number of lines in a vertical column—and the shorter a story looks, the more likely the reader is to start it.

● Break long expanses of gray for easy reading. You may do so by (1) using subheads, (2) inserting slugs of space instead of subheads, (3) indenting paragraphs a pica on the left, perhaps on the left and right, and (4) including some boldface in the body.

● The "woven" look on a page means that no alley of white space or no column rule runs the entire length of the page because horizontal elements weave the page into a coordinated pattern.

● "Smokestacking" refers to the use of several heads of the same size and width piled one atop another, perhaps with a picture also of equal width, for special effect.

● "Catchline" refers to the headlines under pictures to help attract reader attention. They are increasingly popular in efforts to achieve the new light, bright, open, and airy look. If the line is

used above the picture, it is called an "overline."

● If you use double-column leads, do not shift to smaller size type at the same time you shift to single-column width. Either set some lines double column—the number depending on the size of your page—in 10-point type and then in 8-point type before shifting to single column (perhaps seven lines in 10 point and three lines in 8 point) or set all double-column lines in 10 point and then from four to six lines of single column in 10 point before shifting to 8 point.

● To vary the page, some copy may be set double column, as editorials and special features usually are. Other copy may be set double column for special effect, as perhaps in a two-column box. Occasionally copy may be set one and one-half columns wide. Column widths may be varied, too, in the one-up technique.

● Make use of the one-up technique. It is also called the flat-out technique. It means running three legs of type in four columns of space, two legs of type in three columns of space, and so on. The width of the legs of type may be worked out as you like, since the amount of space between the columns need not be the consistent spacing on the page. Also, the first leg of type may be indented a pica or two.

● Check your page to be sure that if you have dropped column rules you have adequate space between columns, at least one pica.

● Avoid long alleys of white that let your page fall apart.

● Generally speaking, one head should dominate an inside page, especially if it is a small page.

Headlines

• The trend is toward downstyle headlines, as they have three advantages: they are easier to write, easier to set, and easier to read. The use of all caps is disappearing.

• Keep heads simple, large in size. One-line headlines and wider horizontals are becoming increasingly popular.

• Avoid "tombstoning" of headlines, that is, placing headlines of the same size and the same kind of type side by side. The term loosely refers to any placing of heads together. Tombstoning is to be avoided as it causes confusion for the reader. Occasionally it is necessary to place two heads side by side—but if you do so, make sure that they are as contrasting as possible in kind of type and in size, and see that the one on the left is short enough that the reader does not read over to the next head.

• With the trend toward lighter heads and one-line multicolumn heads, remember that more white space is needed around them.

• Avoid "armpits": headlines that are run up under another headline, as when a two-column head is used with a story that fills only one column. There should be at least six lines of copy between the two heads except on very small pages.

• Headlines should be written with two considerations in mind: (1) to indicate the relative importance of the story and (2) to give the proper weight and design to work in with the overall pattern of the page.

• Subheads are best centered.

• Kickers are better flush left than centered. Heretofore kickers were underscored, as with a hairline rule. Now, however, many professionals are dropping the underscoring.

• The main head under a kicker should be indented one pica per column width. The point size of the kicker should be approximately half the point size of the main head. It may be contrasting, as italics.

• The reverse kicker, also called a "hammer," is popular because it allows space to the right. It is usually just one word and is set flush left. The reverse kicker should be no wider than half the headline area and should be about twice the point size of the main head, which is indented one pica per column. The reverse kicker should never be less than 24 point.

Boxes

• One-column boxes should be vertical. Two-column boxes are generally horizontal.

• Headlines in boxes: Sometimes no headline is used. If used, the headline is chosen from the regular headline schedule. It may be one line, even one word. If the box is indented at the left only, set the head flush left. If the box is indented on both sides, center the head.

• Boxes are used as are pictures, to break up the gray areas of body type. Usually they are boldface to provide contrast.

• Boxes may be run at the top or bottom of a column but are not run as a "floating" element, surrounded by body type.

About Typography

• In designing layouts, you need to know something of typography. For one thing, you probably have never paid much attention to the body type used for the copy in your paper. The exact size is not particularly important to you, but you do need to know how many lines you can count on per vertical inch of copy and how many character counts you will average per line on the typewriter as you type your copy.

• To ascertain the number of lines per column inch, you simply lay a ruler along a column of copy and then count the lines per inch. It will be about six on some papers and as many as eight or nine on others.

● Fitting copy will be one of your most tedious jobs. But if you give painstaking care to it at first, you will not only become skillful at estimating, you will also enjoy the satisfaction of having your layouts turn out as you designed them.

● Failure to estimate the amount of copy accurately leads to many mistakes and many headaches.

● To ascertain the number of characters you will average per line, you simply count the characters in any body of 12 or 15 lines and figure the average. It is easily done on the typewriter. Once ascertained, the average will determine your typewriter margins. Therefore, if your character count per line averages 30, your typewriter margins will be 10–40. Typed thus, every line of copy will approximate a line in type—and so you can estimate closely the relationship of the amount of copy typed to the space to be filled.

● In addition to body type, you need to know about cutline type, usually enough different from your body type to afford a contrast on your page. As it is usually the same size as the body type, the fit does not pose an additional problem.

● Learn about your headline type, as headlines can be a factor in your success—or they can constantly befuddle your efforts.

● You should have a headline schedule handy for easy reference. It will afford you an overview of every headline used on your paper, with the size of the type, the number of lines, the column width, and the count. Some staffs arrange their headlines on poster board. Others gather them in a booklet or add them to their style book.

● Be sure that you understand about point as a measure for type. Vertical measure of type is figured in points. There are 72 points per inch. Therefore, type that is 72 points high is an inch high. A 36-point headline would require one half inch of space. An 18-point headline would require one fourth inch of space. That of course is for the type only. On your layout you would

need to allow for the extra spacing required above and below your headline in order to give it an airy look. Remember: no crowding these days.

● Important note: You cannot always tell by looking at a letter what the point size is. The reason is that the point size refers only to the height of the little block on which the letter is designed. That is, in all the hundreds of type faces that have been designed, every one that is termed 18 point is on a little block 18 points high. (The measure refers to the face of the block.)

● If you measure the individual designs of any one letter—say the "g"—you will find a great variance in the point measure of the letter itself, even though the height of the block in every instance is 18 points. Therefore, headlines in some 18-point faces would look much taller than others simply because of the variation in the letter design. To repeat, you cannot tell by knowing the point sizes just how the various heads will compare. That means you must be fully acquainted with each headline you use—since a 36-point head in some instances, for example, would look lighter than a 30-point head in another style. The knowledge is important to you as you design your pages and try to balance one head against another.

About Pictures

● Encourage the photographer to try for shapes and content that will give your layout a lift. Those would include deep verticals and very shallow horizontals, both of which will help you gain variety on your pages. Also, good close-ups of any shape will be a welcome contrast to the usual groupings that turn up.

● Suggest that the photographer always try to shoot feature pictures as if they are to run in the upper left-hand corner of the page. Since that is the prime optical area and the space for an attention-getter on every page, the picture, if good, will be suitable for any page.

● Although it is not your responsibility as

layout editor to order pictures, you are free to make suggestions that you think would add effectiveness to your layouts. Unless you suggest ideas for dramatic pictures as you visualize them, no one will.

- Pictures are increasingly important elements in layout.

- Every page should have a picture if possible, or some kind of art or box.

- Pictures run at the top of a page help prevent tombstoning of heads.

- A cutoff rule is used to separate a picture from an unrelated story immediately under it or above it.

- If a picture must be set into body type, then it should be within a paragraph, as most readers skip what lies below the picture.

- When a one-column picture is used with a two-column story, it is better to run the lead and story in the first column and set the picture in the second. The same is true for a three-column headline and one-column picture—or a two-column picture—with picture best in the third column. If necessary, wrap the copy under the picture.

- Normally it is not a good idea to place a picture between the headline and the story.

- If cutlines are indented, they should be definitely indented, otherwise aligned precisely with the edge of the picture.

- Study the use of pictures in magazines and newspapers in an effort to develop a picture sense. Although you are restricted in many ways on a school paper, this very restriction encourages you to be more original by forcing you to devise ways to gain variety and sparkle on your pages.

- Sometimes when a photograph is turned in, someone will say, "I don't see any picture there."

What he means is that there's no story worth noting, no message conveyed. In order to avoid using pictures that are not worth running, try to keep a supply of pictures—suitable for any issue —that *do* tell a story, that are worth the space. By doing so, you will always be prepared, even though the picture you expect does not turn out well.

- Sometimes by studying a photograph that does not turn out as expected, you will find something else in it—perhaps something that could be used as a special feature. That does not happen often, but when it does, it is a pleasant moment. (It is such occasions that keep a layout editor going happily on. In fact, the more pleasure a layout editor finds in his work, the more readable his pages will be. His enthusiasm shows through his work.)

- To use pictures effectively, you study them to see just what the "picture" is—and then you trim away all the unnecessary part. That does not mean literally taking scissors to a photograph, as you never do that. "Trim" is a figure of speech. The word "crop" is used to indicate the selection of the part of a photograph you want to use. You indicate the cropping by making marks in the margins of your glossy print, usually with a grease pencil. Never mark on the face of your picture.

- As an aid in suitable cropping, you will find it helpful to make yourself a pair of cropping L's. These are simple L shapes cut from sturdy cardboard, about an inch or slightly more in width and about ten inches long. Also, to figure enlargement and reduction, a proportion guide is an aid.

- A picture may be reduced without much problem, but enlargement shows up flaws. Therefore for enlargement try to get the best photograph possible. It is not wise to enlarge more than twice the size of the original—and even that can be a poor choice. The "new look" is to crop some pictures close and enlarge dramatically—but for that, you must have a quality photo.

- Handle photographs very carefully, for they

are fragile and are easily damaged. Do not write on the back, except in the margin, do not use paper clips, and do not scratch the surface.

Advertisements

- Advertisements should be pyramided to the right on both the right-hand and left-hand pages.

Editorial page #1—This example is characteristic of *Ranger* editorial pages all year, as the staff worked out a page pattern and followed it rather closely for all issues. This plan is true of most papers, since it is a general feeling that the format for the editorial page should remain constant so readers will know where to find what they follow from issue to issue, as in editorials, cartoons, columns, and regular features. Note that the double-column editorials are in larger type with additional spacing between lines and are in the upper left, the prime optical area. Cartoon and human interest story on the right offer variety in both makeup and content. The column, Ranger Round-up, has a heading designed for contrast. Note that the masthead is set tight and small in the lower right to anchor the corner but not compete for the best reading space. The alignment of the "Fanciful" story and the masthead gives the bottom of the paper color and a neat geometric look.

The reason is that thus using the lower right for the ads frees the primary optical area for the copy and pictures that are necessary to stop the reader on the page and keep him there long enough to read the ads. Also, it means that the columns become shorter as the reader moves across the page, so that he is encouraged.

- Ads should never be piled up to a full column height, as the top of the page is needed for copy to attract the reader.

- Ads should be placed so that every ad is touched by body copy. Motto: "Avoid buried ads."

Editorial Page

- The editorial page can have as much personality as you want to give it. Here you have opportunity to use typography to help you make the page readable. Since the reader comes to the editorial page wanting to read, you can devote your efforts to seeing that he is encouraged to read every word.

- Generally speaking, once you have decided on the format of your editorial page, you do not vary it much from issue to issue. (On other pages you make a special effort to see that there is definite variety from issue to issue.)

- Because editorials are usually your most important copy, you try to run them where the reader will be sure to see them. Usually that will be the primary optical area—which means your best space: the upper left-hand quarter of the page.

- However, by carefully leading the reader's eye, you can entice him from one part of the page to another.

- As a beginner, you will be wise to follow accepted practices and try to do well with them. To try an experiment or to be "original" is difficult even for experienced students.

- "Originality" comes in approaching your

page with fresh, bright readable copy, important copy that stimulates you to display it with bright, impressive photography, or other art, and headline display.

• "Originality" does not mean "just being different."

• Pictures on the editorial page are increasingly popular. They can be informative, or they can create a mood that will make the reader more receptive to editorial copy pertaining to the picture.

• Three guiding principles: (1) Display your editorials and editorial features in your best space. (2) Go horizontal with as much of your copy as you can. (Remember: Think in blocks of copy.) (3) Use plenty of space around headlines and between sections of any stories that are long, as you would subheads, for that prized light, bright, open, airy look popular now.

• That means keeping your staff box as small as possible and using it at the bottom of the page. The information in the staff box is not designed to attract reader attention. Save top-of-the-page space for important copy or "reader bait."

• THEN, when you have had some experience, and developed understanding, give some time to experimenting with new ideas you see in the professional papers and sometime during the year modify your page for a new look, your own look, based on your knowing how to achieve attractive display, inspired by top quality copy.

Sports Page

• By the very nature of sports, the sports page generally has a bolder look than most of the other pages of the paper. Action is the key word in sports, and that action is reflected in the layout with considerable vigor. Also, generally sports editors are more enthusiastic about their coverage and presentation than other editors are. Headlines may be larger and bolder than on other pages and more pictures may be run.

• As always with pictures, the editor should see that they are action pictures when possible and he should insist on a variety of shapes, sizes, and composition. Nowhere is the relationship between the shape of the picture and the subject matter so well illustrated as in sports pictures. Take basketball, for example. It is necessary to remember that vertical space must be allowed for most basketball pictures. If you take a good vertical basketball picture and crop it to fit a square space, or a horizontal, you have not made a square or horizontal picture. All you have accomplished is to ruin a good vertical shot.

• Boxes are a definite help for variety in makeup on the sports page because they are functional.

• On the sports page avoid any feminine-looking headlines. Italics may be used for some contrast, but it is generally better to reserve these for sports features.

• Suggestion: For a sports column, use the standing column head as a kicker or tag and then write a regular headline based on the opening item, if it is a column of miscellany, or on the general content.

• As on all pages except page one, the upper left is the focal point of your page.

Inside Pages

• Advertising may be run on any inside page except the editorial page—and even sometimes on this page, too, if necessary. (If advertising is run on the editorial page, it should be the kind of ad suitable to accompany your editorial copy.)

• Ads may be pyramided to the right, or they may form a well, with copy running to the bottom of the page. Also it is possible to square off the ads in the lower right, either as a horizontal block, or one slightly vertical. Your problem is to be fair to the advertiser and yet to display your copy to advantage.

• The general rule of art or headline in the upper left is based on the reader reaction to any single page. The reader sees the upper left part of the page first. Keep pictures to the top of your page unless you intend to direct the reader down the page, and then back.

• Keep the copy block in mind on inside pages as well as on the front page.

• Avoid single-column heads as much as possible.

Preparing the Dummy

• No matter what printing process you use, your dummy must be prepared carefully. After you have worked from your initial sketch to your own drawing of the exact amount of space for each item to be included on the page, you prepare a dummy sheet for the printer, or for the paste-up man.

• For your preliminary planning, you can use any size sheet you like, merely marking it off into columns. Of course, you must know the approximate length of each story and the size of any art to be used. Those are indicated in proportion on the initial sketch. If you are using blocks of type, you manipulate them by estimating the proportionate amount of space each will occupy.

• If your paper goes to a school or job shop, you may be expected to submit a pasted-up dummy so the paper can be produced to your exact specifications. Some shops, however, prefer a dummy sheet with the indication of stories and art merely penciled in.

• For such a skeleton dummy sheet, the exact length of each story should be indicated, with the lettering on the slug line written in, and in the case of the printed paper, perhaps the galley number. Some shops require you to letter in the headline exactly so there can be no mistake about what you want. The number of the headline according to your schedule should be indicated so that the printer will know the kind and size of type. Also, the content of each art block should be indicated and the exact size given. For that kind of dummy, you must expect the printer to cut stories as necessary for fit. Therefore you must have each story sufficiently long, and you must see that each story can be suitably cut from the end. Also, you need to have some copy suitable to use as filler. Hopefully it will not be triteness but short human interest items appropriate for any issue during the year.

• For a paste-up dummy, you must measure every item included to be sure that your measurement on the paste-up is accurate. When the printer says "accurate," he means EXACTLY— not "almost" or "nearly."

• Always see that the copy is typed according to the correct margins. Make it a rule that every person who types anything for the paper verifies those margins and indicates the number of lines typed.

PART IV

Advisers Comment

CHAPTER XI

REGARDING THE MIMEOGRAPHED PAPER

Of the publications advisers who have contributed examples to this work and accompanying comment, Mrs. Lorine Lay of Chaffin Junior High School, Fort Smith, Arkansas, formerly of Darby Junior High School, has had experience with both printed and mimeographed papers. She writes:

Since our local secondary schools have grown in number from two to six during the past ten years, the mimeographed process has been used for the junior high school papers for several years. Although it does not produce as professional an appearance, it has one main advantage —the students do all the work.

By the time they have written, rewritten, and typed the stories twice (to justify the lines); written and "inked" the headlines; taken the pictures, cut them to size and written the captions; written the copy for the ads, "inked" the copy and pasted it in the proper-sized border; pasted up the four sheets and proofread them; run them on the mimeograph machine; stapled and distributed the finished product, they feel pride in their paper, as it is truly theirs. (The only thing the students do not actually do is cut the stencils, as we use a machine that requires that the stencils be cut electronically.)

Specific Helps

Instead of using styli on the stencil itself, we use a K. & E. Leroy scriber (with different-sized templates and pens) and engineers' technical fountain pens (with different-sized pen points and lettering guides) to write the copy for ads and headlines on a sheet of paper. Then these are cut out and pasted on the paste-up sheet from which the stencil is cut by a local firm.

The least expensive Leroy set includes an adjustable scriber (which makes straight or slanted letters); three templates, sizes 100, 140, and 240 (which approximate 10, 14, and 24 point in print); three standard pens, No. 00, No. 1, and No. 3; and two reservoir pens. The more templates and pens, the higher the price. However, each item can be purchased separately.

We use the Koh-i-noor RAPIDOGRAPH technical fountain pens in three pen sizes— No. 0, No. 1, and No. 2½—and two sets of lettering guides: (1) the Koh-i-noor Rapido-guide, which includes No. 3030 ($\frac{5}{32}$") for the No. 0 pen, No. 3031 ($\frac{3}{16}$") for the No. 1 pen, and No. 3032 ($\frac{9}{32}$") for the No. 2½ pen, and (2) the RapiDesign Hi-Lo Letter set in three sizes suitable for the three pen sizes above.

The Koh-i-noor guides are straight letters; the Hi-Lo letters slant. We use the straight letters primarily for news and the slanted letters for features and sometimes for kickers.

With these sets of lettering guides and the three pens, we can develop fair variety in headlines. With more styles of lettering guides, of course, more variety could be gained. As we use the downstyle in our headlines, however, we must have caps and lower case, and most lettering guides have caps only.

Although the legal-size paper is used in many schools, we feel the letter-size is better proportioned for a newspaper. Because we have a typewriter with smaller type—an Olympia Model SC-3-L, manuscript type #4, with 17 letters to the inch horizontally and seven vertical lines per inch, we changed from a three-column paper to a four-column paper to allow us added variety in makeup. Each column is 10½ picas (29 letters) wide with a one-pica space between. We do not use column rules, as we think the extra white is attractive.

Our nameplate, drawn by the drafting teacher, has shaded letters which give it the three-dimensional appearance. A plate was made of it, and the senior high school printshop prints copies, which we simply paste on the paste-up sheet. Besides a full-page nameplate, we also use a "floating" three-column one that allows variety in front-page makeup.

Functions First

As we plan each page, we try to keep in mind the function of page layout as given by Edmund C. Arnold and Hillier Krieghbaum in *The Student Journalist:* (1) to attract the reader by a pleasant overall pattern; (2) to capture his attention by pictures and headlines; (3) to direct him into body type; and (4) to guide him from one story to another in such a way that he gains maximum information with a minimum of time and effort.

We try

. . . to place stories on the page according to their importance, the big story in the upper right corner on the front page, although it is permissible to use the upper left for the big story in a mimeographed paper.

. . . to anchor the corners with a picture, a box, or a story.

. . . to use contrast and balance so the page is pleasing to the eye.

. . . to use horizontal makeup often, as this type leads the reader from one story to another more easily than does vertical makeup.

We have tried to streamline our pages as much as possible, by eliminating column rules and by using the downstyle headlines (only the first word and proper nouns capitalized), flush left heads with only one deck and often only one line, and the floating nameplate.

The last steps are pasting each story, headline, picture, caption, and ad on paste-up layout sheets and covering any smudge or unwanted marks with Liquid Paper. Using the Liquid Paper before the stencil is cut makes a cleaner, sharper stencil. If any marks should remain on the stencil, however, these can be covered with mimeograph correction fluid. Care must be taken not to cover any of the copy, or it will not reproduce on the finished product.

The following examples with comment are included for illustration of these points.

Editorial Page

The editorial page should have a distinctive and dignified appearance. Some journalists advise a fixed place for editorials, cartoons, and columns, yet the editorial page should vary from issue to issue. Because of the small size of our page this is difficult. We use larger type and two columns for editorials and a different headline style. Some years we have a column head (a drawing), which stays the same in each issue. This year, however, we used the same kicker but a different headline for each column. Separating items in the column with small circles or asterisks gives added white space to make the page more attractive. Our masthead was placed in the lower right column.

The *Cougar Print* dummy: Each page editor plans his page by making a dummy. He measures exactly, saving the proper space for ads, pictures, cutlines, headlines and stories. On the dummy he specifies the size and style of headlines and the number of lines in each story. If the dummy is properly planned, pasting up the stories, heads, etc., is not difficult. If the ads are pasted up first (the width of the page is 45 picas), then the Word Power box at the top (exactly 60 picas from top of page to bottom), it is easier to fill in the stories and heads. Sometimes it is easier to paste up from top to bottom, sometimes from bottom to top, but always from the outside toward the inside columns.

———→

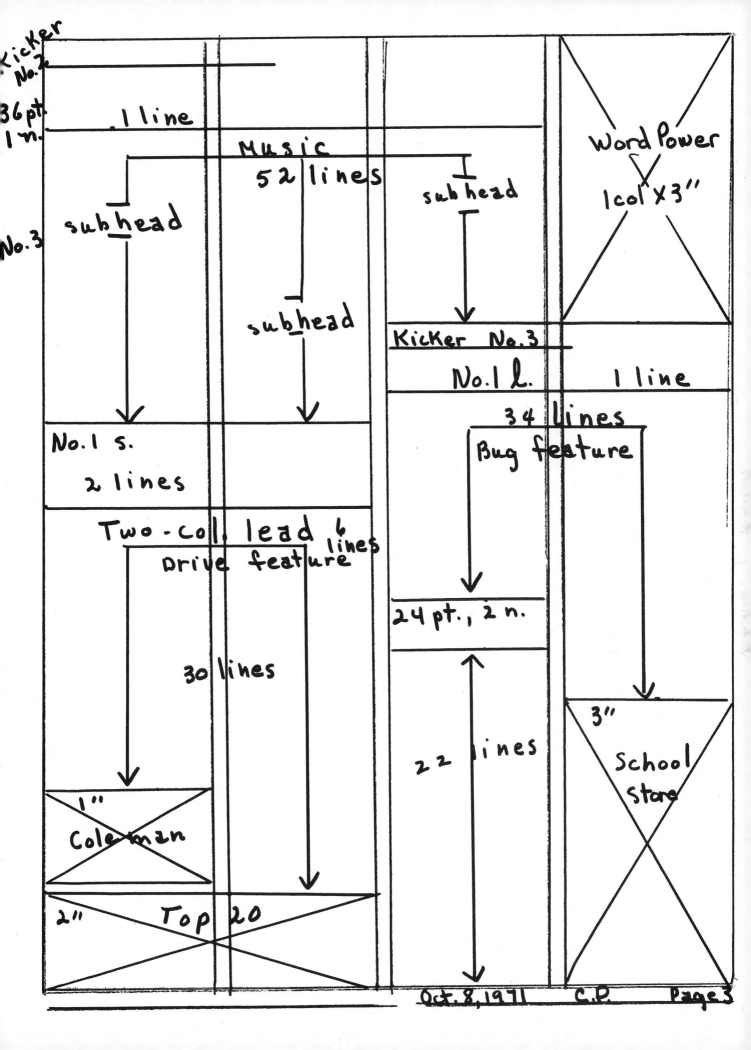

THE RANGER

Vol. 37   Darby Junior High, Fort Smith, Arkansas, October 4, 1968   No. 1

Construction on New Darby underway; unit to have carpet, pods, folding walls

Construction for Darby's new building is now underway. Workers are leveling and scooping dirt for the foundation.

Major changes in curriculum include more teams, no Latin

Two major changes in the Darby curriculum this year are Latin being dropped from the schedule and the increased number of teams.

"Latin was discontinued at Darby," Mr. Frank L. Jones, principal, explained, "because no other junior high in town offers it." Latin is now offered only on the high school level.

Because the new building will be divided into departments, this year each team is composed of two or three teachers in the same department.

Many of last year's changes have been continued because of their success.

Physical education classes are rescheduled for all band and glee club members.

For the second year in succession, the boys' homecraft class was continued. This year, however, there are two one-mod

groups under the instruction of Miss Lillian Gibson and Mrs. Norine Doyel.

"Both groups," explained Miss Gibson, "are learning to make simple household repairs and to use and repair the sewing machine among other things."

Extended opportunity classes are used for a study mod or an extra mod in a regular class for students who need help in that particular subject.

October 7
PTA to have Open House

At 6:45 Monday, Oct. 7, Darby parents will attend Open House and follow their child's daily schedule through 17 modules.

Besides meeting classes, parents will have an opportunity to join the PTA organization. The homeroom with the largest percentage of enrollment will

be awarded a canteen party.

The incumbent PTA officers are: Mr. and Mrs. Henry Walker, co-presidents; Mr. and Mrs. Tom Moore, co-vice presidents; Mr. and Mrs. Brad Thompson, co-secretaries; Mr. and Mrs. Jim Cheyne, co-treasurers; and Mrs. W.C. McLachlan, junior historian.

Pods, carpets and folding walls are some of the features in the new Darby building under construction.

Brennan-Boyd Construction Co. Inc. received the contract in mid-August and began work before school started.

The facilities will be divided into wings. One wing will be a pod made up of five classrooms, one of which is permanent. The other four rooms will be formed with accordian type walls.

"With the accordian walls," Mr. Frank L. Jones, principal, explained, "the walls can be pushed back so a movie can be seen by all four classes at the same time, or a lecture can be given to a large number of students at once."

A conference room, storage closet, lounge and five lockers will be provided for the five teachers in each of the carpeted pods.

"The construction crew is trying to get the main decks and the roof up before bad weather comes," Mr. Jones said "If workable weather prevails, the new building will be ready for use next year."

Though new boilers will be purchased, the present boiler room will still be used. A tunnel from the old building to the new will enclose electrical wiring.

The prayer will be led by Stan Irvin.

Tommy Cheyne to be installed at SC assembly

Tommy Cheyne will be installed student body president in an assembly this morning. He was elected by popular vote last year to replace 1967-68 president, Ricky Cogburn.

"Ricky is expected to be here today to conduct the installation," said Mr. Bennie Deaver, Student Council sponsor.

After his installation, Tommy will conduct the rest of the program, installing the officers, committee chairmen and homeroom representatives.

Other officers are Alan Richardson, replacing Pierce Farris as vice president, and Vicki Winters, replacing Jeanie Martin as secretary.

Chairmen for the standing committees, appointed this year by Tommy, are: David Tedder, Building and Grounds; Diana Burns, student affairs; Brent Pollock, Courtesy; Jackie Baker, elections; Jon Fiehl, Publicity; Kirby Lockhart, Lost and Found; Joyce Rose, scrapbook; Jim Birch, Auditorium; and Bo Baumeister, parliamentarian.

Four seventh graders will explain the four symbols of the Student Council insignia, the torch, scroll, quill and gavel.

Looking over plans for the Student Council installation today are President Tom Cheyne, Vice President Alan Richardson, and Secretary Vicki Winters.

Front page #1—This front page is mainly horizontal makeup (helps reader move from one story to another) with the three-column head for the big story and two two-column heads. Using three lines for the No. 2 head gives that story prominence. The No. 2 story leads into its accompanying picture (at bottom of page), which anchors the corner. This one-column picture and the two-column head in the lower right corner give contrasting balance to the three-line head and the two-column picture at the top. Brace from lower right to upper left gives emphasis to the big story.

A good variety of headlines is used: two lines three column, two lines two column, one line two column with kicker, and three lines one column.

The floating nameplate with headline and story to the side and the use of flush left and downstyle heads give a streamlined appearance even to this small page. The bottom half of the page was not neglected, as it has two good-sized headlines and a picture.

This page could have been improved if the picture in column four could have been above its story rather than below. A cutoff rule should have been used below the building picture even though the three-column head ties it with its story.

News Briefs

In connection with the recent Beat Ramsey day, the jingle winner was Mrs. Audria Bogan's home room 108, and was awarded a football autographed by the varsity football team. Wendall Martin wrote the verse.

Mr. Bill Washum's room, 218, won the Beat Ramsey door prize. Pamela Manckiy and Laurie England designed the decoration which was a picture of a can-can girl with the lettering "We can-can the Rams."

Reginald Moore was elected president of Darby Red Cross; Mike Deranger, vice president; and Ricky Angel, secretary-treasurer.

Willard West was elected vice president of the science club to replace Darrel Findley, who moved to Germany recently.

A total of $33.50 was divided among the winners of the PTA membership drives concluded in November: Mrs. Miriam Hatfield, seventh grade; Mrs. Evonne Fulkerson, eighth; Mr. James Moody, ninth; and Mrs. Jane Davidson's combination eighth and ninth grade.

The week of Nov. 18-22 was officially introduced as TWIRP week by the Student Council. Girls carried boys' books, asked them out on dates and paid their way on all occasions.

Standish projects portray life of early Pilgrims

Many different types of projects have been turned in to Mrs. Mildred Knox and Miss Judy Muller in connection with the study of "The Courtship of Miles Standish."

Some included posters, notebooks, pictures and replicas of the typical house of early Pilgrim times.

"The projects showed hard work and originality," commented Mrs. Knox.

Some of the projects were on display in the trophy case outside the auditorium during November.

SC to sponsor two campaigns

Two up-coming projects of the Student Council are the clean-up campaign and Christmas canned goods drive for the Salvation Army.

David Tedder, chairman of the building and grounds committee, will launch the clean-up campaign Dec. 2. It will continue the entire week.

Large cans outside the building will be painted and labeled by grades, one for the seventh grade, one for the eighth and one for the ninth.

Students will get rid of all their trash in the designated cans, which will be counted and judged by the SC. The winning grade will be presented

a trophy by the Student Council.

The canned goods drive will begin the second Monday of December and continue until the Christmas holidays, Dec. 20.

The room with the most cans will receive a canteen party from the SC and a "Golden Can" from the Salvation Army.

THE RANGER

Vol. 37   Darby Junior High, Fort Smith, Arkansas, November 27, 1968   No. 4

Band to "Wish You a Merry Christmas" in annual concerts for students, public

The Darby band will "Wish You a Merry Christmas" Dec. 13-14 as they present their two annual Christmas concerts.

The first is scheduled for Thursday night, Dec. 12, for the general public and the second will be given the following morning for the student body.

Some of the yuletide tunes will be "Sound of Bells," "We Wish You a Merry Christmas," "Yuletide Fantasy," "Messiah Overture," and "March of the Blazerteers."

"As usual," stated Mr. Ronald Garner, band director, "the concert will end with a

Sing-along."

This part of the program was introduced several years ago and is continued "because the kids seem to enjoy it," Mr. Garner added.

The second band will have its performance preceding the Ranger Band's.

Ranger to aid library at jail

Collecting books for the newly acquired city and county jails is the current project of the Ranger Staff.

"The jail has been in need of something to occupy the prisoners," said Judge Lawson Cloninger, one of the civic leaders who led in founding these small libraries.

Though the library is well stocked at the present time, it is becoming low on reserve books, for paperbacks wear out quickly.

"We appreciate the interest the Ranger Staff is showing in this project," Judge Cloninger said, "and hope the students will respond to the plea for books for the jail."

Westerns and mysteries are preferred by most of the inmates, but other types would be acceptable.

Books may be brought to Room 121 anytime between now and Dec. 20.

"Last year was the first time the second band's program was included in the concert for students," Mr. Garner explained. "They will be included again this year."

On Saturday after the concerts most band students will go to Kimmons to tryout for Regional Junior High Clinic, an annual event.

The members tryout before judges and are selected for one of two bands.

Today three University of Arkansas band professors are in Darby for an all-day clinic. They are Mr. James Jones, Mr. Robert Bright and Mr. Andy Anderson. They will be working with the brass, woodwinds and percussion.

Happiness is:
Two queens?

What's this? Two queens? That's what happened in the recent pancake king and queen contest.

Kathy Criswell from Mr. Nobel Hunt's home room and Daisy Carter from Mrs. Miriam Hatfield's room were chosen.

The reason for two queens and no king was that Daisy Carter was mistaken for Davey Carter. In all the confusion, two girls were awarded a small cup and a plaque stating they were "Pancake Champions."

Front page #2—Floating nameplate with stories above and below gives variety in makeup. News Briefs column allows many short items and adds white space between them. Picture and its story are tied together with a two-column head, and the student is looking into the story. Varied headlines are used, and the lower corners are anchored.

Sherry Cockrell sets up her Miles Standish project.

Editorial page #1—In a four-column format, editorials can be thus effectively set double column in a type size larger than body type. With the standing kicker (note the hairline rule for underlining) and the centered headlines, the upper corner of the page commands attention. This three-column arrangement is balanced in the lower right by the cartoon. The column, with a standing head designed for color in the upper right, is balanced in the lower left by "Dear Editor" and the masthead. Note that "Dear Editor" is aligned with "Eighth grader" headline to contribute to the horizontal look and the geometric effect. Head in italics affords contrast.

Editorial page #2—To make space for a long and important feature story, this basic editorial page format was modified slightly by shorter editorials than usual and by a vertical cartoon below the column. Here the masthead offers contrast and anchors the corner. Subheads centered and surrounded by space break up the expanse of story. Spacing within the story also helps. Asterisks in the column are a favorite device to add color with space in breaking up a body of copy.

It's our opinion

Couple show Christmas spirit

Mrs. Weatherby was a maid for the Browns. In the same building Mr. Rex worked as janitor. All alone in the world, they were both elderly with a small income.

Although they weren't very well acquainted, Mrs. Weatherby had saved all year to buy Mr. Rex a Christmas present, a watch.

On Christmas morning as Mr. Rex was on his way downstairs to sweep the walk, Mrs. Weatherby shyly handed him the pocketwatch. He thanked her. As she started away, he brought out his gift, 8 silk handkerchiefs, for her. As they stood for a moment admiring their presents, tears came to their eyes. Each realized what a great sacrifice the other had made.

But isn't that what Christmas is about, making a sacrifice, as Jesus did, and not expecting anything in return?

Chaffin students share with others

We think it is good for Chaffin students to participate in the Christmas drives-- toys and canned food for the Salvation Army and toothbrush-toothpaste for the Red Cross.

These drives help the needy and the students alike. Participation by students helps them realize how much they have and helps develop good habits. The collected items help those who receive them.

Compassion is what everyone wants and needs. By giving to these drives we show compassion for our fellowman. Because of this someone's Christmas will be a little happier.

Dear Editor
No. 1 Girl say,
日本可乙
(American translation)
HAVE HAPPY NEW YEAR

THE COUGAR PRINT
Published bi-weekly by the ninth grade journalism class of Chaffin Junior High School, Rt. 1, Box 335R, Fort Smith, Arkansas 72901

Editor... Patricia Dickinson
Ass't Editor... Sandra Curtis
Page Editors.. Martha Morgan, Sharla Cate, Barbara Smelley, Sarah Jaber
Sports.. Mike Wortham and Bob Sawyer
Advertising.... Martha Morgan
Photographer.... Mike Wortham
Cartoonist....... Pam Manckiy
Exchange.... Janiesse Kleier
Scrapbook.. Cheryl Bohnenkamper
Adviser...... Mrs. Lorine Lay

Eighth grader makes gift wrapping with cloth, string, paints, crayons

By Catherine McCann

This year I decided to make my Christmas presents exotic. Way out, you know?

I began by taking crayon shavings and pressing them on a piece of shelf paper. First of all, I had too many shavings and the colors melted through the paper.

As that didn't turn out too well, I tried another method. This time I used string, paper and paint. After I had arranged the string, I pulled it out. Not only did the string come out, but paint also.

The only colors I had were orange and yellow, so I decided they weren't Christmasy enough anyway.

I tried a third way, thinking that nothing could possibly go wrong with using felt strips, a white box and glue. I forgot that glue can cause lumps and bubbles!

I finally settled for cloth and made a face design on it. It isn't exactly as exotic as I had hoped, but it turned out bright and jolly, and I can use it over and over again.

WELL, NOW, LITTLE ONE, HAVE YOU MADE OUT YOUR XMAS LIST? / I SURE HAVE SANTA! / HERE IT IS!

It's our opinion

Staircase can be dangerous

A short time ago a girl was injured from a fall down the stairs. Although she broke no bones, she had several bruises, a sprained arm, and pulled muscles in her back and legs. Because of this she had to miss several days of school.

Staircases are usually safe enough when used properly. When students start pushing, shoving and clowning around, however, they can become downright hazardous.

Now you're probably thinking that you're careful enough and that you won't fall, but there just might be that first time, right?

Values of contest enumerable

A speech contest has values that are practically enumerable; however, these values are usually not realized unless one enters the contest.

For instance, a person obtains the experience of speaking before an audience. Also he can express his own feelings about a given topic. In addition, he learns how to present his speech, using proper enunciation and gestures.

We feel entering the oratorical contest is worthwhile.

From capitol steps

I watch first inaugural parade

By Sharla Cate

Everyone loves a parade—especially if it's the very first inaugural parade ever held in Arkansas, and that's the one I saw Jan. 12.

Preparation started for me at 6:45 A.M. when I joined the Southside band for the 187 mile ride to Little Rock.

Published bi-weekly by the ninth grade journalism class of Chaffin Junior High School, Rt. 1, Box 335R, Fort Smith, Arkansas 72901.

Editor... Patricia Dickinson
Ass't Editor... Sandra Curtis
Page Editors.. Martha Morgan, Sharla Cate, Barbara Smelley, Sarah Jaber
Sports.. Mike Wortham and Bob Sawyer
Advertising.... Martha Morgan
Photographer.... Mike Wortham
Cartoonist....... Pam Manckiy
Exchange...... Janiesse Kleier
Scrapbook.. Cheryl Bohnenkamper
Advisor...... Mrs. Lorine Lay

After two hours in my "viewing stand," the parade ended at 3 o'clock, giving me a full hour before time for the bus to leave for home.

The parade started at 1 P.M., came right up to the steps where I was sitting and turned right. The fog, wet and cold were reflected on the face of everyone who marched up the hill, but excitement was also present.

Clowns perform

Clowns are usually a big attraction in a parade, and this one was no exception. Clowns on ponies, mini-bikes and dune buggies weaved in and out between cars, floats and bands.

Two carried a bumper bearing the name of the new governor, Dale Bumpers. Another in an out-house which exploded was sent hurtling through the air in his drawers.

Bands, floats, mayors and county queens made up the rest of the parade with an added attraction for the children, "Smokey the Bear."

Arriving 40 minutes before parade time, I found the best possible viewing seat on the Capitol steps, right in the middle of the fourth step from the top.

I tour Capitol

In the Capitol I found my good friend, Senator W.E. Rainwater, who took me on a short tour of the building. We rode to the second floor, where I was shown the Senate chamber. A bill had just been voted on to extend the 60-day session to 90 days.

We found a reception committee in the next room, reminding Mr. Rainwater that he was supposed to be there. He introduced me to newly-elected Lt. Governor Bob Riley and his wife. I also met Senator Milt Earnhart from this area. Before leaving the Capitol, I visited the House chamber also.

Coming back on the bus, I decided that it had been a beautiful parade and a wonderful day. The only trouble was that it was over too soon.

NO, ROGER, IT'S NOT A NEW HAIRDO, MOTHER JUST LEFT HER SPRAY STARCH ON MY DRESSER.

It's our opinion

A few Chaffin students have already begun driving, and many more are planning to in the near future, so let's look at some facts we found in the Tulsa Daily World recently.

Teens drive

According to the National Transportation Safety Board, 15-to-25-year-old youths are involved in the most accidents. The records show that 31 per cent of highway deaths were in this age group, yet this same group constitutes only 21 per cent of the driving public.

The board suggests that a probationary license be granted those under 21. The probation period would run two years. If the driver has a clean record at the end of this time, he would receive a regular license.

Good safety havits pay off by letting one drive safer, happier and longer. Maybe they could also let one drive sooner.

What's spirit?

What is spirit? The school policy folder that was sent to all junior high students spells it out for us. Spirit may be divided into three categories-- courtesy, pride and sportsmanship.

It can be shown as courtesy to teachers, students and officials. Spirit can be shown through pride in your own accomplishments and in those of your school in anything it may try to do. Spirit can be shown in sportsmanship by being able to lose as gracefully as one wins, and by being loyal to all phases of school.

It sounds reasonable. Let's have spirit.

Clasped Hands
For a good year

Classroom Calamities

By Cathy Linder

Since school opened Aug. 27, we've all changed a little. It didn't take long for the ninth graders to get used to the idea that we're the "big guys."

• • •

The first day, bright faces awaited the teachers. Each day faces have gotten a little less bright. Now they look quite tarnished. Also teachers have begun to smile at us less and less.

• • •

The first week reminded us of that treacherous device called a test, for it was during that week that the civics classes were given a severe jolt, a pop test. So intense was the jolt that some very strange answers were given.

• • •

For instance, did you know that the national anthem is "The Stars and Stripes Forever"? Or that someone thinks the county we live in is the United States of America? (We won't mention the fact that yours truly almost forgot how many stars there are in our flag.)

• • •

After the first few days of school, many apparently felt as Lynn Wintory did when she wrote the following poem:

SUMMER VACATION

Vacation is coming
Oh, how I yearn
To leave the building
Where we do nothing but learn.

I could stay up till midnight
Then sleep till noon.
Oh, how I wish
That it was again June.

I could go to parties
And I could swim,
Then go traveling
To visit my kin.

It's so very hard
To sit here in class
Knowing there are 9 months
Before summer comes at last!

In yardwork

We find 20% fewer calluses

By Robb McDaniel

Yards are getting easier to keep these days. I have 20% fewer calluses to prove it!

The gasoline and the electric lawn mowers have been around for awhile, but have you heard of some of the latest inventions?

For the sidewalk-driveway areas you have the muscle-saving electric edger, which is a neat and tidy way to make your yard look luxurious.

This summer I also had the experience of operating a pair of electric hand-trimmers. All the muscle is in the thumb-motion to give an expert cut to the tall grass and shrubs.

Everything has begun to look like something, electrically, except the sidewalk. That's where miracle No. 4 comes in. It's an electric vacuum cleaner made for the outdoors. It gobbles up sidewalk clutter to the touch of a button.

Now, if somebody would just invent an electric leaf raker..... I'd have it made!

THE COUGAR PRINT

Published bi-weekly by the ninth grade journalism class of Chaffin Junior High School, Rt. 1, Box 335R, Fort Smith, Arkansas 72901

Co-editors.. Lynn Wintory and Robb McDaniel
Business managers.... Michele Nicodemus and Reyn Ellis
Page editors. Barbara French, Robin Hatfield, Leslie Staton, Catherine McCann, Mandee Harper, Caron Smets
Sports... Marc Allen and Gail Hammersly
Columnist....... Cathy Linder
Art... Karen Hutcheson, Cindy Sagely, Sarah Minchew
Exchange......... Janet Brown
Adviser...... Mrs. Lorine Lay

Editorial pages #3, #4, #5—These three examples show how a basic layout can be varied. Heads in the editorial column provide an attractive change from the usual one line above the copy. Note that in each instance the head fits into a uniform space. Slugs of space separate the editorials. (A rule here or row of three asterisks or filled or open circles would serve to emphasize the separation.) The rules in both column headings contribute to the horizontal impression, as do the two- and three-column cartoons, the "Letters to the editor" headline and the "Soothsayer" headline. All three pages show balance of upper right against lower left. Again the masthead, set tight, anchors the lower right corner. Special features like the "Smiley" drawing add color to the page.

It's our opinion

Buses defaced

Because of vandalism on the bus, the city is considering the discontinuance of the Eastgate student bus route. One of the schools this route serves is Chaffin.

By kicking out windows, writing obscene remarks and loosening seats, a few students are jeopardizing the only means of transportation that some students have.

Just as it is against the law for someone else to destroy our property, so is it for us to destroy another's property.

The city is trying to ascertain the identity of those vandalizing the bus to correct this problem.

Chaffin has always maintained a good reputation, but will it continue to do so?

Friend in need

She wasn't exactly my friend. True, I knew her well enough to say "hi" to, but I never did. I was always busy with my school activities, and besides she wasn't in my social group. She had her own friends anyway, or did she?

As I remember, she always seemed to be by herself sitting secluded in the back of the room, and she always went home to eat.

I remember everybody used to laugh at her because she was blind and had to be led around. Even I laughed. Then at night I was conscience-stricken, resolving to make amends with her the next morning. But that was always tomorrow.

She died last week.

An investment in knowledge pays the best interest. --Benjamin Franklin

Ah,
RA-RA
the joy
Hiss-BOOM
of football season!-
BA!
reyn

Classroom Calamities

By Cathy Linder

Recently in Mrs. Rosemary Prescott's English classes, students studied verb compliments. Such difficult terms as OC, DO, IO, PN and PA were used. Now this can lead to much confusion.

When asked what the compliments in one particular sentence were, one befuddled student might reply, "DC, OP and OI."

Now, of course, that isn't right so he must try again "BC, AD and BO?"

And so on it goes until he finally makes the classic reply, "I guess I wasn't paying attention."

* * *

i8m not ve ru good in typkng. When i signge up i didnt no iT woudl be this hard? I a lways spel word s rong; The other Day we wree suposed to typ e "Win as if you8re used to iT." my sentense came out, "sin as if you're used to it" . see wat i me an!

* * *

The gym classes recently went through a trauma. We had a skills test (why do our skills have to be tested?) Have you tried to hold a tip-up five seconds? It's not as easy as it sounds! And five seconds is longer than it seems.

In a tip-up you balance your knees on your elbows and you are up on your hands without your head touching anything. Getting into a tip-up is somewhat like the position of a frog.

* * *

While giving a report in civics recently, a student was interrupted by a loud noise from Home Ec. When the "reporter" was talking about the Food and Drug Administration, this was heard, "Yes, I know it smells good, but...."

It's a fact••

By Caron Smets

As Halloween approaches, the mountains of candy in stores get lower and lower. There's no need to worry though, for the United States makes more candy than any other country in the world.

A wide variety is available with more than 2,000 different kinds, and more are being invented all the time.

In ancient times people ate candy. The Egyptians wrote about their candy and even drew pictures of it. Made of honey, it was shaped in little mounds.

The Romans had some candy, but it was so expensive that only very rich people could afford it.

As a special treat colonial children enjoyed candy made from the sap of maple trees.

THE COUGAR PRINT

Published bi-weekly by the ninth grade journalism class of Chaffin Junior High School, Rt. 1, Box 335R, Fort Smith, Arkansas 72901.

Co-editors.. Lynn Wintory and Robb McDaniel
Business Managers.... Michele Nicodemus and Reyn Ellis
Page editors. Barbara French, Robin Hatfield, Leslie Staton, Catherine McCann, Mandee Harper, Caron Smets
Sports... Marc Allen and Gail Hammersly
Columnist....... Cathy Linder
Art... Karen Hutcheson, Cindy Sagely, Sarah Minchew
Exchange......... Janet Brown
Adviser...... Mrs. Lorine Lay

It's our opinion

Boos booed

After attending the first few Cougar games, we noticed some bad sportsmanship displayed by both cheering sections.

When either football team is penalized, it is not good taste to boo or to cheer, whatever the case may be. By cheering when the other team is penalized, it shows poor sportsmanship because it is actually cheering their mistake. Booing when our own team is penalized could cause us further penalty on the grounds of unsportsman-like conduct.

Neither is it proper to cheer and applaud our national anthem.

Let's work to keep our good reputation.

Humpty dumped

Humpty Dumpty ran down the hall;
Humpty Dumpty had a great fall.
All of his foes and all of his friends
Trod on his toes and jogged on again.

This rhyme pretty well describes the situation in the Chaffin halls. Have we turned into a Humpty Dumpty, his foe or his friend?

A smile is a bit of sunshine added to the face, and like the sun, it warms the heart of those who experience it.

Letters to the editor

'plause 'n' claws

Dear Editor,

In elementary school and in high school we have pictures taken. Why can't we have them in junior high?

Just Wondering

(Mr. Alverson: According to the administration policy handbook, the school board suggested that school pictures not be taken in elementary and junior high school. The exception is when the PTA decides to have it done and chooses a local licensed photographer.)

Dear Editor,

Since the rest of the school is air conditioned, why can't the gym be air conditioned also?

Hot in P.E.

(Mr. Alverson: You don't air condition a gym. It isn't used as a study place; it's for exercise.)

(Editor's note: If the doors are propped open the gym is much cooler. Could this be a solution?)

misery is:
getting contacts s
that you can se
better, and the
having to keep
your eyes close
because they hur

The soothsayer predicts

fall can be fatal

By Cathy Linder

The stars are bright this month. They definitely say, quite clearly, "October is a doom-filled month." (But what month isn't?)

LIBRA– the "Weight Watcher" (Scales) Beware of any "ayds" a friend tries to give. All troubles will be pounding in on you.

SCORPIO– the "Stingin' Swinger" (Scorpion) Your friends will tend to avoid you because all your criticism will have stung them with remorse.

SAGITTARIUS– the "Robin Hood" (Archer) Watch for evil while walking through a forest. There are spies everywhere.

CAPRICORN– the "Kid" (Goat) Caution! A hungry friend could eat you out of house and home.

AQUARIUS– the "Water Fountain" (Water Bearer) This month everyone will think you're a big drip. Be careful or you'll find yourself in hot water.

PISCES– the "Perch" (Fish) Beware of any lures or bribes this month. Try to get off the hook in math.

ARIES– the "Sheep" (Ram) Don't let a well-meaning friend crying "wolf" fool you.

TAURUS– the "Cow" (Bull) Don't let anyone try to sell you a bunch of bull. Avoid all bells.

GEMINI– the "Twin Man i Moon" (Twins) At the beg this will seem like one step for school, but it giant leap for educati

CANCER– the "Grough" Stop that consistent n or it could mean a sulk ober.

LEO– the "Cougar" (Your troubles will be m Lyin' only makes it wor it is.

VIRGO– the "Bachelor" (You will tend to want alone this month. Don near any rice. It could for you.

THE COUGAR P

Published bi-weekly ninth grade journalis of Chaffin Junior High Rt. 1, Box 335R, Fort Arkansas 72901

Co-editors.. Lynn Wint Robb McDaniel
Business managers.... Nicodemus and Reyn E
Page editors. Barbara Robin Hatfield, Lesl ton, Catherine McCan dee Harper, Caron Sm
Sports... Marc Allen a Hammersly
Columnist....... Cathy
Art... Karen Hutcheson Sagely, Sarah Minche
Exchange......... Jane
Adviser...... Mrs. Lor

Inside Pages

The inside news and feature page generally has the main story in the upper left corner, especially if the ads pyramid to the right. Other than that, the same principles of makeup apply to inside pages as to page one. Because of the small size of the paper, pages two and three are planned together so they will look good as a unit.

The following suggestions for mimeographed papers are offered by Mrs. Marjorie Robinson, adviser of *The Redbird* of Loudonville High School, Loudonville, Ohio.

Guidelines for improving mimeo makeup:

(1) Edit copy sharply because of space limitations. Justify to make right margins even.

(2) Carefully plan a full-sized dummy sheet for each page.

(3) Use a three-column plan except for the editorial page or special pages. Use 8½ x 11 paper. Lay out the page so that each column counts down to line 60 (61).

(4) Prefer elite type to save page inches, but try pica type for eye-catching lead paragraphs, subheads or editorials.

(5) Vary page makeup with some two- (or three-) column headlines, and lead paragraphs two columns wide with the rest of the story dropping into one column.

(6) Keep the nameplate small and simple in design. A two-column nameplate that can be shifted on the page allows more variety and flexibility.

(7) Include name of school, city, state, volume number on page 1 dateline. (Also in masthead on editorial page.)

(8) Place name of paper, date, and page number on each page. A streamlined technique is to put this dateline at the top or bottom of one column. Even page numbers are arranged to the left, with odd numbers to the right.

(9) Try to include at least one picture (cartoon, illustration) per page. Vary pictures one, two, or a half column wide. Use more original cartoons related to lead stories and less artwork that is merely decorative.

(10) For headlines use letter guides with capital and lower case in various sizes—⅜ inch, ¼ inch, 3/16 inch, and ⅛ inch—in both roman type (straight up and down letters) and italics (slanted letters). Cursive or script (like handwriting) should be used only sparingly, perhaps for a column head.

(11) Separate headlines by pictures and boxes to avoid bumping (tombstone).

(12) Avoid breaking stories to the tops of columns. The top of every column should have a headline or a cut.

(13) Break up gray areas by the use of subheads, indented paragraphs in caps, use of small stories with small headlines.

(14) Avoid having the top half of a page too heavy by balancing it with a spread head beneath the fold. An occasional boxed story or a boxed head lends distinction to the lower section of the page.

(15) Make up inside pages as facing-page units rather than as single pages.

(16) Use "30" dashes and cutoff rules or replace them with white space. Trend is toward omission of column rules and dashes.

* * *

Our front pages have a number of characteristics in common:

(1) Short but distinctive nameplate with essential information. Size makes it easy to float in the upper third of page. Printing in red adds a note of color.

(2) Two-column, two-line headline over main story. Occasional three-column, one-line banner for variety.

(3) Reasonably large cartoon or sketch with a point and cutlines usually to play up a major story, or perhaps a season or holiday.

(4) Headlines and copy below the fold. We prefer a two-column head and story here, but do not always have the space.

(5) Kicker on second most important story for white space, contrast. Use of boxed headline or box around short, important story for contrast or highlighting a particular item.

(6) Carefully justified right margins and even top and bottom margins.

(7) No column rules and sparing use of cut-off rules and dashes give page lighter, whiter look.

(8) Capital letter paragraph lead-ins in place of subheads in longer stories.

(9) Carefully counted flush left headlines and use of simple, related headline types. Some heads could be a bit shorter to add white space.

(10) Attempt to anchor the corners—picture, box, strong headline, short story.

(11) Lead story is often in the traditional top right corner, but sometimes we reverse this for variety in makeup.

(12) Headlines, art define the reading diagonal.

(13) Elements of makeup arranged to avoid tombstoning.

These characteristics in common ensure consistency from issue to issue and develop the personality of the paper.

Mrs. Verna E. Powers, formerly adviser of *The Hi-Spot*, at Waverly High School, Waverly, Nebraska, summarizes suggestions for layout in the mimeographed newspaper as follows:

For each page there must be a basic plan indicating outside margins, column width, and the number of spaces between columns. The staff at Waverly uses special layout forms—mimeographed sheets that have lines numbered to correspond with the lines on the stencil. The arrangement of this form is optional, but it should be consistent throughout the paper and from issue to issue.

In no instance should copy be typed any higher on the page than line 2 or below line 62 on an 8½ x 11 inch sheet of paper. If *elite* type is used, the margin stops for the first column should be 9 and 35; second column, 38 and 64; and third column, 67 and 93.

For *pica* type, use a 22-space line for columns, with the following margin stops: 7 and 29; 31 and 53; and 55 and 77. This leaves two spaces between columns instead of three.

A three-column format has more versatility and gives better-looking pages than one of two columns.

Decide upon the number of lines between headlines and copy, between decks of a headline, between heads and a by-line, and between by-line and copy. We leave one line in each case. This allows for "breathing space" on the page and at the same time eliminates wasted white space, a fault of so many duplicated publications.

Front Page

The front page is the show window of the school. Just as the show window of a local clothing store shows the latest in wearing apparel and the coming fashions, so, too, should the first page of the school newspaper display the latest in events and give some indications of coming attractions. The stories and features must be arranged in an attractive way so that people will want to read them.

The most important single element on the front page, and the item so often neglected, is the nameplate. An attractive, functional nameplate can do much to vitalize front-page makeup of the mimeographed paper. Our nameplate is two columns wide and nine lines high. We use it in various positions from issue to issue. This not only gives more variety to our front page but

Front page #1—Use of the two-column title plate in the upper left with the two-column lead story emphasizes the importance of the story as the other heads—"Students," "Faculty," and "Juniors—form a brace. Art in the second column breaks up the gray, the corners are anchored, and the entire page has a neat look. Every story is easily seen. Cutoff rules add to the horizontal look. The kicker "Can See" allows for pleasing white space. The "Students To Canvass" story has prominent display and is neatly aligned above the two-column "Faculty" story with the cutline of the cartoon. All this care in detail creates an effective page.

THE REDBIRD

Loudonville High School
Vol. XXIII, No. 8   Loudonville, Ohio   Feb. 23, 1968

Science Fair, Art Show Combine With Senior Buffet March 12

The annual Science Fair, art show, and senior smorgasbord will share triple billing March 12 at LHS.

Although the Science Fair will again feature some 240 projects in all areas of science and mathematics, this year something new may be added, according to Mr. David Bick, chemistry teacher.

"I HOPE to be able to use the members of our Science Club to help put up the exhibits and to serve as guides for the parents," commented the youthful teacher.

"Also this year we would like to have a telescope displayed outside since the moon should be nearly full by March 12. The Science Club will take charge of this, too," he added.

Judges for the projects, which are required of all students taking a science course, will be Loudonville teachers and other

(Continued on Page 2)

Juniors Take Test

Forty-two juniors will be taking the National Merit Scholarship Qualifying Test Tuesday.

Results of this test will be used in determining National Merit Scholarship finalists, semi-finalists, and commended students.

Who needs a telescope to look at the moon?

CAN SEE PUPILS' JOBS

Faculty To Visit 2 Industries

School will be dismissed at 1 p.m., March 27, so that Loudonville-Perrysville teachers may tour two area industrial plants.

Tours of Mansfield Sanitary Incorporated and the Flxible Company will be conducted starting at 1:30 p.m. and lasting for about two hours, said Miss Peggy Booze, LHS assistant guidance director.

All faculty members will attend. About half of the group will go to the Flxible, while the others will visit Mansfield Sanitary.

These tours are being scheduled to help teachers visualize the jobs many of their students will hold

and to prepare them better for these jobs.

"Because of the length of time the tours will take, I assume we will inspect each part of these businesses," said Miss Booze.

Annual Adds Color

Because of increased income from advertising and yearbook sales, this year's annual will take on a colorful new look.

In addition to black and white, red will be used in the sports section, blue in the activities section, and four full-color pictures in the newly established introduction.

Students To Canvass Area For Heart Fund

Fifty LHS students will canvass the Loudonville-Perrysville area Sunday afternoon for the annual Heart Fund Drive.

Each student will be assigned to cover a part of the town. At each residence the canvasser will pass out free literature and collect donations.

"Unique is the fact that all the money donated goes directly for research instead of salaries or wages," explained Mrs. David Dalton, general chairman of the drive in the Loudonville vicinity.

"And many persons in this immediate area are benefiting daily from medicine and drugs provided from Heart Fund money," she added.

Front page #2—The elements on this page illustrate a kind of occult balance. The two major stories balance each other, and the picture balances the half box headline. Although the "Tests" and "Band" headlines are adjacent, the reader does not read from one into the other, because of the contrast in headlines, the half box, and the fact that the "Tests" story begins two lines above the "Band" story. Although it is usually suggested that stories not be continued to other pages, this layout proves that the appearance of the page is improved by jumping a story in order to maintain the geometric look. By jumping front-page stories, you can control the appearance of the front page. Running stories above the title plate gives them special significance.

Tests Set Tomorrow

Sixty LHS students will travel to Ashland College tomorrow to participate in the Ohio Tests of Scholastic Achievement.

Only the three students who ranked highest in each subject in the preliminary tests take the finals.

Science, math, social studies, language, and business subject areas will be covered in the day of testing.

Band, Choir Concert To Feature Sacred, Musical Comedy Numbers

Music will fill the air Sunday when the LHS band and choir present their combined spring concert at 3 p.m. in the Budd Auditorium.

The choir, under the direction of Mrs. Marjory Peck, will sing four sacred numbers: "O Sing Praises"; "Breath of God," one of the contest numbers;

"In the Shelter of Thy Arms"; and "Every Time I Feel the Spirit."

"In the Shelter of Thy Arms" features a fugal portion where one section begins a theme and then goes on to a counter theme while another section takes up the main theme. The lively spiritual, "Every Time I Feel the Spirit," will present junior Eric Koppert as a bass soloist.

*

AFTER appearing in robes for the sacred numbers, choir members will then wear spring clothes for six popular numbers.

They will sing a modern love song called "What's New," a Pete King publication. They will also perform "Scarborough Fair Canticle" by Simon and Garfunkle and a new song,

(Continued on Page 2)

THE REDBIRD

Loudonville High School
Vol. XXIV, No. 11   Loudonville, Ohio   May 2, 1969

National Merit Who's Who Lists 2 Local Outstanding Seniors

Seniors Sue Kick and Dean Stitzlein have been chosen outstanding teenagers by Merit's Who's Who Among American High School Students.

Merit's Who's Who is an annual publication devoted to honoring outstanding graduating high school seniors throughout the nation.

Only students who have demonstrated leadership in the fields of academics, activities, athletics, and awards competition are chosen for this honor. Less than three per cent of the graduating seniors in the country are selected for this recognition every year.

Students selected for this honor are required to fill out a Biographical Data Form which includes their high school activities and their future plans and career.

Information provided by this form will be used for a personal biographical sketch of each individual named in this book.

Paper Wins Medalist

For the 10th consecutive year, the REDBIRD has been awarded a Medalist rating in the 45th annual contest of the Columbia Scholastic Press Association.

Scoring 952 out of possible 1,000 points, the REDBIRD earned the highest rating given by CSPA.

The judge suggested making news leads more complete, but praised the make-up as "consistently excellent."

"You have an excellent newspaper which you and your staff must be proud of!" summarized the judge.

AS THE PROM DRAWS NEAR...

Boys are shyer.

Girls are more forward.

THE REDBIRD

Loudonville High School
Vol. XXIV, No. 7   Loudonville, Ohio   Feb. 7, 1969

LHS DATELINE—
Feb. 7 . . Clear Fork Game
Feb. 16. . .Winter Concert
Feb. 18. . . . Merit Tests
Feb. 25. . . .Science Fair

Concert To Feature Contest Selections

Members of the LHS Concert Band will present "Winter Concert '59" Feb. 16 at 3 p.m. in the Budd Auditorium.

Under the direction of Mr. Curt Torrey, the band will feature "Bellerophon," an overture by Whear. This is the required number for all Class B-2 bands at the District 7 contest.

Various instrumental sections will be highlighted with brief solos when the band presents "Introduction and Allegro" by White. This selection will also be performed at the district contest.

Excerpts from the Broadway show "My Fair Lady" will include the well-known show tune "On the Street Where You Live."

No admission will be charged for the concert.

Sue Kick Attains High DAR Score

With a test score of 98, senior Sue Kick has won the local Good Citizens Contest sponsored annually by the Daughters of the American Revolution.

Sue will receive a Certificate of Award, and her paper is now eligible to compete for state and national awards.

In 1964 alumna Karen Krenrick tied for fourth in the state and received a $25 savings bond.

SMORGASBORD   CS

"We are running out of food, Fred. See if you can get some frog's legs from the Science Fair."

Science, Art Shows Share Billing With Class Smorgasbord Feb. 25

Scheduled about a month earlier than in recent years, the annual Science Fair, senior smorgasbord, and art show, will take place Feb. 25 at LHS.

Several area residents will judge some 200 projects Feb. 24 in Building II; the display will then be open to the public the following day until 9 p.m.

"Students who receive superior ratings will have an opportunity to compete in the district contest at Ashland College," commented Mr. David Bick, chemistry teacher.

As HAS become a tradition, the Senior Class will sponsor a smorgasbord the same night in the LHS cafeteria, according to Mr. Robert Cassill, senior class advisor.

Prices are $1.25 for adults, and 75 cents for sixth graders and under.

In the halls of Building II, art students will exhibit their paintings and drawings.

Mrs. Nancy Crow Stitzlein, an LHS graduate and college art major, will display ceramics at the art show, said Mrs. Mary Strouse, art instructor.

Rotary Foots Bill For Science Trip

Sponsored by the Loudonville Rotary, Mr. David Bick, chemistry teacher, and Jim Albertson, LHS junior, will attend the Junior Science and Humanities Symposium in Columbus, next week end.

Mr. Bick remarked that this symposium "allows high school seniors to present oral reports of research projects which they have carried out."

Teachers and students who attend the convention will also tour several industries in the vicinity of Columbus.

Front page #3—The two-column title plate to left is balanced by two-column art, headline, and story to right. All one-column stories have two-line headlines. The corners are anchored. The boxed head adds contrast, separates calendar from title plate. Two-column art highlighting the major story emphasizes the horizontal look. This page lacks a two-column spread below the fold.

Front pages #4 and #5—Perhaps too much space is given here to seasonal artwork, but these pages illustrate two ways to use artwork to indicate a special issue. On the Christmas page we experimented with printing outlines and background of pictures in black, then adding red and green. It is difficult to get perfect registry, but we like the effect better than the picture drawn and printed in a single color. We prefer a kicker with a one-line headline like the one on the "Mr. Jordan" story. (Note that this head is poorly spaced.) Also, we prefer two-line headlines over one-column stories, but space is often too limited. Although we prefer not to jump stories from page one to inside pages, sometimes there is no choice, especially with large areas of artwork.

Lutheran Intern To Speak At Assembly Today

Featuring Mr. and Mrs. Santa Claus; Mr. Jack Pealer, intern of the Loudonville Zion Lutheran Church; and the Senior Choir, the Future Homemakers of America will present the annual Christmas assembly today.

Debbie Cowen, senior, and Donna Baldner, junior, will dress the parts of jolly old St. Nicholas and his merry wife.

Mr. Pealer will deliver the Christmas address, and

FHA members will read poems.

Mrs. Marjory Peck, LHS choir director, has selected five numbers from the choir's Christmas concert for the assembly.

They are "Fanfare"; "Lullaby," a Korean melody; "The Angel's Song" by Tschesnokow; "Break Forth, O Beauteous, Heavenly Light," a Bach chorale; and "Christmas Eve Prayer" by Oliver.

THE REDBIRD

Loudonville High School
Vol. XXIV, No. 5   Loudonville, Ohio   Dec. 20, 1968

High Winds Rip Roof From Gym; Insurance Covers All Repairs

Winds gusting at 40 or 50 miles per hour ripped portions of the gymnasium roof apart during a recent gale.

After being told that sheets of roofing paper

Girl Wins In Wool

Susan Ramser, a junior, is the winner in the junior division of the District Wool Contest.

With all her expenses paid for the week end, Susan will travel to Columbus next Friday to compete in the state wool contest.

Competitors will be involved in the final judging at the state level their first morning in Columbus. That night they will attend a banquet.

Unassisted, all girls had to construct a dress, suit, or coat from wool.

Oh, boy, just what I needed--aspirin!

were blowing from the top of Building IV, Mr. Carl Hardesty, head custodian at LHS, climbed to the roof to investigate.

Over the northwest corner of the gym, an area of roofing about 15 feet wide and 50 feet long had come loose, and, in some places, was peeling away.

COMPOSED of five consecutive layers of roofing paper, each covered with tar, the area was missing about three layers of paper. In several places all of the roofing was blown off to expose the actual ceiling layer of the gym.

After examining the damage, Mr. Hardesty called Supt. Richard Jordan, and the Edwards Roofing and Heating Company in Orrville was contacted. This
(Continued on Page 2)

Congratulations

THE REDBIRD

Loudonville High School
Vol. XXIV, No. 12   Loudonville, Ohio   May 23, 1969

Baccalaureate Set For Sunday Night

Baccalaureate services for the 1969 graduating class at LHS have been scheduled for 8 p.m. Sunday at Redbird Gymnasium.

The Rev. Richard D. Freseman of Zion Lutheran Church will deliver the address on the subject, "Two Wishes for Your Future."

Members of the Concert Band will play, and the LHS choirs will also present special music.

Other local ministers who will participate in the service are the Rev. James Bennet, the Rev. Forest Carter, the Rev. Jay Keiser, and the Rev. Clifford J. Leach.

Top 4 Honor Students To Speak At Graduation for 99 Tuesday

Ninety-nine seniors will receive their high school diplomas at Loudonville's 90th annual Commencement Tuesday at 7 p.m. in Redbird Stadium.

Curtis Ramey, senior class president, will lead the pledge of allegiance to the flag.

Four honor students, Pam Conrad, valedictorian; Sue Kick, salutatorian; and Connie Snyder and Cindy Dudte, who placed third

and fourth scholastically in their class, will speak.

Principal John Boich will make the awards to these four girls and announce the Best Citizen awards that go to the boy and girl selected from the previous Good Citizen winners.

Supt. Richard Jordan will present the class to Dr. Charles McMullen, president of the Board of Education who will distribute the diplomas.

Members of the Concert Band will play the prelude and recessional. The combined choirs will sing "O Praise God in His Sanctuary" by Matthews, "Salvation Is Created" by Tschesnokoff, and "Go Song of Mine" by Cookson.

Mr. Jordan Quits To Work On Ph.D.

Supt. Richard H. Jordan has resigned to accept a fellowship to work on his doctorate at Ohio University where he will begin classes in June.

As one of four candidates picked from several hundred applicants, Mr. Jordan will spend one year on the OU campus in the education department.

Consisting of two parts, his scholarship grant will provide a tax-free government subvention from the United States Office of Education and the payment of all tuition and fees by OU.

Although ordinarily the earning of a doctorate requires about two years, Mr. Jordan is now taking some courses at Ohio State University which will be transferable, thus enabling him to graduate next June.

The superintendent explained that although he has mixed emotions about leaving the Loudonville-Perrysville School System, the fellowship has given him the chance to fulfill his ultimate goal. "I want my doctorate as preparation
(Continued on Page 2)

Girls Win Grants

Three LHS seniors have already been awarded scholarships to the colleges which they plan to attend.

Both Pam Conrad and Sue Kick received grants to Capital University, while Peg Rader was awarded a scholarship to Ohio State University.

Front page #6—This page shows the nameplate centered, with ears to draw reader's attention to inside pages. Note how the banner head frames the picture and story, how the kicker head affords contrast, and how boxed story adds interest to bottom half of page. The use of asterisks and capital letter lead-ins are attention devices. (The headline in all capitals is not consistent with our style, but no lower-case letters are available for this guide.)

Front page #7—This is an example of column-and-a-half, double-column, and two-column body copy blocks. The two-column story at the bottom balances the two-column nameplate. (This page might have looked better had the "Learning Lab" story been set one column wide and then arranged in two columns. We like the white space between columns and ordinarily avoid large blocks of double-column type.)

Front page #8—With the nameplate and main story in the upper right, this layout affords space for two more important stories and two lesser ones, plus a picture. The headlines "Legion Women," "Play Dates," and "Fowler Wins" define the reading diagonal. The two-column Easter story balances the two-column main story. Note the extra width of line in the Easter story and the variety afforded by the vertical drawing. Again the cutoff rules help define the geometric look and the horizontal effect. (The picture was printed in purple.)

VIP
Alumni
—See P. 3

THE REDBIRD

Man vs.
Machine
—See P. 10

Vol. XXIII, No. 7   Loudonville (Ohio) High School   Feb. 2, 1968

2 Chosen Outstanding Teen-agers Of America

CS

He wouldn't "make the scene" at LHS. See Page 4.

Seniors Karen Coates and Gary Conrad have been selected as Outstanding Teen-agers of America and will receive certificates at the Recognition Day assembly.

EACH YEAR the Outstanding Americans Foundation, a nonprofit group dedicated to honoring, inspiring, and encouraging young people to take full advantage of the opportunities in America, sponsors this awards program.

"These two students measure up to the criteria of this honor, which are academic leadership, school citizenship, and participation in activities," commented Mr. John Boich, LHS principal.

Karen and Gary belong to a number of LHS organizations. Karen is a member of the Senior Honor Society and is active in the band, Spanish Club, and FTA. Gary is in the Senior Honor Society and is a varsity football letterman.

*

THESE TWO students will now compete with other winners in the state for the Governor's Trophy awarded annually to the most outstanding teen-ager.

They may also become eligible for one of the top 10 national awards and a $1,000 college scholarship made available by the Outstanding Americans Foundation.

TO STUDY COMMUNISM

Rotary Picks 2 Girls For Trip

For the first time, two senior girls have been selected to represent the local Rotary Club at the 22nd annual World Affairs Institute.

Karen Coates and Rose Anne Johnson will travel on an all-expense-paid trip to Cincinnati March 15-16 to attend the institute, which is sponsored by the Cincinnati Rotary Club and the Cincinnati Council on World Affairs.

*

THEY WILL hear speakers on this year's theme, "The Challenges of International Communism Through the Seventies," and will participate in round table discussions on "Communism, Today and Tomorrow."

Karen and Rose Anne were chosen on the basis of their total academic record, especially in social studies.

"The purpose of this institute is to enlighten students in matters of international concern," remarked Mr. John Boich, LHS principal and a local Rotarian.

Last year's LHS delegates were Nancy Nowels and Steve Frank.

Pupils To Register

Student registration for the 1968-69 school year will begin March 1.

Mr. Elmer Boyer, LHS guidance counselor, will explain registration at class meetings in February. Students will register with Mr. Boyer individually during study halls.

CONCERT CHANGED

The LHS band, under the direction of Mr. Robert Everhart, has rescheduled its annual winter concert for this Sunday at 3 p.m. in the Budd Auditorium.

Included in the variety of numbers on the program will be "Air and March," a composition by Henry Purcell; "Jedermann," a Civil War piece; and "Toccata" for Band," featuring the woodwind section.

Because weather conditions prevented practice, the concert was changed.

THE REDBIRD

Loudonville High School
Vol. XXIV, No. 10   Loudonville, Ohio   April 11, 1969

LHS DATELINE
April 14. . . VICA Banquet
April 25.All-Sports Dinner
April 26. . . . NOSPA-Kent
April 30. . . .FHA Banquet

Faculty Picks 4 Juniors For Boys', Girls' States

Faculty members have chosen four juniors to represent LHS at the 23rd annual Buckeye Girls' and Boys' States.

Dana Frye and Susan Ramser will attend Girls' State at Capital University from June 14-22. Their alternate is Kathryn Wise.

Dave Krenrick and George Winters, with Jim Albertson as alternate, will represent their school June 12-20 at Boys' State, which has traditionally been held at Ohio University in Athens.

Outstanding representatives of their class, the girls chosen must have high moral character, good leadership potential, and a definite interest in American government.

Besides believing in the ideals of God and Country on which the American Legion is founded, the selected boys must possess leadership, sportsmanship, scholarship, patriotism, and courage for service.

The American Legion Post 257 and the Legion Auxiliary will sponsor these students.

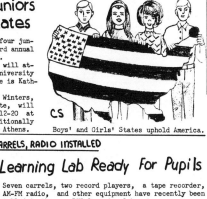

CS

Boys' and Girls' States uphold America.

CARRELS, RADIO INSTALLED

Learning Lab Ready For Pupils

Seven carrels, two record players, a tape recorder, an AM-FM radio, and other equipment have recently been installed in the new LHS learning laboratory.

According to Mr. Robert Cassill, head librarian, this equipment, which has been installed in the former seminar room of the library, is now available to students for extra study and class assignments.

*

EACH CARREL, which is like an individual booth, is equipped with a light, a small viewing screen, electrical receptacles, and earphones.

The carrels are connected to the main control center where the record players and tape recorder are located.

By turning a dial, the student can select what he wishes to hear, and several students can listen to different sources at the same time.

*

"THE SEVEN carrels should be adequate for our high school enrollment of 500," said Mr. Cassill. "Many larger schools plan only 8-10 units. However, we have plenty of room for expansion," added the librarian.

Paper Earns All American Rank

The REDBIRD has received an All American Honor Rating in the 80th All American Critical Service conducted by the National Scholastic Press Association at the University of Minnesota.

Earning the highest honor rating for the first-semester issues of this school year, the REDBIRD improved upon the previous semester's First Class Rating. This is the 37th All American Rating in the paper's history.

"The REDBIRD is among the most thoroughly newsy papers in this group, and its production standards are hard to match," summarized the judge, Mr. H.S. Stensaas.

Legion Women Pick 2 For Girls' State

Chosen by the local American Legion Auxiliary, two LHS junior girls will attend Buckeye Girls' State, June 19-27, at Capital University in Columbus.

Barbara Derrenberger and Martha Guinther were selected as delegates and Marjorie Wigton and Betty Wigton, as first and second alternates.

Both Barbara and Martha have worked on the REDBIRD staff and are in the National Honor Society. Barbara was awarded the Citizenship medal in the ninth grade, while Martha received it in the 10th grade. Martha has been on the District-State Scholarship team for two years.

Delegates to Boys' State will be announced later.

Concert Substitutes For Easter Assembly

Because of the rescheduling of several major spring events, LHS will not observe Easter with the traditional school assembly.

Instead, the Ontario High School Band will present an exchange concert for Loudonville students Tuesday morning.

An assembly schedule with short morning classes will be followed Tuesday.

Directed by Mr. Lanny Hisey, the Senior Choir will sing three numbers at the community Sunrise Service in the Budd School auditorium at 6:30 a.m. Easter Sunday.

All high school and college students are invited to a breakfast in the McMullen cafeteria following the Sunrise Service.

Tickets, on sale in the office, are 50 cents.

THE REDBIRD

Loudonville High School
Vol. XX, No. 10   Loudonville, Ohio   April 9, 1965

63 Local Students Will Enter Final Scholarship Tests May 1

Sixty-three local students will travel to Ashland College to compete in the Final District-State Scholarship tests May 1.

Three LHS students will enter each subject area this year.

Those who ranked in the 95th percentile, or above, in the Preliminary District State Tests were:

GENERAL Science, Gary Conrad; Biology, James Conrad; Chemistry, Joe Taylor; Algebra II, Nancy Nowels.

American History, John Arnold; World History, Jim Wright; Senior Social Studies, Dave Brightbill, Phil Glasgo, Eric Laser, and Jim Wright.

English XI,John Arnold; English XII, Jim Wright; Latin II, Marlene Miner; French I, Tom Drouhard.

STUDENTS rating in the 90-94th percentiles were Phil Glasgo, Physics; Christina Cramer, Algebra I; Connie Zehner, Plane Geometry; Cynthia Joseph, Nancy Nowels, Linda Roberts, and Teresa Smith, English 10; and David Wigton, French II.

Play Dates Reset

Cast and crew of the junior class play have resumed rehearsals, but production dates have been changed.

"Brother Goose," a comedy, will be presented April 30 and May 1.

Rescheduling was due to the illness of Mrs. Lucille Hastings, play director.

Fowler Wins Grant

Mr. Ken Fowler, math teacher, has won a National Science Foundation grant to study at Miami University, June 21-Aug. 6.

Forty teachers, or one out of 30 applicants, were accepted for this summer institute for mathematics instructors.

Guitar-Strumming English I Teacher To Retire

By Cindy Dudte

Decked out in velvet breeches and a white satin blouse and strumming on the guitar she held in her hands, a solitary enter-tainer filled the Cleve-land Public Auditorium with strains from an old Italian song.

Who could guess that this young soloist, having some of the fun which has filled her life, would become a familiar figure at L H S--Mrs. Evelyn Mann, freshman English teacher?

HOWEVER, in the next few years her face will be seen only occasionally in the classroom because Mrs. Mann plans to retire at the end of the school year to devote more time to her family and to music.

Fifteen years of teach-ing in the Loudonville-

And to think I gave this all up for teaching! Perrysville School System has occupied only a part of the life of the fun-lov-ing teacher, who has also enjoyed rearing two daugh-ters and one son, direct-ing school plays, a n d singing continuously.

Oddly enough, when she was graduated from Wooster College in 1931, Mrs. Mann did not have the proper credits to go into a teach-

ing career. When asked to consider teaching, she de-clared, "Heavens, I could-n't teach school! I never even thought about teach-ing."

But, with her family grown and the need for teachers increasing, the ambitious mother enrolled in summer school and night school at Ashland College and completed correspon-dence courses from Ohio University in order t o take up education.

"Even though I was old-er than most of the other college students, I didn't have any problems," Mrs. Mann explained. "We got along all right."

AS A MEMBER of her col-lege glee club, Mrs. Mann was originally ambitious to be a singer, rather than a teacher.

"I wanted to be a blues-singer. O u r glee club would travel all around putting on musicals, and I used to sing all those old torch songs. We had a lot of fun!" reminisced the happy, gray-haired woman.

"When I look back on it now, I don't know how I ever had the nerve to do what I did!"

For the past 25 years Mrs. Mann has either sung in or directed the Perrys-ville Baptist Church Choir. She also sings solos at various church occasions. I've buried and married so many people," said the English teacher, who mar-ried her own husband, Clay-(Continued on Page 8)

Local Citizen Donates Potter's Wheel For Making Ceramics In Art Classes

Donated by Mr. Hugo Young, a local resident, a new potter's wheel has ar-rived for use in LHS art classes.

Mrs. Mary Strouse, art instructor, explained that this new electric wheel with two speeds is a "good one that is well-made."

"Plaster throwing heads and the round plates that the clay is put on and molded can be removed easi-ly from this wheel, so ce-ramic pieces do not have to be cut off immediately and perhaps disfigured.

Since the process of drying and firing may take

weeks, the wheel won't be u s e d extensively until next year, according to Mrs. Strouse.

But senior art students will have an opportunity to use the wheel since Mrs. Strouse believes t h e y should have this chance be-fore they graduate.

"I believe there will be more interest in ceram-ics next year because of this new, good, working wheel," added Mrs. Strouse.

Mr. Forest Swank, indus-trial arts teacher, and Ken Babcock, j u n i o r , worked on the base for the wheel.

Inside page #1—In general on feature-news pages we try to achieve attractive top-of-page treatment with a two-column story below the fold. Here the kicker head three columns wide frames the story and picture (run in green). Note that the main head is indented about a letter's space at the left. The by-line is centered with one line of space above and one below. The story was jumped to another page rather than cut because it was considered better than average. Long stories are broken with capital letter lead-ins. The two-column, two-line headline draws attention to another important story. Cutoff rules are important here. Note the effectiveness of the dateline.

Inside page #2 and #3—These two pages are vari-ations of the basic plan for inside page #1. Loud 'n Clear is really a column. It needs a more distinctive head to indicate that it is a humor column and not just a light essay. A half-column cartoon of the author set into the first column would make the top of the page more interesting.

Research Paper Woes Plague English Students

By Greg Shreve

Pop Phot 52: 49-63 Mr. '63
il Mod Phot 27: 60 Mr. '63

Can you decipher the hi-eroglyphics above?

One hint: they are like-ly t o b e found while searching for information to write a research paper.

They are, obviously, ex-cerpts from the Reader's Guide to Periodical Liter-ature, found in all major libraries.

If you missed the first one, try this one.

What is an appendix?

Clue: it likewise has to do with research papers.

Also: it's not a little thing in y o u r stomach which goes bad sometimes.

An appendix is, accord-ing to a well-known En-glish language textbook, an addition of supplemen-tary material at the end of a research paper.

If you have taken, or are taking, any junior or s e n i o r English courses, you learn all kinds of t h i n g s like deciphering hieroglyphics and defining appendix.

If you are planning to sign up for any of these courses, which you proba-bly are, since they're man-datory anyway, by a l l means go ahead.

You'll find the answers to these and many other questions of alleged impor-tance to college-bound stu-dents. For instance, the vertical file is a course in itself.

"Hey, how do you find stuff in the vertical file?"

"It's arranged in alpha-betical order by subject."

"Good. Then it'll b e easy to find what I'm look-ing for."

"Not really. Most o f the things are lying on top of the cabinet in no particular order at all."

A nother lesson y o u

learn in writing a re-search paper is the impor-tance of careful checking.

A f t e r completing a stack of bibliography cards, you triple - check them with a high-power mag-nifier against every known correct example you can ob-tain. T h e n proceed to English. Here, before hand-ing them in, you find an average of 2.6 mistakes per card.

"Huh? But I never saw that before" is your only comment.

Yes, sir, research pa-pers are really fun. They fill in the space between first and second semester tests, while competing for your time and effort with science projects and other less exciting pastimes.

Juniors Discuss World Affairs

Thirteen LHS juniors, supervised and assisted by Mr. Frederick Boston, Amer-ican history teacher, are exchanging ideas on world situations.

At 7 p.m. o n e night each week, the students

meet in the history room at LHS to discuss a single topic.

To prepare for the dis-cussion and obtain back-ground information, they read a section of Great Decisions 1969, devoted en-tirely to that night's sub-ject.

"There are eight sec-tions in the book," ex-plained Kathryn Wise, one member of the group. "They each deal with a particu-lar world problem, ranging f r o m Cuba's Castro to Southeast Asia."

Eight issues are out-lined in the book, and the program will last for eight weeks.

Junior Revives 'Lost Art' With Spinning Wheels

By Cindy Dudte

Decades ago it was prob-ably customary to see a spinning wheel occupying a space near the fireplace in almost every log cabin.

But, in this age of perma-press fabrics and syn-thetic materials, spinning wheels and spinners are "getting kinda scarce"--ex-cept at the home of Susan Ramser, a junior.

Here, at least, spin-ning is not an ancient practice because Sue not only owns t w o spinning wheels, but she also knows how to use them.

EVEN THOUGH she isn't planning to spin her own Easter outfit this year, Sue has spun yarn for a few sample pieces of cloth.

About seven years ago at the Loudonville Free Street Fair, Sue got inter-ested in this pastime from watching a Mrs. Baughman demonstrate spinning.

Then, when Susan bought a small spinning wheel to refinish as a 4-H project, she was on her way to dis-covering a new hobby.

MADE BY a company in Canada, t h i s spinning wheel stands about 2½ feet tall and is called a flax wheel because it is used mostly to spin flax.

Almost six feet tall, Sue's other spinning wheel is an antique she bought near Loudonville. It is called a wool wheel be-cause it is used primarily to spin wool.

"Actually, spinning the wool takes practice and muscles," commented t h e six-year member o f the Stitches and Chatter 4-H Club from Knox County.

"It takes strength to straighten the fibers and pull them apart i n t o threads. This is done by moving two pieces of wood,

which are called cards and are covered with metal spikes, over the wool," ex-plained Sue. "The spinning wheel is used to twist these fibers into threads."

SUSAN AND Sue Snively, another junior, demonstra-ted spinning at the county fair for 4-H and later went on to the state fair. Susan has also demonstra-ted to Brownie S c o u t troops and friends.

"I enjoy spinning a lot because it is an unusual hobby. It is interesting to think that a couple of centuries ago women had to know how to spin in order to clothe their families," she added. "Now we don''t need it anymore. It's kind of a lost art."

Teacher Committee To Write Policy Governing Student Activity Program

Extra-curricular activ-ities are being reviewed at LHS.

Fifteen local teachers make up a committee that will evaluate these activ-ities and create a written policy for participation in the student activity programs in the h i g h school. Such a policy is required by the state.

By April 17, when its report is due, the commit-tee will form guidelines for future organizations and determine the adequacy of existing groups.

Recently the committee had members of the student body fill o u t activity questionnaires. They found out that, in general, up-perclassmen tend to go out

for more school activities than underclassmen, accord-ing to Mr. Alton Lance, committee chairman.

Fifty-six per cent of all LHS students belong to at least one school organ-ization; 10 per cent be-long to three o r more organizations.

Hop, Bake Sale Set

The Freshman Class will sponsor a record hop in Room 101, tomorrow night from 8-11 p.m.

Saturday morning, March 29, the sophomores will hold a bake sale in the Legion lobby. In the after-noon they will sponsor a car wash a t the water works.

CALLS IT 'SATURN'

Grad Builds Car Like Astro I

By Jim Hunt

Because he "likes to make things," a Loudonville alumnus has built a three-wheeled vehicle that did 65 m.p.h., made a 12-gauge pistol at home, and is currently working on a sports car he designed himself.

Mr. Richard Smith, who was graduated from LHS in 1950, builds such things as sports cars at his home on Rt. 95, outside McKay.

*

THE CAR he's working on now is called the Saturn 444. "I named it Saturn, because it's out of this world," explained the automobile mechanic as he applied a piece of gooped-up fiberglas to the wire body of the machine.

The car is made of hardware cloth and fiberglas built around a Corvair chassis. It has a 1965 Corvair engine that Mr. Smith rebuilt. "The basic design is like the Chevrolet Astro I," added Mr. Smith.

This car should be finished in a couple of months, according to Mr. Smith. When it is done, he may take it to an auto show in Cleveland. "I built it as a showpiece," related the builder as he continued work with the fiberglas.

*

MIKE Smith, LHS junior and the nephew of Mr. Smith, sometimes helps with the work on the Saturn 444. Mike disclosed a special reason for wanting it finished soon. "I want to drive it to the Prom, Mike said with a laugh.

"You? Ha! I'll get the lead!"

Sympathy—

Members of the REDBIRD staff, faculty, and high school students extend their sincere sympathy to Mrs. Clayton Mann, freshman English teacher, whose brother died Monday.

Cast Of 15 Juniors Start Rehearsals For Class Comedy 'A Date With Judy'

Practice started this week for "A Date With Judy," a three-act comedy by Aleen Leslie, to be presented March 28 at the Budd School Auditorium by the Junior Class.

Since they had the biggest group ever to try out,

Mrs. Helen Geiselman, director, and Mrs. Jean Fulmer, seventh-grade English teacher, said they had some difficult decisions in selecting the 15-member cast.

Kay Berry and Eric Koppert, student directors, will assist Mrs. Geiselman in producing the play which shows the headaches as well as the fun of being part of the Foster family or a close friend of the vivacious Judy Foster.

Portraying the Fosters will be Dana Frye, Darlene King, Larry Riter, and George Winters. Steve Glasgo and Becky Welsh will play Judy's close friends.

Supporting members of the cast are Jeff Allerding, Tom Dilgard, Jayne Dubler, Karen Frank, Barb Fisher, Paul Hodge, Pam Jordan, Linda Lozier, and Kathryn Wise.

2 Girls Invade Drafting Class

It's a man's world--or is it!?

At LHS this year, two girls have threatened this traditionally accepted statement.

Velda Montgomery and Pat Roney, sophomores, wanting to further their education in art, have invaded the LHS drafting class.

"I love the class,"

said Velda. "One of the best parts is listening to the boys talk; you can really learn a lot," she continued with a twinkle in her eye.

"Although the boys joke about having girls in the class," said Pat, "they're always very willing to help us."

"Having girls in the class is O.K.," admitted Ron Kettering, one male classmate, "till they get better grades than you!"

8 THE REDBIRD
Feb. 28, 1969

Inside page #4, #5 and #6—The use of a major story with a two-column headline in the upper left forms the basis of this layout. Any number of variations can be worked out if you use as many horizontal headlines as you can and if you arrange your copy and headline (and art if used) in rectangles.

TOPS FOR 20 YEARS

LHS Scores Accredited Rating

Loudonville High School recently received the accredited rating of the North Central Association of Schools and Colleges.

This rating is an evaluative report composed by the Association and is based on facts submitted by Principal J. William Thomas in his annual report.

Policy, organization, and procedure are three general areas covered in the rating; but altogether over 100 checks must be made in subdivisions such as credit hours of faculty members, extra-curricular activities, and per capita library expenditures.

As Mr. Thomas views the rating, its major value is that "the North Central standards are at least one step higher than those imposed by the state minimum laws."

LHS has achieved a c-credited-rating standards for almost all of its more than 20-year membership in the organization.

LOUDONVILLE HIGH SCHOOL

FFA Teams To Vie

FFA members of the State Judging Team will travel to the state contests in Columbus, May 8.

"To instruct students in specialized areas of agriculture production and to gain a better knowledge of the specialized area," is the purpose of the contest, according to FFA advisor Mr. Jack Nowels.

Competition will be in nine events: dairy cattle, farm equipment, horticulture, meat, milk, poultry, wool, agronomy, and general livestock.

2 THE REDBIRD
April 30, 1965

Shop Hosts Dinner

LHS Industrial Arts Department will host the Mid-Ohio Industrial Education Association Wednesday.

The Association will hold a dinner-meeting in the Loudonville High School cafeteria, followed by a tour of the Flxible Company and the local industrial arts facilities.

Arrangements for the Flxible tour are being made through Mr. A. C. Grant, personnel manager for Flxible.

This Association is made up of vocational and industrial arts teachers.

Musicians Rate State 'Excellent'

LHS musicians received Excellent ratings at the Ohio Music Education Association State Band and Chorus Competition at Newark Saturday.

Both the LHS Symphonic Band and Senior Choir qualified to enter this contest by receiving Superior ratings at the district competition.

*

THIS YEAR LHS was competing with the larger B-I schools.

Even though LHS is rated by school size as B-II, contestants are allowed to enter any higher classification in order to increase the competition.

*

THE 75-MEMBER Senior Choir directed by Mr. Lanny Hisey, LHS vocal instructor, received three excellent ratings from its judges.

Ratings earned by the 61-piece Symphonic Band included three Excellent ratings, and a Superior in

sight reading, Mr. Norman Mathews, LHS instrumental instructor, conducted.

Most musical groups enter these contests in order to receive constructive comments for improvement, which are given by the judges in addition to the numerical ratings.

Staff Wins 'Medalist'

"As you have reached your 20th year, you have every reason to celebrate the publication of a Medalist paper!"

So wrote the Columbia Scholastic Press Association judge who awarded the REDBIRD its sixth consecutive Medalist rating, the highest honor given by CSPA.

News stories were termed "complete and well-written"; feature stories, "interesting"; sport columns as "lively as the plays they report"; and makeup, "effective."

'TO ERR IS HUMAN'

Science Club Views Computer

By Peg Rader

Blinking lights, tap-tappings of minute machinery, and constant, tiny buzzing sounds are the characteristic details of a cool, green-walled room at Mansfield Sanitary, Inc., in Perrysville.

In this room is an IBM 360 computer run by Mr. Stanley Ryland, who explained its operation in simplified terms to Kettering Science Club members on a field trip.

*

MR. RYLAND began his lecture in the key punch office where the IBM cards are prepared so they can be read by the computer.

After the operator

transmits written information into "computer language," the card is checked by a verifying machine which will send back imperfect cards.

*

AS SOON AS the computerized cardboard is properly punched, it helps to form a stack of related cards. After being registered in the computer, these cards can be put through again at any time, read, and translated into type at superhuman speed.

Swinging open part of the light blue metal paneling that encases the computer, Mr. Ryland pointed out the wired and cable-tangled sector that reads the cards with a beam of

light. The information is then passed through the memory banks, which can hold 64,000 separate facts.

After information from the cards is correlated with stored information, the computer types it out in the original "human" words. The computer prints a line at a time, 400 lines a minute, 120 letters per line.

*

ANY MISTAKES that are made will be discovered by the computer itself. As soon as the error is found, the computer will stop operating immediately. Guide lights blink on to show where the fault lies hidden.

"One thing to remember," cautioned Mr. Ryland in conclusion, "is that computers can't make mistakes. Only men have that virtue."

29 Boys Make Sparks Fly; Complete Electrical Projects For Shop Class

"Don't touch those two wires together; you'll blow up the whole school!"

This might be one of the comments of Mr. Gail Porter, industrial arts teacher, as he advised 29 second-year shop students about their electricity projects.

"In order to receive a passing grade, the students had to complete a kit or self-designed project," related Mr. Porter.

Although most of the boys chose to order through the school, a few ordered their kits directly from several electronic companies.

Seven boys, Carl Black,

Floyd McIntire, Tom Motz, Marvin Sprang, Steve Stricklen, Lloyd Stull, and Rick Woodring, took soldering guns as their project. Dale Cleghorn, Donald Cline, Terry Disbennett, and Jim Heiser chose V.O.M. meters.

Roger Hans, Roger Lyons, and Jack Spreng made battery chargers; Alan Petty, a tube tester; Jim Russell, a code oscillator; Rick Bilger and Glenn Eggerton, TV listener; Tim Vincent, a walkie-talkie; and John Combs, a tape recorder.

Prices of the kits ranged from $5 to $15. In choosing the kits, the shop boys commented that they tried to select "different and low-cost, but good-quality projects."

8 THE REDBIRD
Feb. 7, 1969

Teacher To Marry

Wedding bells will be ringing for one of the LHS faculty this year.

Mr. Curt Torrey, band director, has recently become engaged to Miss Sara Delkirk of Bedford. She is a junior majoring in art education at Hiram College.

Mr. Torrey and Miss Delkirk were introduced in December of 1965 by the girlfriend of Mr. Torrey's brother.

Firsts Keep School On Map, Improve Conditions

"There's always a first time for everything," and LHS has more than proven this famous saying this year.

On the sports scene fans watched the LHS football squad beat rival Fredericktown for the first time in 17 years.

*

And after being placed in front of Building IV by the Class of 1968, the new victory bell rang for the first time when the local gridders defeated Smithville in the season finale.

*

Turning to basketball, the LHS reserve team copped the No. 1 spot in the JAC conference, and the FFA basketball

team lost only one game during its regular season.

This year also saw the FFA travel to Northwestern Clark High School to participate in a new tri-state invitational judging contest, at which local boys took eighteen honors to become one of three teams dominating the event.

The library was opened for student use on Wednesday nights for the first time this winter, and students began using the new learning lab several weeks ago.

*

Recently junior Greg Shreve became the first LHS student in many years to win a superior rating at the state science fair in Columbus.

*

With these accomplishments under its belt, LHS has continued to strive for excellence, not only in honors for the school but in improved conditions for its pupils.

Activities Rush Pupils

Preparing for the Prom, working on science projects, cramming for final exams, finishing of research papers, serving on banquet committees, studying of daily assignments. . .

That is the dilemma which faces juniors and seniors each year during the second semester. After a relatively quiet first-half a school year, students find themselves swamped with things to do and little time to do them in.

*

Teachers could help students solve this problem. Some advisors might schedule their organization s banquet a little earlier in the year. As it is now, most of the banquets are planned within a period of four weeks. This is especially rough on the schedule of a student who belongs to several organizations.

Another partial solution might be the assigning of research papers earlier in the year, perhaps during the first semester. Most students could work on these papers longer and more carefully if they were assigned earlier.

*

Teachers are not the only ones who can alleviate the problem, however. Students can help themselves by learning to budget their time wisely and by making an honest effort to finish everything that they have to do.

I worked on my research paper until 4 a.m.

I went to four banquets last night.

Notice how the spring rush makes everyone bright and cheery.

THE REDBIRD

Published every third Friday from September to May by the REDBIRD staff of Loudonville (Ohio) High School.

Vol. XXIV, No. 11 May 2, 1969 Page 4

Member, NSPA, CSPA, NOSPA, JAOS
Subscription: 50¢ a year; $1 by mail

Editor. . . . . .Pam Conrad
Associate Editor. . . . . .Karen Frank
Advisor . . . . . .Mrs. T. H. Robinson

Editorial page #1—With editorials set one and a half columns wide and headlines in italics, the editorial page contrasts with the other pages. A kicker identifies the page. Large block letters are used to dress up the beginning of each editorial. A short masthead is used in all issues except the first of each semester. Note that the name of the paper is a small version of the front page title plate. To make editorials look more interesting, key paragraphs are indented two spaces on each side and set off above and below with stars to provide added white space. Use of a cartoon adds interest to the page, especially when in color. On this page, the two-column headline holds the two columns together.

THE TALENT SHOW WANTS YOU

EA

Citizens Aiding School

Although originally organized before the November election to inform the community o f the school's financial n e e d s, the Loudonville-Perrysville School Citizens' Committee is meeting regularly as a permanent group.

Membership of the committee includes 80 area residents who were originally selected by the Board of Education, any civic-minded individual who may wish to serve on the committee, a teacher representative from each building, the Board of Education, principals, and the superintendent.

One objective of the committee is to inform the citizens of the Loudonville-Perrysville School System about educational problems and so to create public good will.

Also, t h e committee is a direct source of information for the Board of Education which is attempting to discover what kind of an education local citizens want for their children.

This is just one more way in which school officials are attempting to improve school-community relations in this district.

Sympathy

The REDBIRD staff, together with the student body and faculty, would like to express its sincere sympathy to Mr. Forest Swank, industrial arts instructor, whose mother died recently.

Club Reaches Trip Goal

"Where there's a will there's a way" was recently demonstrated anew by the LHS Spanish Club.

After working hard for 10 days, Spanish students ended their candy sale campaign netting more than the sum needed to send a student to South America this summer.

Although nearly all students did an exceptional job, several freshmen and a senior should be commended for the diligent effort which made them the leading salesmen in the campaign.

Also, many area businesses and industries helped to sell the candy. Without their cooperation, the drive could not have been so successful.

One lucky student selected for the Latin-American tour will enjoy an all-expense-paid vacation.

But t h e sense of accomplishment shared by all Spanish students has made the project well worth the work put into it.

GOOD LUCK, TEAM

Redbird fans are optimistic as they await tonight's tournament battle with Norwayne. Feeling confident of a victory, they're behind the team all the way.

THE REDBIRD

Published every third Friday from September to May by the REDBIRD staff of Loudonville (Ohio) High School.

Vol. XXIII, No. 8 Feb. 23, 1968 Page 4

Member, NSPA, CSPA
Subscription: 50¢ a year; $1 by mail

Editor. . . . . .Rob Koppert
Associate Editor. . . . . . .Pam Conrad
News Editor . . . . .Sue Banks
Feature Editors . . . . . .Darla Hannan
                            . . . . Sue Nowels
Sports Editors. . . . . .Joie Drouhard
                         . . . . Lynn McClure
Art Editor. . . . . .Vicki Thomas
Circulation Editors . . . .Elaine Kemp
                            . . . . .Marilyn Peters
Mailing Editor. . . . . .Terry Allerding
Advisor . . . . . .Mrs. T. H. Robinson

Rating System Helps Viewers Pick Movies To See

The awarding of motion picture Oscars Monday will show which of the year's performances and pictures movie people rated outstanding.

But because of its obligation to the public, the Motion Picture Association has established a nationwide voluntary film rating program.

This system is not intended to censor or reveal the quality of a movie. Its prime objective is a concern for persons under 16. It hopes to assist parents "to fulfill their responsibilities" to their families by making available certain information about the pictures that may be shown in the local theaters.

One of four ratings is issued to a movie by a Code and Rating Administration which first views that motion picture. These ratings are:

G--Suggested for General Audiences

M--Suggested for Mature Audiences-Adults and Mature Young People

R--Restricted-Persons under 16 not admitted, unless accompanied by parent or adult guardian.

X--Persons Under 16 Not Admitted.

By learning to recognize these ratings and their meanings, students can make wise decisions about the movies they want to attend.

Paper To Aid Teachers

It's good, and satisfying, to know that a newspaper may be used for something more than just reading.

Having received a request from Mr. William Hartman, professor of journalism at Colorado State College, the REDBIRD's advisor, Mrs. T.H. Robinson, sent copies of the LHS newspaper for study in a class the college is conducting for prospective journalism teachers.

Some stories from these issues may also be printed in a book on journalism called Activities for Journalism to be published by Laidlaw Brothers, the textbook division of Doubleday and Company.

Following is a portion of a thank-you letter received from Mr. Hartman:

"I am impressed with the quality of your newspaper. It shows that students today do much more than just report events. It appears to me that they are doing some real thinking..."

We are pleased to discover that not only can a newspaper keep people informed, but that it can also be used as an aid in teaching young people in the field of journalism.

Staff To Get Typewriter

Everyone likes to receive something new, and the REDBIRD staff is no different!

For the publications office will soon sport a shiny new typewriter, which replaces one purchased shortly before the Christmas of 1954.

Deeply grateful, the REDBIRD staff wishes to thank Principal John Boich, Supt. Richard Jordan, and the Board of Education for making this welcome addition possible.

New hairdo and The rains came.

THE REDBIRD

Published every third Friday from September to May by the REDBIRD staff of Loudonville (Ohio) High School.

Vol. XXIV, No. 10 April 11, 1969 Page 4

Member, NSPA, CSPA, NOSPA, JACS
Subscription: 50¢ a year; $1 by mail

Editor. . . . . Pam Conrad
Associate Editor. . . . . .Karen Frank
Advisor . . . . . .Mrs. T. H. Robinson

Easter Theme: 'Love Life'

You've got to love life to have life, and you've got to have life to love life."

This comment of the stage manager impressed junior English and senior speech students as they recently read "Our Town" by Thornton Wilder. The quotation implies how important the small and seemingly insignificant events in our daily lives really are.

Keeping this thought in mind, the students asked, "What is life, and do we really have it?"

They came to the conclusion that many of us don't live life to the fullest. Right now, when school matters appear to be foremost in life, we don't have time to notice what is going on around us, and we haven't really cared.

We haven't noticed the beauty in nature or appreciated the warmth of close family relationships.

Because we have had everything we've needed throughout our lives, we seem to have taken "food and coffee" and "hot baths" for granted.

But if we stopped worrying about our personal concerns and started thinking about others more often, we just might find what life is and really have it.

Isn't this what Easter is all about?

Easter

"I am the resurrection and the life; he who believes in me, though he die, yet shall he live, and whoever lives and believes in me shall never die."
--John 11:25

Nixon, Kennedy Lead Presidential Poll At LHS

In a presidential preference poll given recently to 188 LHS juniors and seniors, 50 per cent named a Democrat as their choice for President of the United States in 1968.

Preferring a different party, 47.8 per cent named a Republican for the position, while 2.2 per cent named a "third party" candidate.

*

REPUBLICAN RICHard Nixon was the leading candidate for President with 43 per cent of the students' votes, and Democrat Robert Kennedy was second with 31 per cent.

President Lyndon Johnson was the presidential choice of 9.8 per cent of LHS upperclassmen; Eugene McCarthy, 9.2 per cent; "third party" candidate George Wallace, 2.2 per cent; Nelson Rockefeller, 2.2 per cent; George Romney, 1.6 per cent; Charles Percy, .5 per cent; and Ronald Reagan, .5 per cent.

*

IN THE VICE-presidential race, 22.8 per cent of the juniors and seniors polled, named McCarthy; 16.7 per cent, Rockefeller; 14.4 per cent, Reagan; 13.9 per cent, Kennedy; 8.3 per cent, Percy; 7.2 per cent, Romney; 6.7 per cent,

Vice President Hubert Humphrey; and 5.6 per cent, J. William Fulbright.

Most frequently mentioned as a President-Vice President combination was a Kennedy-McCarthy duo with 20.2 per cent of the votes, and a Nixon-Rockefeller combination with 12.2 per cent.

Asked what the key issue in the 1968 presidential campaign would be, 93.6 per cent of the juniors and seniors ranked Vietnam first, while the remainder listed civil rights, inflation, crime in the streets, urban problems, or farm problems.

THE REDBIRD

Published every third Friday from September to May by the REDBIRD staff of Loudonville (Ohio) High School.

Vol. XXIII, No. 10 April 5, 1968 Page 4

Member, NSPA, CSPA
Subscription: 50¢ a year; $1 by mail

Editor. . . . . .Rob Koppert
Associate Editor. . . . . . .Pam Conrad
Advisor . . . . . . .Mrs. T. H. Robinson

Editorial pages #2, #3, and #4—These pages illustrate the various possibilities within the adopted format. Cutoff rules help preserve the horizontal look. Note the pleasing effect achieved by hairline rules with the "Sympathy" headline. The use of the two-column headline across the center of the page makes it possible to run a long story without seeming to monopolize the page. The "Easter" editorial and cartoon form a rectangular block emphasized by the cutoff rule.

THE REDBIRD

SPORTS

Nov. 8, 1963   Page 6

Locals' Early Surge Defeats Hillsdale

After losing a hard-fought game to Rittman, the LHS gridders came back to pull out a 20-16 decision over Hillsdale Oct. 25 on the home field.

In posting their second victory in eight starts, the Red Birds were never headed as they ran up all 20 points in the first half.

Senior halfback Ken Stumbaugh tallied twice on runs of 64 and 28 yards to lead the scoring. Jeff Arnholt scored on a four-yard quarterback sneak, and fullback Ron Harbour picked up a two-point conversion.

The previous week Loudonville was shut out by the Rittman Indians, 22-0. Two early miscues hurt the locals as both were turned into TD's by the Indians.

Red Birds Blast Spartans 28-0

Playing an inspired second half, the Red Birds downed the Millersburg Spartans 28-0 last Friday.

Although they led by only eight points at the half, the locals scored 20 more points after the intermission to insure their third win of the season.

Junior Ron Harbour was the leading scorer for the Birds as he crossed the goal line twice for 12 points.

Quarterback Jeff Arnholt tallied once and threw one TD pass to end Randy Hinkle. Senior Ken Stumbaugh added two extra points.

HOSTS TRIWAY

Grid Team Ends Season Tonight

Out to gain their third straight win, the fourth of the season, Loudonville's Red Birds will host Triway tonight at Redbird Stadium.

The Titans will seek to recover from a 66-0 drubbing by Smithville last week and to avenge last year's 12-8 loss to the Birds.

*

"TRIWAY is better than Millersburg," said head coach Mr. Herbert Hartman, "but the school is a new consolidation and has a morale problem."

Coach Hartman praised a fine team effort at Millersburg and commented, "Unless we have a letdown after last week's game, I think we should beat Triway.

"It should be a good game the first half and all ours the second half—if we play ball the way we are capable of playing."

*

SENIORS Mike Cowen, center; John Paullin, Brad Ross, and Steve Smith, guards; Conway Dudte and Ron Zickefoose, tackles; Jack Arnholt and Glenn Oswalt, ends; and Ken Stumbaugh, halfback; will play their last high school football game tonight.

Not only will the team be gunning for its third straight win, but the boys will also be after their third victory at Redbird Stadium this year.

The season for Hillsdale Was no fun.
They couldn't even win Number one.

Hillsdale's fledgling Falcons closed their season last week with an 0-9 record. It hardly paid them to rent the Redbird football field.

*

REDBIRD hoopsters ought to have pretty "high" chances this year with six candidates topping the six-foot mark.

THE Birds' Nest
BY Bob Weidner

Loudonville fans were glad to see Redbird victory number three. And while these fans could ask for more, I'd be content to settle for four.

Although the gridders will be out to win their fourth victory of the season tonight against the Triway Titans, three will be a more significant number for the Birds.

Sports page #1—Generally sports pages should have a bolder look and heavier headline type than other pages in the paper, and, if possible, action pictures. In mimeographed papers, however, this is often difficult to achieve. Here some variety is gained by the "Sports" heading and by the two drawings. The heading and upper drawing are in color. This arrangement of stories affords space for a long story, and yet the page looks interesting. Capitalized lead-ins and asterisks with spacing give the page variety and a light, bright look.

Sports page #2—This page shows the use of three two-column headlines placed to preserve the horizontal look, aided by the cutoff rules, and to break up areas of gray. The headlines are correctly planned with the most prominent head at the top of the page, the second largest used next, and the lightest head placed lowest on the page. This page lends itself to many variations—and also provides for three long stories.

Sports page #3—This page shows the pleasing effect of balance. With the cartoon at the top, no kicker is needed with the main headline. This makes it possible to use the kicker on the second head and thus gain the advantage of extra white space to brighten the middle of the page. Note that one story has asterisks and spacing, whereas others do not—a simple way to achieve contrast with the other stories and also to break up this long story.

BEATS FREDDIES

Baseball Team Gets 2nd Victory

Recording only its second baseball victory, Loudonville beat Fredericktown after a string of losses in recent weeks.

*

IN A MAKEUP game at Ontario Friday, the Birds collected only two hits off the Warriors' Wayne Motley. Junior Terry Lozier and sophomore Dave Koch pitched the 10-0 loss, while four juniors were attending the Prom.

Two days earlier LHS fell to the same Ontario team, 11-2. Junior Don Carr belted two hits, the second being the first Redbird home run of the season.

*

LOZIER pitched a four-hitter to down the Freddies, 2-1. Carr's two doubles figured in the scoring of both runs.

On a wet Plymouth field, LHS jumped to a 4-0 lead, but a late Big Red rally took the game, 7-5.

Crestview, aided by a three-run inning, defeated the Red Birds and Lozier, 4-2.

Previously, LHS lost games on consecutive days to Crestline and Lexington, 6-3 and 7-3.

A season to remember for years to come.

Golfers Finish 3rd In League

LHS's most successful spring sport, golf, was to have concluded its season on Monday at Briar Hill Golf Course in Millersburg against West Holmes, but the match was canceled.

Going into this match, the golf team had a record of 13 wins and four losses.

*

REDBIRD linksters started the season with five consecutive victories after an opening loss to the Ashland reserves. Victims of this streak were Triway, Clear Fork, West Holmes, Smithville, and Crestview.

Golfers tuned up for the Johnny Appleseed Conference Golf Tournament by defeating Clear Fork, 6-3. Match medalist was Clear Fork's Randy Ridenour with a 37.

Lexington won the JAC Golf Championship at Possum Run Golf Course in Mansfield. Loudonville finished third in the conference with a team total of 347.

*

LOUDONVILLE ran its record to 13-4 by defeating Lexington, 6-3. Local boys' scores were Tom Lavinder, 40; Rick Snyder, 41; Tim Masters, 42; and Doug Rogers, 44.

Going into the last match Lavinder led the team with an average of 42 and a record of 14-3-0. Master had a 43 average and a record of 12-5-0. The No. 3 man, Rogers, averaged 45.5 and made a record of 9-5-2. Snyder, the No. 4 man, had a 48.6 average and a record of 11-6-0.

THE REDBIRD
May 23, 1969   **7**

Losses Don't Dampen Baseball Humor

LHS baseball players, while winning rarely, have accumulated a supply of casual comments and jokes this spring.

March weather produced sore throwing arms and the worries of other minor injuries. After several other players had complained of ailments, sophomore Floyd McIntire was asked how his arm was.

Innocently the tall righthander queried, "Which one?"

Coming into a game as a relief pitcher, sophomore Jeff Haudenschild asked what the signals would be. "What signals?" he was reminded. "You've only got one pitch."

"Where should I throw it then?" Jeff shot back. "Try over the plate," he was told.

Playing on a muddy Plymouth field, catcher Paul Wigton gave his first baseman a concealed pickoff sign. The first baseman, sophomore Jeff Martin, missed most of the motion and stood wondering what had been signaled.

"What did he say?" Jeff mumbled.

"I think he wants you to pick me off," chipped in the helpful Big Red runner.

A little help   Wrong Way

Track Team Drops First Meets

After one week of the regular track season LHS is still without a win.

West Holmes beat the Red Birds 80-47 for LHS's second loss.

Winning first places for Loudonville were freshman Ken Krupp in the 440-yard dash; junior Don Conrad, 880-yard run; and sophomore Rick Wolford, pole vault.

Seniors Rex Messner and Curt Ramey each had seven points to lead LHS scorers.

Ashland High School soundly defeated LHS in the first meet of the season 82 2/3-44 1/3.

Loudonville won only three first places in the entire meet.

Messner won the 120-yard high hurdles, and Ramey took the 180-yard low hurdle event.

Ashland did not enter anyone in the pole vault, so the Birds had a three-way tie for first among Ramey, Wolford, and junior Monty Taylor.

Ramey was high-point man for LHS with 11.

This week the team will travel to Hillsdale Tuesday and Malabar Thursday for dual meets.

GAA Whipped 17-14

"They're tough!"

So admitted senior Maureen Allerding during halftime of the basketball game between the Loudonville girls and Mansfield St. Peter's GAA.

Mansfield made a comeback in the third quarter after being down 4-1 at the half and won the duel by a score of 17-14.

6 THE REDBIRDS April 11, 1969

Golfers Lose Opener To Ashland Reserves

Golf hit the Loudonville sports scene again Tuesday at Ashland as the LHS linksters lost to the Ashland Reserves 5½-3½.

Tom Lavinder, LHS junior, was the match's medalist as he shot a 43 on the back nine of the Ashland Country Club.

Other scores for LHS were senior Tim Master, 47; senior Rick Snyder, 52; and junior Gary McClenathan, 58.

Low scorer for the Ashland team was Jerry Miller who shot a 45.

Next week the golf team gets back to work when it plays West Holmes, Monday; Smithville, Tuesday; and Crestline, Wednesday. All matches are at the Round Lake Golf Course.

REDBIRD'S EYE VIEW

Lexington Picked For JAC Crown

By Jim Wigton

Lexington has been picked in a REDBIRD poll of all JAC baseball coaches to repeat as conference champions this year.

The coaches placed the league in order, excluding Loudonville since there was no Redbird team last year on which to base an opinion.

*

THOUGH Crestline received the most first-place votes, Lexington got the most points due to four second-place votes.

Here is the predicted standings with the points received, and the first-place votes in parentheses:

Lexington (2) 42, Crestline (3) 40, Ontario (1) 37, Clear Fork 22, Plymouth (1) 21, Crestview 12, Fredericktown 11, and Loudonville 0.

*

DEFENDING champion Lexington, which had an 18-0 overall record last year, should again be very tough. The Minutemen have 11 returning lettermen who will see action.

Ontario has only two lettermen back; they are the All-JAC basketball guards, Rick Nichols and Don Heston.

Look for Plymouth and Loudonville to surprise the JAC; both should finish in the first division.

School named for county educator

Mr. L. A. Chaffin, for whom this school was named, taught in the Massard-Barling area for 49 years.

He began his teaching career in 1906 at a school near Fort Chaffee called Pleasant Grove.

In 1929 he taught all eight grades in a one-room frame school building near Massard.

After finally getting a bigger school and another teacher there, his next concern was to transfer students to Fort Smith High School (now Northside) so they could finish their secondary education.

He made arrangements for the school board to provide transportation and pay the tuition for these students. Later, in 1942, he accomplished the same thing for the Barling school and worked out a system for the colored children in the area to attend both grammar and high school in Fort Smith.

Next he instigated a lunch program for the underprivileged children of Barling and Massard. He himself bought kitchen equipment, hired cooks, planned menus and purchased the food.

Mr. Chaffin's interest went beyond the classroom. He encouraged his students to keep their bodies fit by taking part in sports and their minds alert by "finding themselves and their place in life."

Mr. Bill Alverson appointed first CJH principal

Mr. Bill Alverson, former assistant principal and dean of boys at Darby, took over the position of principal of Chaffin Junior High July 1.

A native of Barling, Mr. Alverson graduated from Greenwood High. He received his bachelor of science degree from the College of the Ozarks and his masters degree from the University of Arkansas. He also has 30 hours toward an advanced degree.

Before coming to Fort Smith in 1958, Mr. Alverson was principal of a wing school at Lincoln, Ark., and principal at the high school there.

When Mr. Alverson moved to Fort Smith, he taught math at Darby three years before becoming assistant principal and dean of boys. He held this position for eight years.

Mr. Alverson and his wife, a teacher at Southside High School, have two daughters, Vickie, a freshman at Westark Junior College, and Mary, a junior at Southside.

OPEN HOUSE
for the public
Sunday.... Oct. 19
2 P. M.
PTA OPEN HOUSE
Oct. 20 .... 6:30 P.M.

Vol. 1   Chaffin Junior High, Fort Smith, Arkansas, October 10, 1969   No. 1

To 430 students
Chaffin opens doors for first year

Arrived *according to plan*

Chaffin Junior High School
August 1969

TECHNICAL DATA

Principal.. Mr. Bill Alverson
Team.. The Cougars
Colors.. Kelly Green and Old Gold

ENGINEERED BY

The citizens of Fort Smith and
The Fort Smith Public School System

When Chaffin Junior High opened its doors to the student body Aug. 27, approximately 430 students walked into the building they would call "our school" at least for the year.

The $1,500,000 structure, which took 18 months to build, is situated on a 30.36 acre tract of land facing Massard Road.

It was designed by Mr. Jim Cheyne, architect of Nelson and Associates, and constructed by the Crawford Construction Company.

Chaffin has 86,000 square feet of floor space with 35 classrooms.

The first floor consists of rooms for band, typing, art, special education, drafting, woodworking and a science department consisting of three rooms.

Also on the first floor are the home economics department, library, study hall and a gymnasium measuring 92' by 114'.

On the second floor are social studies, mathematics, general education, English, and language classrooms, each department having an office and a research area.

Mark Saviers chosen president; Lisa Lee wins veep in run-off

Mark Saviers chosen the office of president of the student body without opposition.

Lisa Lee was elected vice president in a run-off against Dean Hutson. The other candidate was Jenny Smoot.

Evan Evans won over his opponent, Robin Price.

Following a campaign assembly Sept. 17, the student body voted in social studies classes.

The following week, seven representatives were elected from each grade. Ninth graders are Cathee Crain, Randy Wagner, Beth Burns, Lucia Hawkins, Jamie Collier, John Mayo and Onnie Hewitt.

From the eighth grade are Bob Gladwin, Cathy Welshans, Sandra Curtis, Cheri Klingner, Paul Rogers, Tony Sherman, and Barbara Smelley.

Seventh graders are Ann Saviers, Cindy Pettit, Elise Bedwell, Kevin Boyd, Robb McDaniel, Dan Bradford and Cindy Sagely.

Front page #1—This is the front page of volume one, number one of a new school paper and shows how the contemporary trends in newspaper makeup are evidenced in the format. The four-column box at the top of the page adds variety to the page by making use of the one-up technique, meaning here three columns of type in a four-column space. In general, the one-up technique means setting columns slightly wider than usual so you have one less column than regular space. Note the rather large amount of space around the floating nameplate and also the light look gained by the space in the center box and the notice at the lower left. The downstyle headlines have a light look.

SC schedules Christmas dance

Holiday spirit will be the prevailing theme when the second annual Christmas dance gets underway Dec. 11 in the school cafeteria.

"Although no band has yet been hired," explained Cindy Sparks, band auditioner, "it is probable that one headed by Neal Pendergraft will play for us."

Part of this same band played at last year's Christmas dance.

Dress will be the same as last year for boys with coat and tie, while girls will wear semi-formal dresses or formal pants suits.

Dates from other junior highs in the city may be invited by Chaffin students, but no high school students will be admitted stated Mr. Benny Deaver, SC sponsor.

Admission will be 75¢ stag and $1.25 drag in advance. Both will be 25¢ higher at the door.

Concerts slated by choral, band for Christmas

Two Christmas concerts, choral and instrumental, are scheduled for early Dec. before students are dismissed for the holidays.

The choral department of Chaffin, supervised and conducted by Miss Therese Miros, will perform a Christmas concert for the Chaffin student body on Dec. 4.

Containing parts of narrators, soloists, and a variety of popular Christmas songs, "The Song of Christmas" will be performed.

The band, under the direction of Miss Leighnora Buchannan, will present a morning concert for the student body Dec. 17, and again that night for parents and the public.

Some of the Christmas numbers are "Have Yourself a Merry Little Christmas" arranged by Gordon and "Winter Fantasy" a Frederick Miller melody of Christmas Song and Silver Bells.

Other concert music will be a march "Henderson Field" by K.L. King, "Hansel and Gretel Overture" by E. Humperdinck, "Air For Band" by Frank Erickson, and "Two Pieces in Folksong Styles" by Hugh M. Stuart.

Vol. 2   Chaffin Junior High, Fort Smith, Arkansas, November 20, 1970   No. 5

News Briefs

CBS Tests taken

The seventh and ninth grade students took the Comprehensive Test of Basic Skills and the Short Form Test of Academic Aptitude Oct. 20-22. This test is given yearly to the seventh and ninth graders.

Citizens chosen

The new citizens of the month are Tom Whitsitt, ninth grade; Dan Bradford, eighth; and John Watts and Chuck Putnam, tied for seventh. Nominations are made by the Student Council and voted on by teachers.

Band marches

Under the direction of Jim Woods, ninth grade drum major, the Cougar Band marched for their first game Nov. 5 when the Cougars played Van Buren.

After several formations, the band played two feature numbers, "Georgy Girl" and "Song from M.A.S.H."

Bean Supper slated

Prior to the Ramsey-Chaffin basketball game, the annual PTA bean supper has been set for Dec. 3 in the school cafeteria. "Prizes will be awarded again this year for students selling the most tickets," stated Mrs. Bob Lane president. Tickets went on sale Nov. 16.

For Salvation Army
SC, staff collect canned goods, toys

Joining together to sponsor drives for the Salvation Army this year, the SC will ask for canned goods and the Cougar Print staff will collect toys.

The SC's second annual canned food drive will begin Dec. 7 and continue through Dec. 18.

The toy drive to help supply children in the local area with toys for Christmas will begin Nov. 30 and continue until Dec. 18.

Last year's SC drive at Chaffin netted 3322 cans, making Chaffin the winner of the citywide contest among junior high schools.

Mr. Larry Schiffner's homeroom won the contest within Chaffin with 758 cans.

"The homerooms worked very hard to make the drive a success," stated Mr. Benny Deaver, SC sponsor, "and we hope the participation is as good this year."

Cans will be turned in to homerooms to be counted and then placed under the Christmas tree in the office.

Boxes for toys will be placed in each homeroom, and journalism students will pick up the toys once each week.

"Since the drive ends only a week before Christmas," explained Patricia Dickinson, editor of the The Cougar Print, "the toys should be in good condition and should not require repairs."

"We hope participation in the toy drive will be as good as last year's canned food drive."

Red Cross representatives collect toothpaste, brushes

Collecting toothbrushes and toothpaste will be the first project of the newly organized Red Cross organization at Chaffin.

The drive will begin before Christmas, stated Miss Gail Lehnen, sponsor, "but the date is not definite yet."

Representatives chosen from each homeroom will collect the toothbrushes and toothpaste and give them to the school nurses, who will distribute them to people in the area.

They are Lynn Wintory, Vicki Lane, Janet Raff, Dottie Weller, Lisa Lunney, Tommy Martin, Jeanette Burks, Dan Bradford, Randy Moore, James Capolina, Michelle Mings, Jon Snider, Cindy Jesson, Mandee Harper, Barbara French, Jackie Koulock, Kathy Treadway, Alan Atchley, Robin Presson, Glen Brady, John Williams, and Marjorie McKee.

Vacation
AEA-CTA MEETING Nov. 23-25
THANKSGIVING Nov. 26-27
No more school until Nov. 30

Front page #2—This page is designed to allow space for four long stories, all of which are prominently displayed. Headlines are arranged to break up areas of gray type, and corners are anchored. Small heads in the News Briefs column attract notice. The three-column box above the floating nameplate makes use of the one-up technique, this time with two columns of copy in three columns of space. More space than usual divides the columns here to attract attention to the copy and offer contrast. Slugs of space are used to divide sections of the story in the righthand column to afford easy reading. When kickers are used with headlines, as in the SC story, the main head is indented one pica per column width of story. Here the kicker is underscored with a hairline rule. Many papers are now omitting the rule. The two boxes afford contrast.

Eighth, ninth representatives elected to SC

The Student Council activities began with the election of eighth and ninth grade representatives.

To give seventh graders more time to become acquainted, the election of their representatives will be held later this month.

Ninth graders elected are Sarah Minchew, Robb McDaniel, Mark Randall, Cindy Sagely, Dan Bradford, Kelly Taylor and Ann Saviers.

Representing the eighth grade are James Bradford, Jay Lane, Phillip Kropp, Vickie Gattis, Lori Lee, Chuck Putnam and Bob Price.

SC officers elected in the spring are Marc Allen, president; Doug Hall, vice president; and Cindy Pettit, secretary.

Mr. Benny Deaver is sponsor. At the first meeting members received a copy of the Constitution so they could become familiar with the way the school government is conducted.

THE COUGAR PRINT

Vol. 3   Chaffin Junior High, Fort Smith, Arkansas, September 24, 1971   No. 1

Over last year's 483
Enrollment increases 82

With 565 students enrolled, Chaffin gained 82 over last year's enrollment of 483. The first year there was 453.

New textbooks adopted this year include seventh and eighth grade English and literature books, and ninth grade algebra books.

A new scheduling system has been undertaken for eighth grade students concerning the reading classes. Each student will have only one semester of reading alternating with one semester of study hall because of the shortage of reading teachers.

One new teacher was added to the staff along with three replacements. Mr. R. D. Ranson, new drafting and history teacher, is from Tulsa, Okla.

Replacements include Mrs. Nicol Wintory, orchestra; Mrs. David Beneux, girls physical education; and Mr. Jerry Bridges, basketball coach.

The band opened with 21 more members, a total of 65. The choral department has 91 students, gaining nine more than last year.

There are 58 boys dressed out for football compared with 43 last year. Chaffin gained one more cheerleader, making its total nine.

The pep squad contains 144 members compared with approximately 60 at the end of last year.

Superintendent's position taken by Dr. Garrison

Dr. C.B. Garrison is serving his first year as the new superintendent of schools, replacing Mr. Chris O. Corbin.

Dr. Garrison obtained his education at Henderson State College, the University of Arkansas, George Peabody College and the University of Illinois.

He holds a bachelors, masters and doctors degrees.

Before coming to Fort Smith, Dr. Garrison served as a teacher, principal and superintendent in the Pine Bluff school system.

He has two children, a son who attends college and a daughter at Southside High.

Magazine, paper staff named for current year

The staffs for the Cougar Print and the Chaffin' Collage were named earlier this month by Mrs. Lorine Lay, adviser of both publications.

Co-editors for the paper in its third year of publication are Lynn Wintory and Robb McDaniel.

Cathy Linder, Sarah Minchew and Cindy Sagely make up the editorial board for the bi-yearly literary magazine.

Michele Nicodemus will be business manager for both the paper and magazine with Reyn Ellis assisting.

Page editors for the paper are Barbara French, Robin Hatfield, Leslie Staton, Mandee Harper, Catherine McCann and Caron Smets. Cathy Linder is columnist.

Marc Allen and Gail Hammersly are in charge of sports. Art includes Karen Hutcheson, Cindy Sagely and Sarah Minchew.

Janet Brown is in charge of exchange and the scrapbook.

The ninth grade journalism class makes up the magazine and the paper staffs. Fifteen of the 17 are second-year journalists.

SMALL TALK

If you see someone without a smile, give him one of yours.

THE COUGAR PRINT

Vol. 2   Chaffin Junior High, Fort Smith, Arkansas, April 29, 1971   No. 14

Sixty girls heed drill team commands to prepare themselves for try-outs

"Mark time, march! Left... right...left..."

Practicing for the Chaffin Drill Team try-outs, not yet scheduled, 60 girls have heard this command over and over the past week.

Twenty girls will be elected from a total of 60 trying out, with 5 to 8 seventh graders and 12 to 15 eighth graders. From these 20 girls, a captain and a co-captain will be chosen.

At three practice sessions before the try outs the cheerleaders taught the candidates pom-pom and dance routines, the correct way to march, which includes stopping and turning around, and how to call drill team signals.

The purpose of a drill team is to arouse more spirit at half-time during football and basketball games. Drill team also gives all girls a chance to participate in more than the pep squad.

The team will also participate in all pep rallies working with the cheerleaders. During track season, the squad will function as a part of the pep squad.

"In addition to coordination and achievement," stated Mrs. Jane Wilson, sponsor, "girls in the drill team must also have and maintain at least a 2.0 grade average."

Nine girls chosen as cheerleaders for next year

Cindy Sagely and Ann Saviers, eighth graders, were re-elected as cheerleaders for next year along with seven new ones.

The seven new cheerleaders are Mandee Harper, Ginger Reed, Janet Taff, Diane Gray and Sarah Minchew, eighth graders; and Tonya Long and Kathy Treadway, seventh graders.

Cindy Sparks, head cheerleader, and eight faculty judges chose the nine girls from approximately 35 trying out.

A head cheerleader and co-head cheerleader will be elected by the girls themselves in an up-coming meeting.

By band, glee club
Concerts planned

Both the Chaffin Band and Glee Club are scheduling concerts for next week. Miss Leighnora Buchanan will direct the band while Miss Therese Miros conducts the Glee Club.

With all three groups performing, the Chaffin Bands will present a concert May 4, at 7:30pm. for the public and again the following day for the student body.

First, the beginning band will play two numbers, "Castles in Spain" and "Holiday" both by Frank Erickson.

Next the training band will play "Activity March," "Close to You," and "Little Irish Suite."

Presenting their part of the program last, the first band will play "Little Champ," "Highlights from 'West Side Story'," "Three Songs of Colonial America," "Festivo," and "Shenandoah."

Based on the featured song, "What the World Needs Now," the glee club concert will begin at 7:30 P.M. May 7 in the school cafeteria. The concert will be directed by Miss Therese Miros.

All girls glee club classes and the boys glee club will combine on the songs "Camelot," "Whatcha' Gonna' Do My Son?" "What Color is God's Skin?" "While We're Young,"

"Hymn of Brotherhood," and "America the Beautiful."

The boys group will sing "Lodi," "Lookin' Out My Back Door," accompanied by Farley Pouland and Pat Echols on the guitar with Paul Catsavis on the drums. Farley Pouland will be as soloist in "House of the Risin' Sun."

Auction, dance planned by SC

Plans for a second dance this year and a Slave Day are being finalized by the Student Council for the month of May.

The dance, tentively set for May 14, will be the final one of the school year. It has not yet been decided which band will play, but an eight-piece group from Northside is under consideration.

Also undecided is the theme for the dance. Dress will be the same as for previous dances. Boys do not have to wear a jacket but must wear a tie. No jeans will be allowed. Girls may wear dresses or pant suits.

A Slave Day, set for the last of May, will have SC members auctioned "off the block" to the highest bidder. The slaves will then do chores for their "master" the rest of the day.

The voting for "Who's Who" took place last Friday. However, the results were not available due to the time it takes to tally the votes. For this reason, this year's ballot is somewhat shorter.

Staffers, journalism students to attend AHSPA convention

Four Cougar Print staff members, along with eight first year journalism students, will attend the Arkansas High School Press Association convention in Hot Springs tomorrow and Saturday.

The journalists will attend group sessions and panel discussions concerning newspaper work tomorrow afternoon and Saturday morning.

The keynote speaker, Mr. William Bowen, Little Rock attorney and civic leader, will give the principal address Friday evening.

Other guest speakers include professional men in the communications field of magazines, newspaper, advertising, and radio.

One of the highlights of the convention will be the presentation of awards for outstanding work in journalism.

Entries have been submitted in 14 catagories.

Mrs. Lorine Lay, adviser of The Cougar Print, will lead two group sessions on editing and publishing the mimeographed paper.

Those attending from the staff are Patricia Dickinson, Sandra Curtis, Bobby Sawyer, and Sharla Gate.

From the eighth grade are Lynn Wintory, Cathy Linder, Robin Hatfield, Leslie Staton, Robb McDaniel, Sarah Minchew, Reyn Ellis and Catherine McCann.

1971-72 Schedule

Aug. 27	School begins
Nov. 22-26	AEA State Convention/Thanksgiving
Dec. 17-Jan. 3	Christmas
April 3-7	Easter
June 2	School closes

Front page #5—With the four-column nameplate this page has the definite horizontal look that makes rather long stories seem shorter and thus more readable. Although there are only three long stories, the News Briefs column affords display space for a number of news items that gain reader attention with the heads. This is an illustration of brace makeup within the geometric block. Note that the News Briefs column is a separate rectangle on the page, which, with the four-column flag, divides the page into rectangles. The News Briefs heading is balanced by the "Small Talk" block.

Front page #6—For variety a two-column nameplate can be used, here affording space for a long news feature story of special importance. The subheads are centered between rules to break up the areas of gray, and the boxed head on "Waffle" is aligned to create a horizontal effect. The shallow story with the three-column headline gives importance to the bottom of the page. Here again the subhead is aligned. The long story is continued to an inside page to control the appearance of page one.

THE COUGAR PRINT

Vol. 3   Chaffin Junior High School, Fort Smith, Arkansas, October 8, 1971   No. 2

NewsBriefs

In economics classes
Social security cards issued

To issue social security cards and to explain their purpose, Mr. Bruce Burkhead, from the Social Security Division, visited Mr. Bill Washum's economics classes recently.

"This," he explained, "is the most important single number you will ever have."

He added that it is used in many ways. For example, they are used for income tax reports, military purposes and savings accounts.

"All social security cards are kept in Baltimore, Maryland, in a room about the size of a football field."

"If a person loses his card, he can be traced through the files by means of information printed on the cards," he explained.

He emphasized that students should take precautions against having two cards, for if this happens, he would have his money and credits listed under two different accounts.

"Then," he said, "you would have to prove you are two different people, and that's not easy."

He also explained various payments, stressing disability.

"If a person should become totally disabled before age 18," he said, "he can draw social security payments for the rest of his life."

He explained that if this occurs, the person is considered a disabled adult child, which means he is totally unable to do any kind of substantial work.

Jesson interviewed

Cindy Jesson, eighth grader, represented the Girl Scouts of Troop 98 in an interview Sept. 28 on Channel 5's noon show, Accent.

Miss Nan Langdin talked with Cindy and representatives of the Boy Scouts and the Boys Club about their organizations.

This year is Cindy's seventh in scouting.

Ribbons, tags sold

Along with beat tags, the cheerleaders are selling spirit ribbons and Cougar football stickers. This is one of their money-raising projects.

Benches provided

Last year's Student Council has provided Chaffin with four benches. The purpose is to provide a place for students to sit during lunch and before and after school.

Coupons donated

Mr. Bill Washum's eighth grade history classes are saving Betty Crocker coupons to donate to Sparks Hospital. They will be used to purchase a kidney machine.

Meetings changed

Pep Squad meetings are scheduled to be held twice monthly instead of every Tuesday so all members can attend both meetings.

Chaffin's Student group discussion

Representatives from Chaffin's Student Council will be leader in a group discussion at the District SC meeting tomorrow at Kimmons Junior High.

Marc Allen, president, will head the discussion on "Objectives of the Student Council."

Seventh grade involvement with student affairs began with the election of their SC representatives. They are Van Martindale, Jan Snider, Tracy Roberts, Steven Sparks, Jim Young and Ella Cooper.

Committees and chairmen were appointed by Marc at the second meeting.

They include Mark Randall, Executive committee; Dan Bradford, Vickie Gattis and Jan Snider, Student Affairs; Ann Saviers, Hospitality; Jay Lane and Steven Sparks, Building and Grounds; Cindy Sagely and Chuck Putnam, Publicity; Robb McDaniel, Bob Price and Tracy Roberts, Elections.

Others are Lori Lee and Ella Cooper, Lost and Found; Kelly Taylor, Van Martindale, Courtesy and Welfare; James Bradford and Jim Young, Student Control; Sarah Minchew,

Council leads at meeting

Lisa Crain, Scrapbook; and Phillip Kropp, Finance.

Money-making activities began with the selling of names for the Cougar calendar, which should be on sale during the first of November, Marc said.

PTA season gets underway with annual Open House

Hosting the annual Open House Oct. 11 at 6:40 P. M., the PTA will begin its regular season of meetings.

Parents will again this year follow their child's schedule and have an opportunity to meet their child's teachers and learn what is expected in each class.

After the last period, mod 16, refreshments will be served in the cafeteria. At that time parents may talk with teachers about his child's work so far this year.

Presiding officers this year are Dr. and Mrs. James Snider, president; Judge and Mrs. Warren Kimbrough, vice president; Mr. and Mrs. Noble Kelton, secretary; Mr. and Mrs. Charles Smets, treasurer; and Mrs. Jimmy Bullington, historian.

They took their pledge of office at the last PTA meeting.

"We usually have a good turnout at the Open House," said Mr. Bill Alverson, principal, "and I feel they both enjoy and profit from meeting their child's teachers and learning exactly what is expected of the child in each class."

SMALL TALK

The gift of silence is the most learned gift.

As seen from blimp
Fort Smith looks like model city

By Marc Allen

THE COUGAR PRINT

Vol. 3   October 22, 1971   No. 3
Chaffin Junior High School   Fort Smith, Arkansas

"Move faster. Come this way. Back up please. Hurry. Now, go!"

I made it. I was in the Goodyear blimp, America N-10a. As the other five passengers got on, I found my seat up by the driver and gazed at the hundreds of instruments before me.

A staff of 22 men held the blimp down by means of ropes but the blimp was never actually still. It floated slightly above the ground the whole time we were trying to get in.

All at once the men let go of the ropes, motors were turned on and up we went. It rose at a 45 degree angle to about 1800 feet before leveling off.

We were over Southside before I knew it, and my first thought as I looked down upon the city was that it looked like an artificial model city on a very small scale.

although I'm not sure they could see me.

The most impressive thing I saw from the air was the Central Mall area, which can be seen the minute you leave the ground in the blimp and from any point over the city.

We swung out toward Chaffin and I saw tiny objects moving around on the football field playing a seventh grade game.

Then we headed back to the airport and circled for a landing. Once he cut the motors off I knew we'd had it, but we just floated there in Turn to page 3

Tiny cars creep

Tiny cars crept along the streets, and swimming pools all over town glittered in the sunlight.

Slowly we moved on toward the north part of town. We passed over Ramsey Junior High and in no time at all we went over Mayo-Thompson field where the Chaffin-St. Annes game was previously played.

The pilot told me that the "America" was the largest of the three blimps in the world and that they had never had a fatality with any of the Goodyear blimps. This eased my mind a little.

Friends wave

We went on around town and I saw scores of people I knew out waving at me. I waved back

Student Council installation to take place this morning

The installation of Student Council officers, committee chairmen and representatives is scheduled to take place this morning in the gym.

Jim Woods, last year's SC president, will formally install President Marc Allen, Vice President Doug Hall and

ACTE publishes students' work

Two students' articles appeared in the annual issue of "Let's Communicate," the Arkansas Council of Teachers of English publication.

They are Cathy Linder and Bill Wilson. Cathy had a short story and Bill an article.

The booklet is composed of works by Arkansas students of all grades. Only teachers who are members of the council may sent entries to be judged.

"We were very pleased with the response and the quality of writings this year in the writing competition," stated Mr. L. C. Leach of the state language-arts department.

Cathy's story was written in the eighth grade and Bill's article in the seventh. Cathy was sponsored by Mrs. Lorine Lay and Bill by Mrs. Miriam Hatfield.

Secretary Cindy Pettit and explain the responsibilities of each office.

Marc will then conduct the rest of the ceremony, by installing the committee chairmen and other representatives.

He will give a chrysanthemum, which represents the light of the Student Council torch, to each committee chairman before the chairmen explain their duties.

Then the seventh, eighth and ninth grade representatives will be given the pledge as a group.

The newly-appointed Fire Marshals and parliamentarian will also take part in the installation.

The Fire Marshals are Clifton Lad, seventh grade; Kyle McDaniel, eighth; and Steven Turner, ninth. Reyn Ellis is the parliamentarian.

Before the installation of the officers, the symbols of the emblem of the National Association of Student Councils will be explained by Jim Young, gavel; Lisa Crain, scroll; Jan Snider, the torch; and Tracy Roberts, quill, seventh graders.

The opening prayer will be given by James Bradford.

Waffle in pocket assures acceptance

Did you know that one of Chaffin's students wears a waffle? A waffle, the kind you just pop into the toaster?

This student explains as he readily offers you a bite, that in order to be in good standing with Doctor Mazzepa you must "smell" like a waffle for a week, then send in the waffle as proof.

When asked who Doctor Mazzepa is, he said, "Oh, he's this cool guy on TV."

What will they think of next?

Speech students to give devotionals

Linda Mahl will be the next speaker to give the devotional for the speech department.

Other speakers for the next few days are Danny Mickelson, Ann Shull, Angel Catsavis, Rosemary Safranek and Marc Allen.

"The main purpose for giving the devotionals," said Mrs. Sandra Newhart, speech teacher, "is to accustom the students to speaking over a public address system."

The source of their topics is from books of various denominations.

Students who have already given devotionals this fall are Tanna Lee, Leslie Staton, Dyke Pair, Carl Beyer, Taricia Gann, Debbie Curry, Kim Kelton, Claudine Giboney, Julie Douglas, Ricky Kline, Sara Kocher, Neal Cowne, Brenda Claghorn, Dale Ragsdale, Stanley Floyd and Barbara Kremer.

SMALL TALK

Beware of stretching the truth. It may snap back and hit you.

often is advantageous, as sometimes one location will work out better than another, depending on the various stories to be used.

The nameplate should set the mood for the paper. It should be economical in size and simple in design, attractive, and in harmony with the rest of the display. It could have a picture of the school, the school emblem or motto, or simply the name of the paper. Basically a nameplate should contain certain information. In addition to the name of the publication, it should name the school, city, state, date, issue, and volume number. A paper without this information on the front page is like a house without a house number.

When the nameplate is used in the standard position in the center top of the page, there is room at the sides for ears. These can be used for promotion of some event, some seasonal motif, or for displaying press association emblems. The nameplate must always be placed in the upper one-third of the page, never below the fold.

Every story or article on the front page should have a headline. Stories should be written so that it is not necessary to carry over a story to another page. The front page is not the place for fillers. The most important stories should occupy the upper left or upper right position and should have the largest heads. The lead story, however, should seldom be an account of something that has already happened. Instead, an advance story on something important about to happen should be featured if possible.

Announcements and short items to which you want to call attention, but which do not have enough news in them to merit a top head, will stand out if they are boxed.

The part of the page below the fold should be as interesting as that above the fold. This can be accomplished by using boxes, two-column heads, etc. Heads below the fold are set in smaller type than those above. Multi-column heads create a horizontal look and open up the page.

Editorial Page

The editorial page should be unique in its appearance and should stand out from the other pages. It should look like an editorial page. One has no trouble turning to the editorial page in the daily newspaper because it has several identifying features. Usually the editorials are two columns wide; the page usually has a cartoon; and it carries the masthead.

We try to set all headlines for editorial and feature copy in italic type. We usually set editorial copy in pica type and two columns wide to make it stand out. In typing the masthead, be as conservative as possible. It is more important to feature what the staff writes than who writes it. Occasionally, however, you should include the entire staff, and most important of all, the adviser, for this gives the paper authority.

The masthead should include pertinent information about the paper, including advertising and subscription rates.

Every issue of the paper should have at least one editorial, but avoid writing on such overworked subjects as school spirit, etc. Every editorial should have a headline, not just a label. Editorials and editorial features should be placed in the strongest position on the page, toward the top. The masthead should occupy a subordinate position at the bottom of the page.

Note in the March 6 issue we have typed the masthead in one-column width and placed it in two columns of equal length. This saves valuable space. Some schools use a two-column width for each line of copy, which wastes space between the names of the members and their positions.

Sports Page

The sports page, like the editorial page, should not need a sign on it to identify it as a sports page. A well-planned sports page is easily recognized through such items as short boxed features, tabulated conference standings, game statistics, and possibly a sports column.

The sports editor of the high school newspaper can get many ideas from the sports section of the local paper. The most important story on the sports page is usually the advance story, which is often placed in the upper left or right. The coverage story, which is usually of less importance, should occupy a less prominent position if less important.

Horizontal makeup is popular on the sports page and can be achieved by running a one- or two-line head over two or three columns. A kicker can be used above the head of a sports column.

As on all pages, keep the lower half of the page interesting with the use of two-column heads, boxes, cartoons, etc. Sometimes action pictures are good to use. These need not be real photos, but do use some line drawings, etc. The purpose is always to make these pages lively and interesting.

Inside Pages

Inside pages—known as inside news-feature pages—should follow the same principles of makeup advocated for good front-page display. These pages should make free use of two-column, two-line heads. Break up long columns of copy by the use of paragraph subheads. Each inside page should have at least four headlined stories. Avoid jumping (that is, continuing) stories from one page to another. If space does not permit the use of subheads in long stories, the monotony of long gray columns can be relieved by typing the first two or three words of each paragraph in all caps.

Sparkle and personality on inside pages is achieved through a balance of straight news, features, and columns. Each kind of story should have its own identity. Straight news stories are usually typed in one-column width. Features can be typed double-column width. Standing columns can be typed either one or two columns, depending on the nature of the format.

Two devices that are often neglected are the "30" dash and the cutoff rule. The dash is used to indicate the end of a story when another story is placed below it in a column. Leave one line of space between the dash and the last line of copy above it, and leave one line of space between the dash and the first line of the copy to follow.

Cutoff rules are lines one or more columns in width used to separate the text of one story from an adjacent story.

If advertisements are used, they should be clear, neat, and legible, have adequate white space, be varied from week to week, contain a selling message—not say "Compliments of . . ."

The most pleasing arrangement of ads is in a single pyramid or stairstep form. In this arrangement, ads are usually and preferably pyramided to the right. (Care should be taken to see that no ad is buried. Always try to see that some copy touches the ad.)

Green, gold take place in football competition

The green and gold of the Chaffin Cougars, the newest colors on the Fort Smith football field this season, had their first test in the local junior high jamboree, participating with Ramsey, Kimmons, and Darby.

This scrimmage game was a new way of competition for Fort Smith ball clubs to help the coaches decide the starting line-up.

The Cougars played against the Ramsey Rams the second quarter and Darby the fourth. The offense didn't score, but the defense held their opponents to low scores.

Chaffin's leading ground gainer was Onnie Hewitt. Evan Evans was good on defense.

Cats drop first

In their first real game Kimmons won 12-0. The Raiders scored on a 53-yard run in the first quarter. The Cubs held them to no more scoring in the first half. In the sec-

ond half the Raiders made a 48-yard run to score again. The extra point attempt was short.

Hewitt made a 28-yard run before the ball went to Kimmons. On their second play John Mayo recovered a fumble. Hewitt was leading ground gainer.

Rams win 13-0

The Cougars lost their first conference game 13-0 to the Ramsey Rams. They held Ramsey in the first quarter, but early in the second the Rams made a drive to score and the extra point was good.

After the Rams' second TD Mayo blocked the try for extra point.

Again Hewitt was the leading ground gainer for the Cougars. Chaffin had 75 yards rushing and completed 2 of 9 passes for 26 yards.

Cougars fight

When two Cougar teams went up against each other, the cats from Southwest passed for three touchdowns to beat the Chaffin Cougars 19-0.

Hewitt again led the offense. The defense was led by Terry Stubblefield, tackler of the week with 10 tackles, three unassisted.

With seven others
Kathy Crow leads cheers

Kathy Crow, head cheerleader, and her seven co-workers, began practicing for their job of leadership last June.

From June 19 until Aug. 1, they practiced twice a week. From Aug. 1 until school began, it became a daily workout.

The seven cheerleaders are Susan McCollough, Lucia Hawkins, Terri Putman, Kay Rappeport and Cathee Crain, ninth grade; Lisa Lunney and Cindy Sparks, eighth.

The girls use a total of 18 cheers, some of which were

Green and gold are everywhere— especially on game day when football players, cheerleaders, pep squad girls and the student body wear the colors to boost Cougar spirit.

Saviers heads Huddle Group; Three guest speakers invited

Mark Saviers is captain of the newly-formed Chaffin Cougar Huddle Group, an organization of the national fellowship of Christian Athletes.

Other officers include Dick Gotcher, captain-elect; John Mayo, secretary; Dean Hutson, treasurer; and Onnie Hewitt, reporter.

The 40-member group begins and ends every meeting with a prayer. At some of the meetings they have guest speakers who will discuss the spiritual relationship between life and football.

Guest speakers at the first three meetings have been Mr.

Floyd Sagely, a professional football player; Mr. Gordon Guest, an ex-Razorback and one of the designers of Chaffin; and Coach Dub McGibboney, coach of the Southside Rebels.

"The team that prays together stays together," Coach McGibboney told the boys.

Chaffin Cubs lose first two

The Cougar Cubs lost the first two games of the season to Kimmons 22-0 and to Ramsey 22-6.

Against Kimmons Larry Lum ran the ball eight times for 23 yards, but the Cub offense couldn't gain enough yards to score.

Chaffin had one first down, one penalty and two fumbles. The Cubs held Kimmons to three first downs. In spite of two penalties and one fumble, the Bandits scored three TD's and two conversions for the win.

In the Ramsey game the Mullets scored in the first half for a 16-0 halftime lead.

Alan Atchley returned the second half kickoff 60 yards for the Cubs' only score. Ramsey scored again in the second half, bringing the final score to 22-6.

Brad Couthron and Bob Gladwin did good work on defense, and Farley Pouland on the offense in the Ramsey game.

Butler elected pep president

Cindy Butler was elected president of the newly organized CJH pep squad in September.

Other officers are Robin Williams, vice president; Beverly Kimbrough, secretary; Beth Burns, treasurer; and Margie Howe, decorations committee chairman.

Other members of this committee are Brenda DeMent, Jenny Smoot, Tina Catsavis, Betsy Randall and Terri Stoufer.

This committee works with the cheerleaders in painting signs and decorating goal posts before games.

The pep squad members, 117 girls, must attend all club meetings, in-town games, and help sell "beat" tags.

"We certainly thank the student body and the pep squad for their support and real Cougar spirit," commented Mrs. Jane Davidson, pep squad sponsor.

Miss Gail Lehman is also co-sponsor of the group.

learned at summer cheerleading clinic at the University of Arkansas.

Five Chaffin girls attended this clinic July 20-25. They are Kay Rappeport, Kathy Crow, Lucia Hawkins, Lisa Lunney and Cindy Sparks.

Besides leading cheers, the girls make posters to promote school spirit and sell "beat" tags.

"Much of this is done during homeroom and first mod," explained their sponsor, Mrs. Jane Davidson.

In city meet
CJH girl tracksters take first

Dedication— proves key to success

Winning the all-city meet, the ninth grade girls finished their track season May 4 at Buck Wells field.

The same day the ninth grade boys qualified for the state meet in two events, the 440-relay team and Evan Evans in the high jump.

The ninth grade girls practically took a clean sweep of their events by finishing first in their events by finishing first and second in the 75, first and second in the 100, first in the 440, first in the 880 and second in the 50.

"The seventh and eighth grade boys and girls made a good showing at the all-city meet," said Coach Wayne Thompson.

The seventh grade girls came in third in the 440- and 880-relays and fifth and sixth in the 50-yard dash.

The eighth grade girls came in fourth in the 440 and fifth and sixth in the 50.

Steve Vance clears another in the 120 low hurdle in the last track meet of the season.

Last track meet brings worry, fear

By Karen Conforti

The day of the last track meet was a very hot one. It was Monday afternoon when we girls piled into our PE instructor's car and started toward Ramsey.

Upon our arrival, the bleachers were rather empty but soon the crowd gathered and the races were underway.

It wasn't long before the speaker announced the ninth grade girls 880-relay. As I was to begin this race, I was rather scared yet excited. But I found that I was lucky, for I was placed on the outside track, my favorite.

When the gun sounded, I dashed ahead. Almost immediately someone screamed my name. Though I was in the lead with no one coming up close behind me, I stopped dead in my tracks, wondering why my name had been called out. I thought for a minute that I had jumped the gun. Unfortunately, the race had started so I dashed ahead again, passed the baton and we came in first place!

Mandee Harper, who entered three events in the last track meet, races to the finish line.

"You've got to dedicate yourself." These words didn't mean much to me last August, the first time Coach Thompson said them, but now I think I'm a little closer to knowing what he meant.

Chaffin athletes are now working on spring football practice and spring basketball practice but these practices won't stop when school is out. They will be encouraged to run, lift weights, and keep in shape during the summer.

Ninth grade athletes planning to play football for Southside and Northside next year will work on weights, agilities and running every day this summer at their respective high schools.

That's dedication.

CJH golfers win tourney, receive SWTR trophy

The Chaffin golf team won the Cedars Southwest-Times Record Junior High Golf Trophy Wednesday, May 6. The top four scores for Chaffin were Billy Sullivan, 86; Jonny Williams, 87; Willard Williams, 90 and Joe Chancy with a 92. Randy Moore and Walt Scales were the other players for Chaffin.

The total of the four lowest scores on each team was tallied with Chaffin ahead by five strokes. Scores were Chaffin, 355; Van Buren, 360; Kimmons, 361; Ramsey, 373 and Darby with 399. Medalist was Mark Secrest of Darby with 84.

Chancy wins 6 ribbons

"Joe Chancy headed the seventh grade boys by earning 6 ribbons," said Coach Thompson. Seventh grade boys also placed first in the discus and the 440 and 880 relays. Leslie King set a new seventh grade record by winning the high jump at 5'0. They also came in second in the high jump, second in the high jump, the hurdles, the mile relay and the 440 dash.

The 440 and 880 relay teams are composed of Joe Chancy, Steve Tichenor, Leslie King and Mike Anderson.

Coach James Myers receives trophy from Willard Williams on behalf of the golf team after winning SWTR tourney.

Cauthron first in discus

Brad Cauthron led the Chaffin tracksters through their first meet of the year, March 19 at Northside, with his first place throw in the discus competition.

Placing fourth in the overall competition with 26½ points, the Cougars had one first place, five third places,

es, three fourth places, and two fifth places.

Others who took the third place were Bob Nunley for high jump with 5, feet 4 inches, Bob Gladwin for the hurdles in 17.8 and David Cousins who leaped 15 feet 11 inches in the long jump.

Sports page #1—Although this page is much lighter than are most sports pages, the arrangement of heads calls attention to every story on the page. Note that the headlines are of diminishing size down the page, with three two-column heads offsetting the two one-column heads. The main story is broken up by subheads and extra space. The "Butler" headline and "Cougar fight" add to the horizontal effect by being aligned. The kicker on the "Kathy Crow" headline creates additional space in the lower part of the page. Note the inset headline on the cutlines under the picture. This page combines roman and italic type for variety.

Sports page #2—Pictures here indicate the value of photography in sports coverage and in layout on the sports page. The three-column headline above the two pictures and copy creates a block at the top of the page balanced by the two-column "Cauthron" head and ad in the lower right. The subhead with rules above and below breaks the long track story and helps achieve the geometric effect. The main head with kicker contrasts with the one-column three lines on "Dedication." As the three-column effect is balanced in upper left and lower right, the one-column vertical effect is balanced in upper right and lower left. This feeling for balance and contrast is the new look in layout—and is very reasonable, since the reader comprehends the page a block at a time.

Sports page #3—With the careful arrangement of headlines and advertising, this page illustrates the brace makeup. As usually done, the ads pyramid from upper right to lower left. The major story occupies the prime optical area in the upper left, with the dominant headline on the page making it stand out. The one-column boxed headline creates contrast at the top and emphasizes the drawing above "Football." The half-column picture and drawing dress up the columns. Note that the "Cougars stand" headline and the top of the picture are aligned—again to emphasize the horizontal effect. Italics contrast with roman type. Because headlines are spaced so as to break up gray areas, no subheads are needed.

Sports page #4—The major story dominates this page. Note that the three-column type is much larger than the other headlines, the kicker adds space for emphasis, the entire story is run down a single column to make it more noticeable, the subheads have spacing around them and are set off from the copy with rules above and below, and the double-column cutline under the picture is a kind of finishing horizontal line. Other headlines are in contrasting type, with the "Athlete" feature in the boxed head breaking up the middle of the page. Note that the bottom of the picture aligns with the "Green team" headline. Ads pyramiding from upper right to lower left emphasize the story in upper left.

Cats scratch Southwest wallop Woodland 21-0

The Cougars defeated both Southwest and the Woodland Cowboys 21 to 0 in the past two weeks.

Les King scored two touchdowns for the Cats against Springdale and Ricky Lux capped a 51-yard drive with the third TD of the game. Lux and Joe Chancey made the extra points bringing the final score to 21-0.

In conference play Sept. 30 the Cats walloped the Woodland Cowboys 21-0. This was a big game for the Cats because Woodland was rated first in season standings.

After less than a minute of play King ran 56 yards to put the Cats on the scoreboard. Chancey kicked the extra point and the Cougars were out ahead.

Later in the first half the Cats got their second chance on a pass completed from Johnny Williams to King for the final TD before the half ended.

In the second half the Cougars marched down field to the Cowboys 6-yard line but penalties foiled the TD attempt. Not until the fourth quarter did the Cats score again when King ran 49 yards to the final TD.

The Cougars defense turned in their best performance as they held the Cowboys to 28 yards on the ground and did not allow a completion.

The Cougars had 254 yards rushing and Williams completed 54 yards in the air.

King had the most yardage for the Cats with 164. He also had 41 yards pass receptions.

Cougars stand 1-2 in eighth grade

Falling to Ramsey 14-6 Sept. 28 brought the eighth grade Cats' record to 1-2. The Cats only score came on a 40-yard pass from Chuck Putnam to Charlie Weindel.

In the second game of the season the Cats ripped Kimmons 30 to 0. Weindel scored first, blasting over the goal line for six points. In the last half Bill Nance and Stuart DeWitt also scored for the Cats.

Boyd elected FCA president; Myers speaks at first meeting

Kevin Boyd heads the Chaffin Huddle group, an organization of the National Fellowship of Christian Athletes.

Other officers include Joe Chancey, vice president; Mark Randall, secretary; Dan Bradford, treasurer; and David Watson, reporter. These officers were elected last spring to serve this year.

The FCA meets every Thursday morning at 7:55 in the gym. Guest speakers are invited to speak to the boys about the spiritual relationship between life and athletics.

Coach James Myers spoke at the first meeting and brought out the importance of a Christian relationship between the athlete and Christ.

At another session Coach Jerry Bridges spoke about mental spirit in relation to life.

"Being a Christian," he said, "helps you not only in sports but in your daily life all of your life."

The group attended the First Baptist Church Sept. 19.

Bird selected president of cougar pep squad

Leslye Bird was elected president of the pep squad at the first meeting of the year.

Ann Gray was chosen vice president; Lisa Crane, secretary; and Missy Lockhart, decorating chairman.

Also new uniforms were selected. They will be flair, gored skirts with matching tank tops of kelly green trigger cloth. A gold "C" will be on the tops. Gold knee socks will be worn.

The officers' uniforms will be the same style, but will be made of gold cloth.

This year committees will be formed to give the girls in the pep squad a better chance to participate. Some of these will be decoration, spirit and transportation.

The cheerleaders and faculty will name the heads of the committees while the members may volunteer to serve on them, stated Mrs. Donna Beneux, pep club sponsor.

Football

By Marc Allen

Seventh graders donned football pads a few weeks ago and are now in full swing of season action. The coaches are receiving help from the ninth grade athletes who transfer from study hall to prepare the seventh grade teams for the up-coming games.

Another football signal is the incomplete pass, which means that the ball was thrown but the intended receiver did not receive it. No penalty, score or yardage is made, but the signal is given. This sign appears as a brisk movement of the arms across each other forming an X.

Are you in the know on football jargon? Did you know....

... GRIDIRON is another name for the playing field?

Cougars No.1

Cats take St. Annes, Central

The Cougars rolled past St. Annes Buffs 35-0 and surprised Springdale Central by a score of 25-20 in recent play.

This action brought the Cougars their fourth and fifth consecutive wins of the season. Chaffin's record stands 5-1-0 for the season and 2-0-0 in the Mountain Conference.

Weindel: 177 yards

In the game against the Baby Buffs Oct. 6, the Cougars racked up 285 yards running, with 177 of it belonging to Charles Weindel, eighth grader, who scored twice.

Johnny Williams completed one out of one pass to Kenny Dougherty for 26 yards and a TD.

Other touchdowns were made by Mike Anderson and Les King. Ricky Lux made a 2-point conversion and Joe Chancey kicked four extra points.

Chuck Putnam had the only interception for the Cats. Chaffin had 16 first downs to the Buffs 9.

Cougars run 285 yds.

Raching up 286 yards, the Cats beat Central Bullpups Oct. 14.

After an 80-yard run and score for the Bullpups on the second play of the game, the Cats came back with a 65-yard drive and score to put them ahead 7-6 at the end of the first quarter.

Chaffin got their second chance when Central fumbled and the Cougars drove 55 yards for their second TD, made by King on a pass from Williams.

The Cats stretched their lead in the third when Williams hit Dougherty for a TD pass.

King's 72-yard sprint accounted for the final TD, ending the game with 25-20 score.

EIGHTH GRADER BILL NANCE sweeps around St. Annes' offense to block McMillen. Buff player carrying the ball after handoff.

Cubs rip Darby, hold 2-3 record

Ripping Darby 34-22 Oct. 12 brought the eighth grade Cubs' record to 2-3. Bill Nance sparked the Cubs with a 70-yard kick return.

Playing the Alma varsity team in the fourth game of the season, the Cubs were overpowered 22-8. Chaffin's only touchdown came on a 49-yard pass from Chuck Putnam to Charles Weindel.

Green team downs Darby seventh

Falling to Ramsey Oct. 12 brought the seventh grade Green team record to 1-3, and the Gold to 0-4.

On their home field Oct. 6, the Green team prevailed over Darby with the fine quarterbacking of Freddy Hudson and the running ability of Jim Young, scoring 20 points to Darby's nothing. Darby beat the Gold team 20-0.

Both Green and Gold went down to Kimmons 30-0 and 18-0 there Sept. 29.

athlete of the month

Les King, No. 44 on the varsity team, was elected Athlete of the Month for October.

The 150-pound halfback has gathered 43 yards this season. Averaging about eight yards a carry, this makes for a good team effort on both the line and backfield.

Also, this season King has scored a total of 66 points, averaging approximately 11 points a game. His longest run has been a 72-yard sprint for a TD against Springdale Central.

Football

One of the most damaging penalties to a team's defense is grasping the face mask. This is a 15-yard penalty and is made with the left hand in the form of a fist four inches in front of the mouth.

DID YOU KNOW THAT ......

... A CONVERSION is the attempt to score either one or two points after a touchdown?

Seven off-season boys are working out for the up-coming basketball season. They are Chris Parker, ninth; James Bradford, Dennis Spahn, Jon Snider, Scott Carty, Jeff Easley and Kenny Kirby, eighth. These boys run laps around the track outside and work on basketball skills in the gym.

General Stand Watie's men fighting two months after Civil War ends

The line of mounted Indians charges across the prairie and suddenly the United States cavalry is retreating before their assault.

Sound exciting?Well, if you could have looked south from a second story window of Chaffin on July 27, 1864, you could have witnessed it, for this was the opening of the Battle of Massard Prairie.

Troops stampeded

The Indians were a unit of Confederate cavalry commanded by Gen. Stand Watie, himself an Indian. The Federal troops were those of Major David Mefford's Sixth Kansas Cavalry.

Charging so suddenly and furiously that the horses of the Kansas troops were stampeded,the Confederate Indians completely surrounded them. Fighting on fott, Mefford's men managed to retreat about a mile to their camp which was located on what is now South Cliff Drive, before being either killed or captured.

So unexpected was the attack that when the Indians reached the old Union camp, a large dinner which was being prepared for the Yankee officers, was captured. Watie and his officers ate it instead.

Camp abandoned

However, Federal reinforcements were already on their way from the U.S. garrison at Fort Smith and Watie and his men abandoned the camp under the bombardment of Union cannon. The Indians then circled Fort Smith with their prisoners,crossed the Poteau River, and camped for the night in Oklahoma.

Gen. Watie's Indian Cavalry was famous throughout the Civil War for the guerrilla warfare it waged against the U.S. Cavalry. Unlike the bushwacker of most border states, Watie's men were so helpful to the Confederate cause that they were praised by the President of the Confederacy, Jefferson Davis.

When Gen. Robert E. Lee surrendered his Confederate Army of Northern Virginia to Gen. Grant in April, 1865, Watie was still fighting the Union forces stationed in this region of Arkansas and Oklahoma.

From then until June the other Confederate Armies were surrendered until by June 23, Watie's men were the only ones still holding out. On this date in 1865, he, too, surrendered ending the Civil War.

* * *

Patricia Dickinson, editor chosen journalist of year

Patricia Dickinson, editor of the Cougar Print, was named Chaffin's journalist of the year for her outstanding work in the field of journalism.

This is the second year the award has been presented at Chaffin and Patricia's name will be engraved on the plaque, following Lisa Lee's, last year's winner.

The plaque, which will be on display at school, is presented by the Northside chapter of the Quill and Scroll, a national journalism organization.

Northside presents the award each year to the outstanding journalist of each junior high to recognize and encourage young writers.

Awards given

GOLF
Walt Scales, John Williams, Joe Chancey and Kevin Layman.

HUSTLING COUGARS
Track—David Cousins, ninth; Joe Chancey, eighth; Charles Weindel, seventh.
Football—Tim McKenzie Basketball— Walt Scales, ninth; Mike Anderson, eighth; Chuck Putnam, seventh.

The Athletic Department gave a plaque to Mrs. Jane Wilson and Mr. Mitchell Wortham, outstanding teachers.

'What's My Line?' played by students

"Are you a service worker?" Questions like this were asked of job holders in Mr. Bill Washum's economics classes. The students were playing "What's My Line?"

Four panelists questioned each individual to try to guess what his job was.

Among the jobs were snake charmers, human cannon balls, bull fighters, mortition, coroner,and female exterminators.

Job holders were given one point for every panelist they stumped. The points will be redeemed for money, to be averaged into their grade.

Mr. Washum's experiment, Eco 214, using "money" for grades is still continuing.

* * *

Next year's head cheerleader and co-head cheerleader were announced at the Awards Assembly, May 7. They are Ann Saviers, head and Cindy Sagely, co-head.

The girls were elected by the new squad.

* * *

The wall outside the art room has been decorated with a variety of art work. Some of the types displayed are designs cut from newspaper and pasted to construction paper, sketches and paintings of flowers, and an array of other objects.

* * *

Mrs. Virginia Peel, who has been hospitalized because of surgery, wishes to thank all students and faculty members who have remembered her with their cards, flowers or visits.

Inside page #1—The two-line italic headline dominates this page, with the long story broken by subheads with rules above and below and extra space. The horizontal look is furthered by the two-column headline and the arrangement of ads. Note that the three-column headline at the top is balanced against the ads. This arrangement of ads is a combination of well and pyramid so every ad will have copy adjacent. (Although most advertising is pyramided from upper right to lower left on all pages, some layout editors pyramid ads on lefthand pages from upper left to lower right.) The "Yearbook photos" headline is a kind of standing head in that the first and last are standing lines in 10-point type, with the first news item headlined in 24-point type. The use of the three suspension points at the end of the first line and the beginning of the fourth help make a frame for the main idea and add depth, which keeps this headline from seeming to butt against another. Note that once again asterisks and spacing break up a long column. Note also that by using the longest item first, the spacing is aligned with the "Patricia Dickinson" headline and contributes to the horizontal effect of the page.

What's happening...
Yearbook photos set for summer
... in Cougar Country

All ninth graders who want their pictures in the Northside and Southside yearbooks next year must be photographed some time this summer.

An appointment card will be sent by Barnett Studio to each student soon. If the appointment can't be met, arrangements for another should be made as soon as possible.

Four teachers new in Chaffin

Ranson, Wintory have IA,music

Two of the four new teachers at Chaffin this year are Mr. R. D. Ranson and Mrs. Nicol Wintory.

Mr. Ranson teaches drafting and seventh and eighth grade social studies.

Since acquiring his masters degree at Oklahoma State University, he has earned additional hours at North Eastern State College and at Tulsa.

He has had 30 years of teaching experience.

Replacing Mr. John Woods, Mrs. Wintory is the orchestra instructor at Chaffin this year.

She obtained her education at Hendrix College and at the American Conservatory of Music in Chicago.

Before taking over the orchestra this year, she formerly taught orchestra after school hours.

A baby in the house

(Dedicated to Mr. and Mrs. Benny Deaver)

Something is different,
What I'm not sure.
But voices are gentle,
Smiles are pure.

Everything is subdued,
Still as a mouse.
Can you guess why?
There's a new baby in the house.

Lynn Wintory

The four teachers new in Chaffin are (front row) Mrs. Nicol Wintory, Mrs. Donna Beneux and (back) Mr. R.D. Ranson and Mr. Jerry Bridges.

Girls selected to form trio

The Triple Trio, a group of nine girls, has been organized this year by Miss Therese Miros, choral director.

The girls are Lynn Freeman, Karen Hutcheson, Leslie Staton, soprano; Brenda Erke, Dianne Gray, Catherine McCann, second soprano; and Dee Ann Sullivan, Cindy Coady, Cathy Coon, alto.

The glee clubs are already preparing for the city-wide choral festival scheduled for mid-October at Northside, although the exact date has not yet been set.

The guest conductor will be Mr. Gene Kinney of Texas Tech University, Lubbock, Texas. A concert will be given by the combined glee clubs of the city schools.

Bridges, Ben'eux in phys ed

The two new teachers in the physical education department are Mrs. Donna Beneux and Mr. Jerry Bridges.

Mrs. Beneux, girls PE instructor, obtained her bachelors degree at Arkansas Tech and her masters at Tahlequah North Eastern State College.

For the past three years she has taught girls PE and geography at Darby.

She is taking the place of Mrs. Jane Wilson.

Mr. Bridges succeeds Mr. Wayne Thompson, who is coaching at Alma High School.

He, too, received his bachelors degree at Arkansas Tech and his masters at North Eastern State College.

He has boys PE and coaches the football team. Before coming to Chaffin Mr. Bridges was in the PE department at Ramsey.

It's a fact..

By Robb McDaniel

While visiting in cotton country this summer, I learned some information I had not known.

For instance, did you know that cotton is the world's most absorbent fiber and, when wet, is stronger than structural steel?

Also, cotton was first woven into cloth more than 5,000 years ago, and only the high priests were allowed to wear it as clothing.

In ancient India, sheer cotton muslin was woven so fine that 73 yards weighed only one pound.

Later, the early desert nomads wore layer upon layer of cotton...to keep cool! And it's still the coolest clothing fiber today.

Another fact, although many people like the fabric, moths don't, so it is free from harmful bugs and insects. A comforting thought, huh?

Robb McDaniel elected 71-72 band president

Robb McDaniel was chosen president and Dan Bradford, vice president of the band at the organizational meeting this month.

Other officers include Cindy Pettit, secretary-treasurer; David Laubach, Mark Harper and Jerry Landes, quartermasters; Tina Deal, head librarian; Betsy Hardin and Cindy Jessen, assistant librarians.

Band representatives are Steve Turner and Marsha Perry, ninth grade, and Kyle McDaniel and James Bradford, eighth grade.

The duties of the president and vice president are to head the newly formed band council, which consists of the officers and two representatives from each grade. It serves as a leadership group, a communications link between the director, the band and the band parents.

The secretary-treasurer keeps an account of band money and has charge of the merits record.

The quartermasters organize the band room each morning and make certain all equipment is packed for trips.

The librarians, appointed by Band Director Miss Leighnora Buchanan, distribute and file the music.

Representatives attend all meetings of band parents and the band council and serve as main spokesmen for the band.

Inside page #2—This page illustrates the use of a blanket headline to tie together several related items. The headlines on the two stories thus become second decks for the main headline. The story below the picture has a boxed headline to separate it from the picture above. For contrast, the headline in the upper right and the heading for the poem are in italics. Type on this page is a little tight but is somewhat relieved by the ads. By careful editing, a story can usually be condensed enough to allow for spacing. This page has a definite vertical look.

Inside page #3—Another illustration of the blanket headline here includes three separate stories following a summary lead. A one-line headline is used for each story, the same type as the kicker for the main headline. All heads on the page are surrounded by space, increased on three stories by the by-line. "Word Power" adds color to the top of the page, anchors the corner. A double-column lead on the "I gain" story is 10-point type to add interest below the fold. Note that the end of the double-column lead aligns with "It's a fact." Ads form a well.

Inside page #4—Two three-column headlines give this page a definite horizontal look and provide space for two long stories. Note that the "Hammerschmidt" story is broken up by subheads, centered, and that the "Colony days" story is divided by slugs of space. Kickers for two heads add extra space to the page, as well as contrast. Note that the kickers are italics, with the main headline in roman. The boxed headline provides variety on the page. Also, the use of the picture adds interest below the fold. The headline properly extends above the picture. Ads, pyramided, reflect the shape of the main story. This is one of the most common and most usable of all basic plans for inside pages.

After clinic, elections

Musical department underway

With band and orchestra members attending camps and the choral and band parents organizing, the music departments are underway for the year.

Kropp best drummer

Phillip Kropp, eighth grader, was chosen best drummer at the junior high band camp at Russelville this summer. He was one of 10 Chaffin band students attending.

Other first band members include David Laubach, Tina Deal, Tomya Long, Betsy Hardin, Cindy Jesson, Kathy Treadway, Bruce Gammill, John Watts and Bill Hansen.

Miss Leighnora Buchanan, Chaffin band director, served as a judge and instructor for the woodwind section.

Mr. and Mrs. Jerry Bogoslavsky, new presidents of the Chaffin band parents have named committee chairmen.

They are Mr. and Mrs. Al Swan, concessions; Mr. and Mrs. Willard, telephone; Mrs. Chris Johnson, hospitality; Mr. and Mrs. Leo Olsen, pancake; Mr. Bill Harper, publicity; and Mr. and Mrs. Bill Hickson, Mrs. A.C. Bradford, Mrs. Ron Pettit and Mrs. Marvin Vann, wrapping paper sales.

Choral officers elected

Mr. and Mrs. Charles McRay have been elected president of the Choral Parents Club.

Other officers are Mr. and Mrs. Robert McCann, secretary and Mr. and Mrs. Eugene L. Staton, treasurer.

Orchestra

Three orchestra students represented Chaffin at a string clinic at the University of Arkansas in September.

They were Nanci Hinds, Becky Mickle and Kevin Boyd. They were shown several techniques to use when playing and ways to relax when playing.

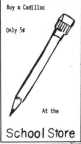
Science student

Bugs not my bag

By Catherine McCann

Whoosh! "I've got it. I've got it," I scream excitedly.

"Gee," I say to myself, "my very first one! That makes 79 more to go."

This was the beginning after my science teacher said we had to have 80 insects by the end of October. All 80 must be labeled as to order, genis, species and common name.

I began my search in the jungles of my own back yard, but soon discovered that the insects which had swarmed around me all summer were now nowhere to be seen.

At first progress was slow. However, by the third week I had about 45 insects. Wow, was I proud of myself! But I didn't have 80.

When the temperature dropped and cool weather set in, I began to worry. Going out in a field of weeds right after a rain just isn't my thing.

By the end of the fifth week I had 20 more with only 15 to go.

Then my teacher casually remarked, "Let's make that 50 insects."

Oh, well, such is life.

It's a fact..

By Caron Smets

Pencils are a necessity. At least to the student. Did you know that on the average, 12 pencils are used each year for every person in the United States?

Even the Romans nearly 2,000 years ago used pencils. Theirs consisted of sticks of lead.

About 400 years ago graphite was discovered and was mixed with sulphur.

This mixture was used by Casper Faber when he established the first pencil factory some 200 years later in Bavaria.

In 1795 a Frenchman named Conte mixed the graphite with clay, producing the mixture which is still used today.

I gain practical expreience on parking lot, back roads

By Leslie Staton

It all started in the Chaffin parking lot. It was hard for me at first, but without my good friend, my companion, my buddy, I never would have learned how. Then when I began to get the hang of it, I liked it and went there almost every evening.

Then I grew bolder. My buddy and I decided to try another place to go. We chose wooded areas, for who needs people!

I was learning, but I still made a mistake every now and then, and it would really have embarrassed me if I had been seen.

Becoming more confident and even bolder, we left the wooded areas and took to the highway. It was difficult at first to have all those people around but I soon began to get the feel of the thing and I didn't let people bother me.

Then came the hardest decision of all. We decided if we could "do our thing" in all those other places, why not "go for broke" and take to the Super Highway? So we did.

At last came the day I had been working toward all these months. We walked up the courthouse steps.

I couldn't wait to get my driver's license!

From Washington

Hammerschmidt 'hitches' ride to city

By Patricia Dickinson

"I seem to be hitching a ride from Washington D. C. to Fort Smit frequently," smiled Congressman John Paul Hammerschmidt in a recent interview.

Congressman Hammerschmidt's latest trip to Arkansas came on Oct. 23, when he attended the Freedom Shrine dedication at Chaffin while Congress was in a 20-day recess.

"Since I do have one of the highest votes in Congress," he remarked, "I don't like to miss any day when Congress is in session."

Visits twice

The trip to Fort Smith was the second this month for Mr. Hammerschmidt. At the beginning of October, he flew here from Washington D.C. with Vice President Spiro T. Agnew, who was campaigning for the Republican Party.

"I've also come in with President Richard Nixon and former Vice President Hubert Humphrey in the past."

Mr. Hammerschmidt will be running for re-election to the third district in the November general election against Democratic Donald Poe from Waldron.

Services are campaign

"I don't get much chance to campaign," said Mr. Hammerschmidt, "so I guess my service to the people in my last two terms will have to speak for me as my campaign."

In Congress, Mr. Hammerschmidt serves on the Public Works committee and the Veterans Affairs committee.

"The Public Works committee is involved in Federal construction," he explained, "and exercises legislative control over the Corps of Engineers."

Aids veterans

The other committee works with legislation of vital interest to veterans, their widows and orphans.

Mr. Hammerschmidt's home is in Harrison although he spends nearly 11 months each year in the nation's capital.

"Since my only son is away at college," he remarked, "I don't have as much reason to go down to Harrison except on weekends as I used to when he was younger."

Alverson attends NASSP meeting in nation's capital

Washington D.C. will be the site of the 54th annual convention of the National Association of Secondary School Principals, which Mr. Bill Alverson, principal, will attend in December.

The trip will include a sightseeing tour of the city and a breakfast with Arkansas Congressmen and Representatives.

Mr. Alverson will also visit the John Fitzgerald Kennedy High School and the Colonel E. Brooke Lee Junior High, both in Silver Spring, Maryland. These schools use the modern team-teaching approach.

Colony days reconstructed in satire

Who were the first settlers to come to Plymouth Rock on the Mayflower? Why, Chaffin eighth graders, of course.

Pilgrims from Mrs. Mildred Knox's English and speech classes will bring a few new ideas when they present "The Courtship of Miles Standish Up-to-Date."

The play, a satire, will be given March 1 in an assembly program.

The setting of the play is Plymouth Rock. The time is just after the first hard winter when the Mayflower starts its trip back to England.

Portraying Miles Standish, the Captain of Plymouth, will be David Tedder.

Other main characters include Priscilla, Marci Smith; John Alden, Jim Birch; Elder Brewster, Brent Pollock; Pecksuot, Roger Carter; Eramus, Wendal Goodman; and Katonda, Holly Mudget.

Three lonely young maidens of the colony will be played by three eighth grade girls: Mercy, Leslie Jones; Charity, Kathy Thames; and Patience, Kerry Brown.

Two handsome young men will be portrayed by Bill Corrough and Kenneth Ewing.

Linda Swearington, Jane Ayers, Marsha Law and Susan Walker will become four pretty bridesmaids in the play.

Brent Pollock (left) scolds Wendel Goodman as they rehearse for the March 1 play.

With red, white, blue

Glee clubs show patriotism

Surrounded by decorations of red, white and blue, Chaffin's vocal department gave a patriotic concert last night in the school cafetorium.

Under the direction of Miss Terese Miros, the girls glee club combined with the ensemble to sing "Freedom Isn't Free," "Let There Be Peace on Earth," "I Believe in America and "I Like the U.S.A."

The ensemble alone sang "America Our Heritage" and "It's a Long Road to Freedom."

Decorations, made by the glee club girls, included a large flag of chicken wire and napkins for a backdrop, silhouettes of George Washington and Abraham Lincoln, a mural of the Statue of Liberty and the Washington Monument and a United States map.

Whoosh
Cycles roar, gun fires, flag lowered

The warm-up lap is practically over. In the distance stands the man with the checkered flag. As you approach him, you hear the fire of a gun. The flag is lowered and the cyclists are off.

"This particular race is the flat track," explained Mike Kilgore, ninth grader, who is motorcycle racer himself.

Mike has been racing just one year, but has won first, second and third places in three amateur races, all in Little Rock, where races are held every Saturday and Sunday.

His first was won two weeks after he started. His second and third were won three weeks after the first. His average speed is 60 miles per hour.

"Another kind of race," continued Mike, "is the motorcross, which consists of a much more difficult race over rough territory."

Races are divided into classes. First is the mini-trail for the smallest cycle, next is 100 class, then the 250 category and the largest is the Harley-Davidson. Each class is composed of an amateur and a professional division. Mike races in the 100 class.

"The amateur division," he went on, "is for those fairly new in racing and are interested in learning how to race professionally."

Each class contains nine or ten heats which are guided on the track by a leader. Each heat is approximately 25 or 30 minutes long.

"The leader of the pack is not necessarily the winner, for an accident can happen at any time," Mike added.

He has had four accidents when he flipped over while racing over rough terrain, but he was not really hurt.

Blimp (Cont.)

the air. It seemed peaceful and calm, just drifting.

The airship "America" is 192 feet long and 60 feet high. It weighs 12,320 pounds— over six tons— but it just floats in the clouds by itself.

The car underneath can hold the pilot and six passengers at one time. The car is only seven feet wide at the ceiling and four and a half feet at the floor. Its maximum speed is about 55 miles per hour.

Blimp blinks lights

At night the blimp gives a "light" show, which consists of five different colors. For the 105-foot sign there are 80 miles of wiring. The sign can be read from a mile away.

The blimp was in Fort Smith for the United Fund drive and from here it went to the Cotton Bowl to cover both the Texas-OU game and the Dallas-New York game on film from the air.

The blimps travel an average of 200,000 miles a year and have been around the world several times.

Needless to say, it was quite a trip.

Library word puzzle

By JANICE CRAWFORD

```
L P D C R O S S R E F E R E N C E L T Q S M
R I L Z N S P G H F D A D U T Z Q A C P R N
Q Y B W I E R T U L A M I C E D A C E Y U I
O H P R A N S D F I G H J K L I T I J Z X C
V P B N A M D Q W E D R T Y D C A H B C L A
U A I O P R A E S D C E F E G T B P U I A L
M R D R N E Y L X I A Z P Q W I L A S S C M
X G Y P B F D F H L L O K G A O E R F U I A
M O W D Q E R Z L C L V B I M N O G N M T N
N I Z R N R X V L C N B Z N R A F O Z O E A
O L W O I E B C Y N U C B F M R C I I L B C
I B T W Y N S C N C M I I O I Y O B T P A E
T I B Y S C N M R P B P T R N C N I B P H W
C B T E S E M T O L E O Y M N F T O Y K P Z
I R Z K E A T E H S R T P A R O E I N M L T
F L X D S R L P T R T B I T A L N G O J A S
N K R P Z I L T U Z B U M I D K T L D N M E
O W C I P O T D A X Z S Q O P X S T R P X W
N M E L V I L D E W E Y N N C V Y F B M W K
X A M Y T O L B R A K G O L A T A C D R A C
```

The following words pertaining to finding information in the library can be found in the square above. Can you find them?

LIBRARY	SUB TOPIC	ALMANAC	CROSS REFERENCE
INFORMATION	GUIDE	ATLAS	ALPHABETICAL
MELVIL DEWEY	AUTHOR	MUSIC	CARD CATALOG
DECIMAL	SUBJECT	INDEX	BIBLIOGRAPHY
CALL NUMBER	TITLE	REFERENCE	TABLE OF CONTENTS
KEY WORD	FICTION	DICTIONARY	BIOGRAPHICAL
TOPIC	NONFICTION		ENCYCLOPEDIA

Laubach, J. Bradford chosen drum majors

Selected for drum major this year is David Laubach, ninth grader, with his assistant, James Bradford, eighth grade.

David's duties are to guide and conduct the band while marching on the field and at times to direct in the place of Miss Leighnora Buchanan, director.

Selecting David and James from the seven who competed for the position were Band Council members Dan Bradford, Marsha Perry and Cindy Pettit; Miss Buchanan and Mr. Bill Alverson, principal.

The determining factors in the selection were how well the band responded to his commands and how he game oral commands. He must, too, be qualified in knowing the fundamentals of marching.

David was scheduled to lead the band through a routine and several songs Thursday at the Darby game. Selections included a rock number, "Brothers and Sisters."

Inside page #5—Headlines on this page are noteworthy. The "Whoosh" headline is an example of a reverse kicker. This is especially effective here with the kicker in roman and the main headline in italics. The story is broken up with slugs of space. The "Blimp" headline is a jump head. This means that it designates a story carried over, or jumped, from another page. A jump head usually is the first word or a major word in the original headline so the reader can find the continuation easily when he seeks it. The subhead in the continued story is body type size but is attractive because surrounded by space and set off from the story by rules. Most subheads are centered, as this one is.

Mr. I. E. Clark submits the following front page from *The Shorthorn*, of Schulenburg High School, Schulenburg, Texas.

With this, he includes the layout sheet that was prepared for this page to show exactly how much space is to be allowed for each story and exactly where lines of spacing are to fall.

The rough draft prepared by the typist provides a preview of the story before it is typed for the final paste-up or stencil. Note that the typist uses a column 22 spaces wide. The copy is typed with normal spacing and then diagonal lines to show spaces unfilled or exclamation marks to indicate the need for crowding in the line in the final typing. This care in making the first draft and then correcting for spacing make the justified margins possible and achieve the neat appearance of the page.

Front page #1—The boxed nameplate and the picture are arranged on this page to break up the long stories and present a readable page without carrying any copy over to other pages. The full headline on the Roundup story is planned to be the width of the nameplate. Note the information within the nameplate box. Also note that the Spanish carols headline is almost aligned with the lower edge of the picture for a horizontal effect. Spacing around the headlines and picture and frequent paragraphing make this page easy to read.

SANTA PARADE TO BEGIN HOLIDAYS

Santa Claus will arrive in his sleigh today at approximately 2:30 PM.

The Bishop Forest Ranger Band will lead Santa to the railroad park, followed by the Shorthorn Band. This event will mark the beginning of the holidays for SHS students.

From 12:45 to 1:45 PM today an assembly program will be put on by the band and choral club. Following this performance, everyone must go back to sixth period classes and the band will be excused immediately after roll check.

Classes will be dismissed at 2:15 PM and everyone is required to parade to the railroad park.

"After the students arrive at the park, they are free to go," said Prin. Stewart Bosl.

In the event of rain, the parade will be canceled.

—shs—

THE SHORTHORN

Schulenburg (Texas 78956) High School
December 22, 1971 Vol. XLII No. 8 Page 1

'ROUNDUP' KEEPS A SECRET

Watch your step or you might find a funny picture of yourself in the 1972 ROUNDUP!

The 25-member ROUNDUP staff has been instructed to take pictures of everyone and everything that happens at SHS' for the yearbook.

This year's staff is led by seniors Paula Schwartz, editor; Tim Patrick, assistant editor; juniors Barbara Bucek, business manager; and Ray Grasshoff, assistant busi-

PAULA WILL SHOOT YOU

ness manager. Mr. R. G. Phillips, librarian, is the sponsor.

The theme of this year's annual will be kept a secret until it arrives in August.

The 1972 ROUNDUP may be ordered from Babette Haba, senior. The yearbooks are $5; $2 may be put down as a deposit.

SPANISH CAROLS SET

"Feliz Navidad y Buen Ano Nuevo" is the greetings of Mr. Bill Butts's Spanish classes.

The Spanish students will go carolling tonight, singing traditional Christmas songs in Spanish.

After that, Mr. Butts's Spanish students will celebrate the holiday season with a dinner composed entirely of Mexican food.

EXAMS COMING

Students will have a long weekend to rest from mid-term exams which begin Monday, January 10.

The week begins with fourth period exams Monday.

First period exams will be given Tuesday, with fifth period exams taken that afternoon.

Second period exams begin Wednesday morning, and sixth period exams will be held that afternoon.

Third period exams will be given on Thursday. That afternoon seventh period exams will be held.

Friday, January 14 and Monday, January 17 are holidays for the students. The faculty will use the time to complete their semester work and prepare for the new grading period.

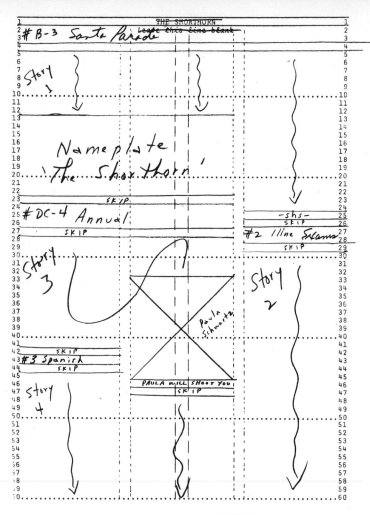

#B-3 Santa Parade — leave this line blank

Story 1

Nameplate 'The Shorthorn'

SKIP

#DC-4 Annual

SKIP

#2 1line Exams

SKIP

Story 3

Story 2

Paula Schwartz

SKIP

#3 Spanish

SKIP

PAULA WILL SHOOT YOU

SKIP

Story 4

STORY 1:

1]2345678901

1234567890123456789012

Santa Claus will ar- !
rive in his sleigh to-
day at approximately//
2:30 PM.

The Bishop Forest//
Ranger Band will lead/
Santa to the railroad/
park, followed by the/ —— to Col. 2
Shorthorn Band. This/
event will mark the be- !
ginning of the holidays !
for SHS students.

From 12:45 to 1:45/
PM today an assembly//
program will be put on
by the band and choral —— to col. 3
club. Following this/
performance, everyone/
must go back to sixth/
period classes and the
band will be excused//
immediately after roll
check.

Classes will be dis- !
missed at 2:15 PM and/
everyone is required//
to parade to the rail-
road park.

STORY 2:

1234567890123456789012

Students will have/
a long weekend to rest
from mid-term exams///
which begin Monday,///
January 10.

The week begins with !
fourth period exams///
Monday.

First period exams/
will be given Tuesday,
with fifth period ex-/
ams taken that after-/
noon.

Second period exams ▓
begin Wednesday morn-/
xillxmxg
ing, and sixth period/
exams will be held that
afternoon. !

Third period exams/
will be given on Thurs- !
day. That afternoon//
seventh period exams//
will be held.

Friday, January 14/
and Monday, January 17
are holidays for the//
students. The faculty
will use the time to//
complete their semester !
work and prepare for//
the new grading period. !

STORY 3:

1234567890123456789012

Watch your step or/
you might find a funny
picture of yourself in
the 1972 ROUNDUP!

The 25-member ROUND- !
UP staff has been in-/
structed to take pic-/
tures of everyone and/
everything that happens !
at SHS for the year-//
book.

This year's staff/xxxxxxxx
xxxxxxxxxxxxxxxxxxx
la Schwartz, editor;// —— to Col 2
Tim Patrick, assistant
editor; juniors Bar-//
bara Bucek, business//
manager; and Ray Grass- !
hoff, assistant busi-/
Put
ness manager. Mr. R./
G. Phillips, librarian, !
is the sponsor.

The theme of this//
year's annual will be/
kept a secret until it
arrives in August.

The 1972 ROUNDUP may !

1234567890123456789012

be ordered from Ba-///
bette Haba, senior.///
The yearbooks are $5;/
$2 may be put down as/
a deposit.

STORY 4:

"Feliz Navidad y///
Buen Ano Nuevo" is the
greetings of Mr. Bill/
Butts's Spanish class-
es.

The Spanish students !
will go carolling to-/
night, singing tradi-/
tional Christmas songs
in Spanish.

After that, Mr.////
Butts's Spanish stu-//
dents will celebrate//
the holiday season with !
a dinner composed en-/
tirely of Mexican food. !

1234567890123456789012

"After the students
arrive at the park,///
they are free to go,"/
said Prin. Stewart////
Bosl.
////
In the event of rain
rain, the parade will/
be canceled.
-shs-

CHAPTER XII

REGARDING THE FOUR-COLUMN PAGE

In school papers, the four-column format is becoming increasingly popular. For one thing, many papers are choosing a smaller sheet size in the consideration of expense and the use of the offset process, as well as other duplicating methods. In most cases, this means additional pages.

Also, the combination of wider columns and the geometric look has created a new enthusiasm for the four-column page.

Four-column format poses problems in achieving variety of makeup. The following examples, offered by Miss Elizabeth Hurly, adviser of *The Little Harvester,* Pampa High School, Pampa, Texas, may afford some help in designing these pages.

The Little
Harvester

Tornado Warnings

What To Do

(See Story Page 2)

Vol. 21, No. 25   Pampa High School, Pampa, Texas   Friday, April 25, 1969

John Duggan Wins Presidential Election

(Photo by Robert Moultrie)
COUNCIL OFFICERS MAKE PLANS---Jackie Gindorf, vice-president, Linda Brumley, secretary, and John Duggan, president, newly elected Student Council officers, plan for the coming year.

Jackie Gindorf, Linda Brumley Named Student Body Officers for Next Year

John Duggan will be student body president next year, and Moss Hampton will represent Pampa High as president of the Texas Association of Student Councils.

Other student body officers will be Jackie Gindorf, vice-president, and Linda Brumley, secretary. Linda succeeded as secretary after Brenda Duncan resigned when she was elected cheerleader.

Officers were installed in an assembly Tuesday by Principal Cameron Marsh.

OTHER CANDIDATES for president in the election April 11 were Moss, Robert Davis, Randy Marsh and John Worley.

Other secretarial candidates besides Brenda and Linda were Carolyn Brown, Jan Elder, Susan Maguire and Mary Ratliff.

Moss's four main objectives were to activate the Student Forum, involve all students in school affairs, encourage active participation in TASC, and initiate more school pride.

Randy's slogan was "Progression through Unity."

John Worley presented a four-point platform that dealt with "political involvement," student forum, student traffic committee and traffic court, and formation of a group for better assembly programs.

ROBERT ADVOCATED doubling the productivity and putting

(See ELECTION, Page 7)

(Photo by Robert Moultrie)
TASC LEADER--Moss Hampton, Junior Class vice-president, will represent Pampa as president of the Texas Association of Student Councils next year.

Hot Disputes in Student Council

Hampton to Head TASC

Moss Hampton was elected figurehead president of Texas Association of Student Councils of which Pampa has been elected president school.

Hampton defeated Robert Davis and Tim Doke in the Student Council election last Friday. Each candidate spoke to the Council for three minutes.

In his speech, Hampton stressed the need for action. "Frankly," he said, "I think we all worked hard and did a good job"

Senior Class Picnic Set in Park May 1

Senior Class picnic will be May 1 in Central Park at 7 p.m. Only seniors may attend, and they will bring their own food.

Senior Follies will be May 2 in assembly.

in getting elected president school. But now that we are president of the association, we need action to carry out our platform."

On recommendation of Moss in a Student Council meeting Tuesday, Debbie Veale was named TASC corresponding secretary.

Davis stressed student involvement in his speech to Student Council. "We will try to get as many students as possible involved in the action of TASC," he said. After all, every single person in this school is president. Why not let them work as such?"

In his speech, Doke pointed out the responsibilities of the

DAYLIGHT SAVING TIME STARTS SUNDAY

(See Story Page 3).

office. "Pampa High is now facing

(See TASC, Page 8)

Former Teacher to Speak At Honors Night April 28

Mrs. Ruth Holladay, former Pampa High School English teacher and now teaching in Olton, will review "Five Fathers for Pepe" at Honors Night April 28 at 7 p.m. in the high school auditorium.

Approximately 139 students will receive certificates for advanced English II, III, IV grammar and literature; advanced American History; advanced plane geometry, trigonometry, elementary analysis; advanced biology, chemistry, physics;

Latin III and IV, French III and Spanish III.

Certificates will be presented by Principal Cameron Marsh and Dr. James Malone school superintendent.

Valedictorian and salutatorin will be announced by Mr. Marsh.

Music will be presented by band members Gayle Miller, Hugh Jones, Jim Herring and Yvonne Dowdy.

A reception in the cafeteria will follow the presentations.

Front page #1—When space limitations push important stories inside, the ear beside the nameplate may be used to direct readers to a particular story on an inside page. Note also the boldface item at the bottom of the second column, a device not only adding color to the page but helpful in directing the reader to other important stories that follow. Boldface lead-ins substitute for subheads to break up long stories in order to avoid gray areas of type.

Robert Davis   John Duggan   Jackie Gindorf   Moss Hampton   Randy Marsh   John Worley

The Little
Harvester

Cast

Your

Ballot

Vol. 21, No. 24   Pampa High School, Pampa, Texas   Friday, April 11, 1969

Student Body President Voted on Today

(Photo by Robert Moultrie)
PHS DEMONSTRATORS---Participating in the political rally for TASC President in Amarillo March 28 are Carolyn McKinley, Judy Brown, Joe Roth, Billy Thomas and Joe Daniel, all seniors. Pampa defeated San Angelo Central in the race for president.

At TASC Convention

Pampa Wins SC Presidency

Pampa High School was voted Texas Association of Student Councils president March 29.

According to John Karr, student body president, the convention began with a keynote address. "Hear Us," from TASC president, Marilyn R u e p i n g from Forest Park High School in Beaumont.

"Pampa High School will give next year's keynote address," he said.

On Friday, Helen Hill, South African AFS student represent-

ed Pampa on an AFS International Panel. Both days 45 Pampa High School students campaigned.

Saturday morning, Brenda Duncan and Randy Marsh, David Irwin, and Moss Hampton, juniors participated in a discussion group, "How to Improve Student-Faculty Relations."

Voting took place Saturday afternoon. Plainview was voted vice-president and Monterey is parlimentarian.

A student to represent Pampa

as president will be chosen April 15 at a Student Council meeting, according to James Hulett, sponsor.

"Student Council discussed the election of a representative Tuesday," he added.

Mr. Hulett and the representative will attend the national meeting at Baltimore, Maryland, in June.

Trap!

The best laid plans of men for mice are oft unsprung.
— Jim Burnham.

Sophomores and Juniors Elect Leaders From Six Junior Candidate Choices

Juniors and Sophomores will vote today for student body president for next year.

Candidates are Moss Hampton, Randy Marsh, John Worley, John Duggan, Robert Davis and Jackie Gindorf.

In order to narrow the number of candidates Scotty King was eliminated by student vote Monday.

Student body presidential candidates and managers will present their speeches at the campaign assembly today at 8:30 a.m. in Harvester Field House.

After speeches, students will report to first period classes and the voting polls will immediately open.

Junior voting booths will be located on the first floor main hall at the extreme west end of the building.

Sophomore voting booth will

be located on the extreme east end on the first floor, in front of room 122.

Polls will be open during the morning and noon hour but will close at the beginning of fifth period.

When a student votes, he must report to his class to his class booth and have his name checked off the list. His name must be on the class list to vote. He will then vote for his choice of president and student body secretary. There will be separate ballots for president and secretary.

If no candidate receives a majority vote, one more than one-half the votes cast, there will be a run off election the next school day for candidates receiving the majority of the votes cast. Thus, the candidate receiving the most votes will be president, and the second receiving the most, vice-president.

Teachers will serve as election judges.

Student body officers will be installed April 18.

Students to Mark Another Test Week

Students again will face fifth six-weeks tests next week.

Third and fourth period tests will be on Monday; first and second period tests will be on Tuesday; fifth and sixth period tests will be on Wednesday. Report cards will be issued April 23 in homeroom.

Because of the tests, there will be no issue of the Little Harvester next week. The next edition will be April 25.

Front page #2—Even in a four-column format, the nameplate may be floated to allow more variety in makeup. Features, or in this case, pictures, may be used at the top of the page. The nameplate may be a three-column with an ear, as here for a timely promotion, or it may be four columns wide. Note the use of the second deck (the two-line, two-column head) with the four-column banner. The kicker with the three-column head adds important white space. In a head as wide as this, it is correct to have the kicker wider than one column.

Editorial page #1—Pictures as well as cartoons brighten an editorial page. In this layout, the picture ties in with the editorial. A cartoon may occupy this space to tie in with a front page story or editorial. Variety of column widths gives the editorial page a distinctive appearance, even though variety of makeup is limited by the four-column format. Note the boldface in the column and the indented cut-lines under the picture at the upper right.

BOSSAY'S BOX

By STEVE BOSSAY

A few weeks ago, The Little Harvester carried an editorial by Wes Izzard, editor of The Amarillo News and Globe Times. In the editorial entitled "Pampa's Year," Mr. Izzard reiterated some of the events that had made the year a successful one for Pampa, and especially the high school.

Mr. Izzard mentioned the fine performance of the band and choir on national television, the winning of the National Debate Tournament in Florida by the men's debate team, and other contributions by students that have brought respect to their school.

Pampa High students can again win respect for their school in perhaps a smaller personal way, but in a much greater overall way.

March 25 Pampa citizens will vote on a $900,000 bond issue which would provide enormous improvements for the school system, with a majority of the money going for improvements within the high school. Simply because they stand to gain more if the bond issue passes, high school students should be more concerned than anyone else.

It is important that high school students become concerned with the bond issue and transmitt this concern to their parents, who will be voting. The bond issue is vital for the advancement of education in Pampa, and students should be the first to recognize this.

If the bond issue passes March 25, it will be not only another link in the chain of events that have made it "Pampa's Year," but the greatest link. The improvements which the passing of the bond issue would entail could provide a cornerstone for a path of better education in Pampa. It would be the first step in making every year "Pampa's Year."

FACE TALK . Bill Nidiffer

My success? I went to a Career Clinic.

Career Clinic Presents Aspects of Professions

Now that childhood dreams of growing up to be a glamorous actress or a fire chief have faded, the reality of choosing a career enters the scene.

The majority of students have in mind the the professions they are interested in. Yet, just how much do they know about that career? What are its advantages and disadvantages? What educational preparation is needed? As time grows shorter, more questions arise.

The Career Clinic is designed to help the student decide and ask questons about a career. It introduces many vocations. It provides a chance for one to decide on a career or change his mind to a profession better suiting him.

The consultants put out their best to answer all kinds of questions and help clear up misunderstandings about professions. They have had valuable experience in their profession.

Also, the Career Clinic helps a student to decide on a major in college. Too many graduates in college discover they are working toward a vocation in which they are not interested.

The College Workshop provides representatives who can give important information about their school's predominant fields, requirements and financial aids.

Truely, the Career Clinic and College Workshops are opportunities. They are not just a holiday from classes. They are a first step into a world requiring much more education and responsibility on the student's part. Students may be surprised how valuable the information from these clinics is.

Only Those Interested Should See Assemblies

There was much rudeness displayed in last weeks choir assembly.

Obviously those making the noise didn't care about being at the assembly.

Why were they there? Teachers made them go.

Why should assemblies be required? Wouldn't it be better if only those interested attended the assembly.

International Quill & Scroll

TEXAS HIGH SCHOOL PRESS ASSOCIATION
Founded 1923

The Little Harvester is published weekly except during examinations and holidays by students of Pampa High School, Pampa, Texas 79065. The paper is a member of Texas High School Press Association, Interscholastic League Press Conference, Columbia Scholastic Press Association, Panhandle High School Press Association, Southwest Conference of School Publications and Quill and Scroll.

Editor-in-Chief ---------- Steve Bossay
Sports Editors ---------- David Irwin, Tim Doke
News Editor ---------- Janet Braden
Feature Editors ---------- Candy Cole, Karen Wallis
Copy Editor ---------- Doug Carmichael
Business Manager ---------- Tim Haigood
Advertising Manager ---------- Rosalie Kurtz
Photographers ---------- Sherrel Land, Randy Maness, Pat Corcoran
Robert Moultrie, Jimmy Gage, Donnie Jones
Exchange Editors ---------- Jessie Fick, Kay Foster
Circulation Managers ---------- Jim Cole, Charlie Barker
Sports Assistants ---------- Jim Burnham, Barry Bowman
Adviser ---------- Miss Elizabeth Hurley

(Photo by Sherrel Lanl)
PLAN CAREER CLINIC PROGRAM---Mrs. D. B. Jameson, left, Altrusa Club coordinator of the Career Clinic, and Mrs. Pete Erwin, secretary in the counselor's office, check the list of consultants who will speak at Career Clinic roundtables Wednesday.

MINORITY RUINS

Immaturity Is Factor In School Destruction

By KAREN WALLIS

Who started the fires in the trash containers; who wrote on desks; who wrote the obscene words on the walls of the boys' restrooms?

In an interview with Weldon Trice, assistant principal, he said, "I can't understand what makes students want to deface school property.

"Of course," he added, "I realize it is only a small minority."

Most Pampa High School students and teachers think vandalism is a sign of immaturity.

"It shows hom immature some students are," said Linda Dyer, senior.

"Yes," added Laurie Dingman, sophomore, "At first, I thought some elementary school children must be doing these things."

Carol Haynie, sophomore, added bluntly, "I thought you had to be 15 to get in this school. Not two."

Some blamed disrespect for the defacing of school property.

"The vandalism only shows real disrespect for our school," said Rhonda Miller, sophomore.

"Students should have more school pride," said Ernest Clay, science teacher.

Coach Swede Lee, athletic director, said "false pride" contributes greatly to school vandalism and always has.

"False pride," he explained, is when students are loyal to their school but at the same time are afraid to expose someone who isn't.

What can be done to stop this destruction?

Mr. Trice said the majority should stop the minority.

"Students don't like these things to happen, but they won't do anything to stop the vandals."

"Vandalism can be stopped," said Mrs. D. D. Spoonemore, history and English teacher, "but only then those doing it are caught and punished."

Mr. Trice said that "if students want a school to be proud of, they will have to do something about reporting vandals."

Editorial page #2—Boldface lead-ins and boldface indented paragraphs used in the editorial and the feature avoid unrelieved areas of body type. This device should also be used in the column. The cartoon ties in with a timely feature story. Note the miniature nameplate in the masthead. Note also the contrast in headline type—the serif italic used on the same page with the sans serif. Note also slugs of space in the long feature.

Student Council Elects TASC Representative

The contested question is settled, and Pampa's representative as president of the Texas Association of Student Councils has been elected.

About two-thirds of the student body feel they got a "raw" deal. But who dealt it? They did. They were dealing when they elected their homeroom representatives last fall.

MOST STUDENT COUNCIL members are conscientious, hard-working individuals; however, it takes only a few flies in the fudge to spoil the batch.

When informing his homeroom about council meetings—the vital function of a representative—the homeroom president who fails is depriving students in his homeroom of a voice in school affairs.

HOW WERE the "flies" elected? Like sheep, some of us thoughtlessly elect a popular "folk hero" because he is handsome, "cool" or comic but too involved in other activities to attend council meetings.

Student Council is the "congress" of our school, composed of representatives elected by their classmates. The council elected a leader to represent the school as TASC president. The least we can do is support him and fulfill our campaign slogan, "Progression Through Unity."

OUR SCHOOL constitution and its election code, a minor reason for the controversy, should be examined for possible changes. This Student Council is now doing.

Next year perhaps students will choose their homeroom representatives more wisely.

Memory Relies on Action

Silence is golden? Not always. You can never learn to communicate if you don't express your opinion. People are known for their actions. If you remain silent, you will be forgotten quickly. Will yours be a forgotten memory?

— The Shiloh, Johnston High Sihool, Austin, Texas

The Little Harvester

VOL. 21, NO. 25 - PAMPA HIGH SCHOOL - PAMPA, TEX.

The Little Harvester is published weekly except during examinations and holidays by students of Pampa High School, Pampa, Texas 79065. The paper is a member of Texas High School Press Association, Interscholastic League Press Conference, Columbia Scholastic Press Association, Panhandle High School Press Association, Southwest Conference of School Publications and Quill and Scroll.

Editor-in-Chief ---------- Charlie Barker
Assistant Editor ---------- Tim Doke
News Editors, Barry Bowman, Jean Ann Hawkins
Feature Editor ---------- Anne Dingus
Sports Editors ---------- David Irwin, Jim Burnham
Circulation Managers ---------- Jim Cole, Jessie Fick
Business Manager ---------- Tim Haigood
Advertising Manager ---------- Rosalie Kurtz
Exchange Editors ---------- Kay Foster, Dana Shepherd
Copy Editors ---------- Steve Bossay, Doug Carmichael, Candy Cole, Karen Wallis
Photographers ---------- Sherrel Land, Randy Maness, Robert Moultrie, Donnie Jones
Senior Adviser ---------- Janet Braden
Adviser ---------- Miss Elizabeth Hurley

CHARLIE'S CHANNEL

BY CHARLIE BARKER

Much of personality is shaped by appearance. Today, hair seems to be a major factor in appearance and personality.

The subject, hair, has such gravity that an avant-garde theatrical production presented by The Living Theatre, has been named after it. Sometimes people view hair in an evil light as in a mane, such as Margaret O'Hair, Austin atheist, who alledgedly is working for the removal of telephone poles because of their inferences as crosses. Mrs. O'Hair believes the poles are pushing religion on others.

Most schools have some locks length rules. If this were not established there would be some who never shave nor get a haircut according to Weldon Trice, assistant principal. Mr. Trice said these school regulations were supported by the school board and are about the same throughout the system.

Believing hair rules to be an invasion of privacy, it is quickly seen that using the same logic one cannot appear naked in public and claim privacy.

A most ridiculous argument, long hair denotes hippies, yippies and other deviates is usually as illogical as those people who utter it.

What is hair coming to? Sometimes the shoulders. Perhaps like the Walnetto, zoot suit and knickers, long hairs shall stumble onto the past.

However, a certain amount of hair is good. A few years ago, a young man was expelled from an eastern school because he had his head shaved.

In the course of school activity the student body is usually refered to as students in public address anouncements and at assemblies.

Looking at restroom doors, "Boys" and "Girls" could not be replaced with students or there would be complications.

Perhaps "Men" or "Women" placed on the respective doors would remedy some of the "false pride" in ourselves and our school.

Told to act like adults, why shouldn't the doors bear it out.

A Penny Saved!

Zeroing in on finance and big business, John English had some advice for his senior English students.

"All of you are capable of making one million dollars by the time you are 30," the instructor said, in jellied tones.

"Of course," Mr. English added, "when you make your million, I want you to remember that I was the person who told you about it."

FACE TALK . . . . Bill Nidiffer

. . .in the eye of a tornado.

SIRENS BLARE

Tornado Precautions Assist in Protection

By ANNE DINGUS

Though Pampa has never been hit by a tornado, students should know what to do in case a tornado does occur.

The only true protection against a tornado, according to the Texas Division of Defense and Disaster Relief, is an underground excavation.

Weldon Trice, assistant principal, said that if a tornado hits during school hours, students on the first and second floors should go into the hall, sit facing the lockers, and put heads down. Students on the third floor should go to the basement lobby and sit toward the inside walls with heads lowered.

Students in Vocational Agriculture-Metal Trades buildings should assume the same position against the inside walls of that building. This positon offers the best protection against flying glass, Mr. Trice said. Large, open rooms should be avoided.

If in open country, people should take cover in a ravine or ditch. The best shelter in cities or towns is against the inside walls of the basement of a factory, office building, or home. If the building has no basement, one should be under a heavy piece of furniture against an inside wall.

"We would like to have a (tornado) siren on each school," said Mr. Trice, in citing the need for a tornado warning system. "If this plan were used, any one siren, when turned on, would simultaneously turn the others on."

At present, in case of a tornado, the Pampa Fire Department would call the high school, which would convey the warning to elementary and junior high schools by telephone, Mr. Trice explained.

Sirens on all three Pampa fire stations, as well as the air raid and storm warning siren atop the Hughes Building, will be turned on if a tornado is approaching Pampa, according to Assistant Fire Chief J. V. Pirkle.

A continuous ringing of bells is used in all schools as tornado alerts, Mr. Trice said.

Key Clubber to Run For Vice-President

Tim Doke, junior, will be a candidate for endorsement for vice-president of Key Club International at the annual Texas-Oklahoma District convention to be held in Houston this weekend.

Cast Works For Contest

Awaiting March 29, day of contest play presentation, the sixth period drama class is rehearsing Oscar Wilde's "The Importance of Being Earnest."

Working during sixth period and after school, the cast is still uncertain about a school performance according to Mrs. William Sargent, director.

The cast includes Herbert Smith as Algernon Moncieff, Susan Maguire as Gwendolyn Fairfax, Mike Hayes as John Worthing, Dawn Hills as Lady Bracknell, Dale Mahler as Merriman, Reggie Thompson as Dr. Chausible, Mary McBride as Cecily Cardew, and Janet Young as Miss Prism.

Helen Hill, American Field Service student, is assistant director.

Publications Adviser Attends Convention

Miss Elizabeth Hurley, publications adviser, is attending the Columbia Scholastic Press Association at Columbia University in New York this week.

Miss Hurley will conduct a session on news coverage.

Sophomore director of the Pampa club last year, Tim served as lieutenant-governor of Division Six this year. If he receives the endorsement of this district in Houston, he will become a candidate at the Key Club International convention in Miami Beach, Fla., in July.

John Karr will be his campaign manager.

Eighteen boys and two adults will attend the convention in Houston. Voting delegates will be David Irwin and Barry George, president and secretary for next year. Tom Neslage and Teddy Trice, vice-president and junior director for next year, will be alternate delegates.

Don Barnhill will enter the oratorical competition.

Others who will attend are Mark Gething, Terry Ward, Ricky Redus, Gary Gattis, Kenny Thompson, Haney Robertson, Ken Vaughn, David McLennan, Butch Wilkerson, Grant Gikas and Barry Bowman.

55 Inducted Into Honor Society

Fifteen seniors and forty juniors were inducted into National Honor Society March 11.

The program included speeches on the four requirements for membership. Joe Daniel spoke on service, John Karr presented leadership, Mary Bearden discussed character and Terry Pulse elaborated on scholarship.

NHS will hold one more meeting in April. Junior initiates will elect officers for next year in May.

(Photo by Sherrel Land)
KEY CANDIDATE---T i m Doke, junior, looks over a speech he will make at the Texas-Oklahoma District convention this weekend in Houston, where he will be a candidate for vice-president of Key Club International.

St. Pat's Celebration Changed to March 15

St. Patrick's Day activities will be celebrated March 15 instead of March 17 in Shamrock.

Jan Autry, senior, will represent Pampa in the Miss Irish Rose contest.

9 to Attend Austin Meet

Nine publication students will a t t e n d the Interscholastic League Press Conference Convention in Austin March 21-22

Students attending the convention are Candy Cole, Karen Wallis, Mona Tyrrell, Mark Buzzard, Randy Maness, Susan Maguire, Robert Moultrie, Lynn Lunsford and Debbie Veale. Advisors attending are Miss Hurley and Bill Haynes.

Warren K. Agee, dean of the William Allen White School of Journalism at the University of Kansas, will be keynote speaker.

Miss Hazel Pressan, author of "The Student Journalist and News Reporting," will participate in both newspaper and yearbook sessions.

Miss Elizabeth Hurley, Little Harvester adviser, will conduct a newspaper session.

Sessions for newspaper, yearbook and photography will be held all day Saturday. Individual achievement awards and results of the annual rating of newspapers will be announced at the Awards Banquet Saturday night.

What's Happening

Student Council will end the year with an assembly May 9 and a dinner in the cafeteria May 13.

John Karr, student body president, Joe Daniel, parliamentarian, and Carolyn McKinley, treasurer, will speak at the assembly.

Prom Set for May 10

The all-school prom will be May 10, 9 p.m. to 12 midnight in the girls' gym.

Jay Johnson, student body vice-president, is in charge of the prom.

4 Bands Will Perform

The four Pampa bands will perform at the Band Spring Festival held in the Field House on the evening of May 8.

Donald Baird, baritone teacher and soloist from West Texas State University, will be accompanied by the High School band.

Choral Festival Set May 16

The Choral Festival is set for May 16 at 8 p.m. in the Field House.

The three choirs from high school will join the junior high and grade school choirs for the festival.

Pep-ers to Give Banquet

Pep-ers will have an end-of-school banquet May 10 at 6:30 p.m. in the Starlight Room of Coronado Inn. Tickets cost $2.50 each and will be sold to anyone wanting to go.

Miss Sweetheart and Miss Spirit will be named, Linda Henley, president, said.

Tri-Hi-Y to Visit Ranch

Tri-Hi-Y will go to Boy's Ranch May 4. Fran Hobbs, president, said members will attend church and eat there.

SPUDNUTS!

Top Sellers This Week

1. Aquarius/Let the Sunshine In Medley	11. Hawaii Five-O
2. You've Made Me So Very Happy	12. Don't Give In To Him
3. Hair	13. Brother Love's Traveling Salvation Army
4. Galveston	14. Gimme, Gimme Good Lovin'
5. It's Your Thing	15. Sweet Cherry Wine
6. Dizzy	16. The Boxer
7. Only The Strong Survive	17. Traces
8. Rock Me	18. First of May
9. Twenty Five Miles	19. You Gave Me A Mountain
10. Time of the Season	20. I Can Hear Music

TARPLEY'S MUSIC STORE
117 North Cuyler   Phone MO 4-4251

(Photo by Randy Maness)
MINI-MANOR PLACES AT CANYON---Darrel Sublett and Steve Taylor, architectural drawing students, put finishing touches on one of the model homes built as a class project. The class built two model dwellings which placed second and third, along with other drawing winners, at the Industrial Arts Fair in Canyon last weekend.

Pampa High School Named Runner-Up At Arts Fair

Pampa High School was named first runner-up in the high school division at the Industrial Arts Fair in Canyon April 25-26.

Fifteen architectural drawing students entered two model houses and won second and third places. The houses were entered in the miscellaneous divisions of group projects.

Those working on the models were Clifford G a g e, D o n Smithee, Don Willis, Tony Teakell, Darrel Sublett, Steven Taylor, Jeff Morris, Jack Rose, Max Miller, Tommy Swindle, Jerry Ferrell, Sam Virden, Ervin Hall, Morris Powell and David Noe.

Students placing in individual competition in mechanical drawing I Level 3 were Jeanne Turner, first, and Jerry Fife, third; mechanical drawing II Level 3, Floyd Hatcher, first, and Michael Hargus, second.

Other students placing were Richard Hall, first; John Stokes, second, and Gary Jenkins, third in Leather Level 3; Chester Jackson, first, and Orville Rob-

inson, second, in Plastics Level 3; and Vicki Webb, first; Larry Taylor, second, and Sam Virden, third, in Plastics Level 4.

Those placing in Wrought Copper Level 3 were Connie Thut, first; Carol Haynie, second, and Jim Jacobs, third. Winners in Wrought Copper Level 4 were Mike Cooper, first, and Beryle Brister, second.

Club Installs New Leaders

Dr. Leon Hill, Methodist minister, will speak at the eleventh annual Key Club Installation banquet tonight at 7 p.m. in the Coronado Inn Starlight Room.

Lt.-Gov. Mike Housman of Tascosa will install new leaders. David Irwin will succeed Joe Daniel as president, and both will speak. Tom Neslage will become vice-president; Barry George, secretary; Bryce Michaels, treasurer; Teddy Trice, junior director, and Moss Hampton, senior director.

Sandy Nininger, Key Clubber of the Year and Student Leader of the Year will be presented.

Hole in the Head

People who whistle in assemblies usually pucker their lips, but make the whistle by letting wind blow through the holes in their heads. — Charlie Barker.

Sports page #1—Limited by a four-column format, this sports page shows how careful layout planning can provide space for a picture, two news stories, a column, and baseball standings, as well as advertisements. Note that the column heading is not merely a label. Boldface lead-ins on the column items add brightness to the page.

Sports page #2—On a four-column sports page, a one-column basketball picture accompanying the lead story allows room for a feature story and cage standings. A two-column picture with the story would fill up the page and limit effective makeup.

SPORT COMMENTS

Prospects Conduct Gridiron Workouts

By TIM DOKE

After four days of rigid spring training drills, the steps of many Harvester athletes may seem quite a bit slower. Each afternoon from sixth period to approximately 5:30, about 100 football hopefuls are going through maneuvers in an effort to give the coaches an idea of prospects for the 1969 football season. Varsity basketball coach Sterling Gibson has joined the gridiron coaching staff as he works with the defensive secondary during this three-week spring workout.

FANS HAVE an added attraction in store for them May 24, the night of the Green-Gold football game. Coach Swede Lee has scheduled this intersquad clash to officially end spring football workouts. However, a new rivalry will come into focus during halftime of the Green-Gold clash as the Pep-ers meet the Truteens in what might turn out to be a powder-puff gridiron classic.

SENIOR BASKETBALLER Edward Moultrie recently received word from Lubbock Christian College that he has been awarded an athletic scholarship to that school. He joins other graduating seniors Jim Hollis and Johnny Epperson on the scholarship list at LCC. Billy Thomas has the gleam of Texas Tech in his eye, but as of yet, no official word concerning scholarships has been received.

ATHLETES INVOLVED in minor sports are also receiving recognition from colleges. Joe Mack Millican, senior netter, has received a tennis scholarship to Frank Phillips College in Borger. Swimmer Jim Cole is making plans to attend Texas Tech on a four-year swimming scholarship.

Pep Squad Sets Banquet

The Pep-ers' "Sweetheart" and "Miss Spirit" will be revealed at the Pep-ers banquet tomorrow night at 6:30 p.m. at the Coronado Inn.

Officers and team captains for next year will also be announced, according to Mrs. Dona Cornutt, sponsor.

Jamilou Schaffer, Mistress of Ceremonies, will introduce Dr. James Malone, superintendent, and Jan Osborne will present the invocation by singing "The Lord's Prayer."

Mrs. Cornutt said, "This is the last activity of the year for the Pep-ers, and new members will be initiated."

Big As A Stick

Teachers teach softly but carry a big grade book.

(Photo by Robert Moultrie) WINNING FORM--- Senior Dan Carlton delivers a pitch against Caprock April 29 in Optimist Park. The Harvesters fell to the Longhorns 4-1.

Baseball Season Finishes; Monterey Clinches Crown

By TIM DOKE

District 4-A baseball season ends this weekend with makeup games postponed by rain earlier in the season. Pampa's game with Tascosa at Amarillo Tuesday was postponed to Thursday. The Harvesters had a 2-15 district record going into their final contest.

Monterey clinched the district title last week with a 13-2 record and three games to play this week. The Plainsmen were followed by Tascosa at 12-6.

In a muddy contest, Pampa was edged by Plainview 2-0 in a Saturday contest. Dan Carlton went all the way for the Harvesters as he kept the Bulldogs to five hits and fanned four. Kerry Eaves won for the Dogs

Too Many 'Friends'?

H. L. Hunt, Texas multi-millionaire, can't even keep up with the people he knows.

Proof of this is seen in the fact that David Webster, senior, jokingly sent him a graduation invitation though David has not seen Mr. Hunt.

A few days later, a package arrived for David. It was a set of $15 cufflinks which Mr. Hunt sent to David as a graduation present.

as he allowed four Pampa hits and tallied six strikeouts.

Pampa was shut-out last Friday by Coronado in a 3-0 romp. The Harvesters could only get two hits, a double by John Jenkins and a triple by Jay Johnson. Sammy Heasley went the distance for Pampa, allowing only five hits and striking out four. Mike Bryne won the game for the Mustangs as he fanned 11 Harvesters.

Caprock Longhorns came to Pampa April 29 to hand the Green and Gold their first defeat of the week. Pampa's nine managed to get nine hits off Caprock's Kerry Morgan but could only make one trip across the plate. Dan Carlton allowed two earned runs for Caprock, but the Longhorns managed to score two more on Pampa's three errors. The game ended in a 4-1 victory for Caprock.

BASEBALL STANDINGS

DISTRICT STANDINGS
(Through May 3)

TEAM	W	L	PCT.
Monterey	13	2	.867
Tascosa	11	6	.647
Coronado	9	8	.529
Plainview	9	8	.529
Caprock	8	8	.500
Borger	8	8	.500
Amarillo	7	8	.467
Lubbock	7	8	.467
Palo Duro	6	9	.400
Pampa	2	15	.118

Harvesters Tackle Rebels In Amarillo

By DAVID IRWIN

Coach Sterling Gibson's Harvesters will travel to Amarillo tonight to tangle with he undefeated winners in the first round of District 4-AAAA basketball play, the Tascosa Rebels.

If the Harvesters downed Caprock last Tuesday, they will stand 5-0 for second half play going into tonight's game beginning at 8 p.m. Both teams will have their hands full as the Rebels just barely squeaked by the Harvesters in first half play, 48-46.

THE HARVESTERS will battle the Lubbock Westerners here Feb. 11 in Harvester Field House and the next Friday travel to Lubbock to face the Coronado Mustangs. The Harvesters had no trouble with either of these teams in first half play as they downed the Mustangs 65-59 and defeated the Westerners 63-48.

In a game played in Amarillo last Friday, the Harvesters

downed the Amarillo Sandies 57-51. The game was fairly tight all the way until the last of the game when the Harvesters pulled out in front to stay. Although both teams were relatively cold from the free throw line, the Harvesters tallied the higher percentage to give them the needed margin.

Leading scorer in that game was Jim Hollis with 22 points which boosted his district scoring lead to over 20 points per game. Jim Gallman added 13 points in the game.

IN A GAME AGAINST Monterey in Harvester Field House Jan. 28, the Harvesters had an easy time with the Plainsmen, defeating them 70-55.

The Harvesters had a amazing free throw percentage in that game by connecting with 34 of their 37 attempts. The local cagers also had a good night from the field, hitting 18 of 33 of their field goal attempts.

Leading scorer in that game was Billy Thomas with 25 points. Hollis dumped in 20 points along with Johnny Epperson's 12 points.

Withering Thought

Like an athlete's legs, the human mind soon withers if it is not used. — Charlie Barker.

(Photo by Robert Moultrie) FROM THE CORNER—John Epperson (22) takes a jump shot for a score against Monterey here Jan. 28. The Harvesters defeated the Plainsmen 61-51.

NATURAL SWIMMER

Cole Finds Water Sport To Be Routine Inhibition

By DAVID IRWIN

For some people, swimming is natural. It's just a case of jumping into the water and getting warmed up. And some people can do anything. Such is the case of Jim Cole, senior.

All the practice that Jim has put in during these past years in swimming has begun to pay off in more ways than one. Jim has a trophy case full of awards that he has won in the various meets that he has entered. Many of them are first place trophies.

JIM SAYS HIS favorite entry is the breast stroke which is one of the hardest strokes to master because of its fatiguing nature. However, he also swims the freestyle in competition.

Jim has returned from the University of Texas Invitational Swimming meet for high school

boys in Austin which was held Jan. 31 and Feb. 1. He placed 10th in the breast stroke out of 63 contestants representing 50 schools. Upon returning home this week, Jim will compete tomorrow in the Midland Swimming Meet at Lee High School.

Future meets for Jim include the 18th Annual Phillips 66 Swim Meet at Bartlesville, Oklahoma, and the Dallas State High School Boys Meet, March 21 and 22.

SOME OF JIM'S higher awards include being high point man in the Lubbock and Snyder meets last summer, and receiving the Men's Open High Point trophy in the Golden Spread Invitational in Amarillo. Jim has also swum in the Mexico-Texas Dual Swim Meet for all stars for the last two years and has received 2nd in the 100 yard free style relay against the Mexico Olympic Team.

When asked about possible Olympic competition Jim said, "I would sure like to swim in the Olympics, but I have a lot of work to do before I can even think of that."

CAGE CALENDAR

GAMES TONIGHT
Caprock at Pampa.
Tascosa at Borger.
Amarillo at Plainview.
Monterey at Palo Duro.
Lubbock at Coronado.

GAMES TUESDAY
Pampa at Tascosa.
Monterey at Amarillo.
Borger at Lubbock.
Borger at Palo Duro.
Plainview at Caprock.

RESULTS LAST WEEK
Pampa 70, Monterey 55.
Pampa 57, Amarillo 51.
Tascosa 69, Lubbock 44.
Borger 72, Amarillo 60.
Palo Duro 58, Plainview 55.
Coronado 77, Caprock 45.
Tascosa 71, Coronado 59.
Borger 45, Caprock 38.
Plainview 50, Monterey 46.
Palo Duro 92, Lubbock 54.

DISTRICT STANDINGS
(Second Round Thru Jan. 31)

TEAM	W	L	PCT.
Pampa	4	0	1.000
Tascosa	4	0	1.000
Borger	4	0	1.000
Amarillo	2	2	.500
Palo Duro	2	2	.500
Coronado	1	3	.250
Monterey	1	3	.250
Caprock	1	3	.250
Plainview	1	3	.250
Lubbock	0	4	.000

*First Round Winner—Tascosa.

(Photo by Robert Moultrie)

NEW BASEBALL COACHES—Tommy Lindsey, right, new head Harvester baseball coach, stands with his assistant, Coach James Pullen, to watch an afternoon workout. Lindsey played baseball at the University of Oklahoma and has played with Chicago Cub farm teams.

Shockers to Test Rebels Tonight in Second Round

Pampa's Shockers go on the court tonight for the second time this season against the Tascosa Rebels in Amarillo. In first round action, the Shockers defeated the Rebels by a score of 51-43.

The Junior Varsity was scheduled to go against the Caprock Shorthorns here Tuesday. They defeated the Shorthorns by a score of 55-50 in first round action.

The local cagers had a rough week, starting off with a 54-45 loss to Monterey. Mike Jordan led the Shockers with 24 points.

Traveling to Dumas for the Dumas Tournament Thursday night, the Shockers had their only victory of the week when they defeated Dumas 56-50 with Doug Thompson heading the attack with 22 points. Saturday,

the Shocks were outscored by Borger 54-35.

Friday night, between tournament games, the Shockers were defeated by the Amarillo High junior varsity by a score of 58-41.

The Shockers are scheduled to go against the Lubbock High's "B" team next Tuesday. The Shockers came out on top in their first meeting, 60-56.

Don't Plant Seeds

Like a weed, hate grows quickly and is hard to kill.
— Joe Organ.

No Off Season for Them

Athletes Build Muscles

By TIM DOKE

For 52 of Pampa High School's athletes, there is no "off season."

These athletes are currently in a specially designed program with the intent purpose of developing them physically. The program consists of 18 different weight and agility stations and one quickness station. Each station has its own specific purpose in developing the athletes.

The weight stations are nine individual steps designed to build up the athletes' muscles and to increase their physical strength. The boys start working out with the maximum weight they can handle. When they have mastered this, they increase the amount ten pounds.

THE AGILITY STATIONS are also a nine-point program designed to develop the ability of athletes to make quick changes

is direction. On one of the agility movements, the athletes are timed. These times are kept on record to measure their development.

The athletes perform at each station for a three-minute interval. Sophomore and junior

football boys work out in this program each Monday, Wednesday and Friday. Tracksters join them in workouts on these days.

Baseball players take advantage of the program on Tuesdays, Thursdays and Saturdays. For the first time at Pampa High School, the coaches are working with the freshmen, the boys who will make up the Shocker team next year. These boys work out on Tuesdays and Thursdays.

THE PROGRAM HAS only been operating for eight weeks, but the results have been most favorable, according to Coach Marvin Lay. Each player is measured every six weeks to check his development.

The coaches have seen an increase in both sizes and weight and hope that this additional size will be beneficial in putting the "Best in the West" back on top in football standings next year.

As the World Burns

Brenda Johnson, senior, was discussing a letter she read in "Dear Abby" in Sterling Gibson's first period government class.

When Coach Gibson asked her if she really read it, she answered, "Of course."

With a look of dismay, 'he said, "That's as bad as watching 'As the World Burns'."

Get a fistful of authority.

The only way you can spell that is H-u-r-s-t, the shifter that's known on every strip and oval in the country as No. 1. You've a choice of Competition Plus 4-speed, the Dual Pattern 3-speed with Syncro/Loc, or the money-saving 3-speed Mystery Shifter. They're steel-hard jewels, precision made, guaranteed forever and you get them right here.

MOTOR INN AUTO SUPPLY INC.

416 W. Foster
Phone MO 4-8466

(Photo by Herb Smith)
WORKING ON WEIGHTS—Paul Johnson watches as Marc Ginn performs at one of the nine weight stations set up for athletes in the girls' gym.

Sports page #3—A three-column feature story with one-column picture is used effectively below the two-column picture and two-column story at the top of the page. This provides a more interesting sports page. A featurette and epigram are used as fillers to brighten the page. The vertical advertisement with the picture is a great help in making this page attractive. Note the importance of contrast in the type used in this ad.

FOR FURTHER HELP

Publications of a wide variety are available in the field of scholastic journalism. Some of them are free with membership in certain organizations. Press associations have been organized on national, regional, state, and local levels to serve the needs of the student journalist and the beginning adviser. Many staffs join as many of those press groups as are open to them in order to have the publications offered, no two of which are alike. Prices are available upon request by nonmembers.

National organizations:

Catholic School Press Association, College of Journalism, Marquette University, 522 North 13th Street, Milwaukee, Wisconsin 53233—Magazine: *The Catholic School Editor*.

Columbia Scholastic Press Association, Box 11 Central Mail Room, Columbia University, New York, N.Y. 10027—Magazine: *The School Press Review*.

Future Journalists of America, H. H. Herbert School of Journalism, University of Oklahoma, Norman, Oklahoma 73069—Bulletins.

National Scholastic Press Association, 18 Journalism Building, University of Minnesota, Minneapolis, Minnesota 55455—Magazine: *Scholastic Editor Graphics/Communication*.

Quill and Scroll International Honor Society for High School Journalists, School of Journalism, University of Iowa, Iowa City, Iowa 52240—Magazine: *Quill and Scroll*.

The National Yearbook Association publishes *Photolith* for both newspapers and yearbooks. Address: Suite 201, 732 Mt. Moriah Road, Memphis, Tennessee 38117.

For advisers only:

Columbia Scholastic Press Advisers Associa-tion—Magazine: *CSPAA Bulletin*. For information, write CSPA.

Journalism Education Association—Magazine: *Communication*. For information, write NSPA.

One of the advantages of subscribing to the above services is the opportunity to be on the mailing list to get information about new publications and also to see book reviews, as most magazines and some bulletins carry book reviews as a regular feature.

Suggestions for additional help and ideas:

Build up a classroom library of a variety of materials. Keep a collection of the brochures, advertisements, and the like that come in the mail to use for staff discussion and study. Professional layout people and artists and photographers call such a collection their "swipe file." They refer to the collection as a kind of stepping-stone in the search for fresh ideas.

Make a scrapbook of clippings—articles, advertisements, photographs, and such—that you find attractive. In fact, a collection of clipping books is a valuable addition as a classroom reference source. Since advertising agencies especially are vying for the reader's attention, they make use of numerous devices that newspaper and yearbook staffs can use to advantage.

Subscribe to an unusual publication now and then. Newspaper staffs will benefit by collecting copies of newspapers from a wide range of sources.

Develop an exchange list so that you can see what other schools are doing in their publications. Yearbook staffs will find it helpful to build up a library of books by exchanging with other schools. Since some schools have built up a reputation for attractive yearbooks over the years, their books are in great demand. Therefore, a staff who would like one of the books should offer to buy a copy, as books are so expensive that few staffs can order more than what are paid for in advance. Newspaper staffs usually can exchange publications more freely than yearbook staffs can, but here again expense may be a factor. Requests for exchange should be by letter so that they can be handled in a businesslike way.

Newspaper staffs will find helpful materials available from the Newspaper Fund Inc. Address: P.O. Box 300, Princeton, New Jersey 08540.

Also, the American Newspaper Publishers Association makes various materials available to newspaper advisers. Address: 750 Third Avenue, New York, 10017.

Mimeographed and other duplicated papers are offered aids by the various companies producing duplicating equipment and supplies. Among them is the A. B. Dick guide for the mimeographed paper.

Various publishing houses provide special helps designed to aid in yearbook production. They vary greatly from company to company and are usually available only with a contract.

Many staffs are taking advantage of the expanding workshop program. A variety of helps is offered by the workshops, ranging from instruction to free publications. The purpose is twofold: to help the beginner get started on the publication year in advance of the opening of school and to give the experienced staff members suggestions and new ideas for improved publications.